Cahokian Dispersions

Melissa R. Baltus • Sarah E. Baires
Elizabeth Watts Malouchos
Jayur Madhusudan Mehta
Editors

# Cahokian Dispersions

Diasporic Connections
in the Mississippian Southeast

Previously published in *Journal of Archaeological Method and Theory* "Special Issue: Cahokia Dispersion" Volume 27, Issue 1, 2020

 Springer

*Editors*
Melissa R. Baltus
Department of Sociology
and Anthropology
University of Toledo
TOLEDO, OH, USA

Elizabeth Watts Malouchos
Illinois State Archaeological Survey
University of Illinois
COLLINSVILLE, IL, USA

Sarah E. Baires
Eastern Connecticut State University
WILLIMANTIC, CT, USA

Jayur Madhusudan Mehta
Florida State University
TALLAHASSEE, FL, USA

Spinoff from journal: "Journal of Archaeological Method and Theory" Volume 27, issue 1, March 2020

ISBN 978-981-19-7367-3

This Springer imprint is published by the registered company Springer Nature Singapore Pte Ltd.
The registered company address is: 152 Beach Road, #21-01/04 Gateway East, Singapore 189721, Singapore

# Contents

**Creating and Abandoning "Homeland": Cahokia as Place
of Origin** ....................................................................................... 111
M. R. Baltus, S. E. Baires: Journal of Archaeological Method
and Theory 2019, 2020: 27: 111-127 (10, December 2019) DOI:
10.1007/s10816-019-09433-x

**Angel Ethnogenesis and the Cahokian Diaspora** ......................................... 128
E. W. Malouchos: Journal of Archaeological Method and Theory 2020,
2020: 27: 128-156 (30, January 2020) DOI: 10.1007/s10816-020-09443-0

Journal of Archaeological Method and Theory (2020) 27:1–6
https://doi.org/10.1007/s10816-020-09447-w

# Diasporic Connections: Cahokia and the Greater Southeast

Melissa R. Baltus[1] · Sarah E. Baires[2] · Elizabeth Watts Malouchos[3] · Jayur Madhusudan Mehta[4]

Published online: 12 February 2020
© Springer Science+Business Media, LLC, part of Springer Nature 2020

The rise of Cahokia, the largest pre-Columbian Native American city north of Mexico, and the rapid spread of Mississippian culture across the midcontinental and southeastern USA after AD 1000 has long been a focus of archaeological inquiry. Trade, political control, and emulation constitute some of the theories used to examine the wide distribution of Cahokian artifacts and architecture. Early cultural historical interpretations focused on migration and diffusion as the mechanism by which Cahokian objects and practices spread, a position heavily critiqued by processualists. Mounting archaeological evidence, now supported by technological advancements in materials-sourcing and isotope analyses (see Emerson and Hedman 2016; Slater et al. 2014), has brought back theories of migration, with attendant processes of hybridity and creolization (see Alt 2006, 2018; Millhouse 2012), to characterize Mississippian interactions and movements. These movements highlight the diverse cultural interactions that worked to, in part, create this Native American city—one that informed the spread of Mississippianism beyond the American Bottom.

For this special issue, we invited our colleagues to consider the possibility and role of a Cahokian diaspora to understand cultural influence, complexity, historicity, and movements in the Mississippian Southeast. Collectively, we trace how the movements of Cahokian and American Bottom materials, substances, persons, and non-human bodies converged in the creation of Cahokian identities both within and outside of the Cahokia homeland. Drawing initial inspiration from theories of diaspora, our goal in organizing this collection of papers was to explore the dynamic movements of human populations by critically engaging with the ways people materially construct or deconstruct their social identities in relation to others within the context of physical movement.

Chapter 1 was originally published as Baltus, M. R., Baires, S. E., Malouchos, E. W. & Mehta, J. M. Journal of Archaeological Method and Theory (2020) 27:1–6. https://doi.org/10.1007/s10816-020-09447-w.

✉ Melissa R. Baltus
melissa.baltus@utoledo.edu

[1]   Department of Sociology and Anthropology, University of Toledo, Toledo, OH 43606, USA

[2]   Eastern Connecticut State University, Willimantic, Windham, CT 06226, USA

[3]   Glenn A. Black Laboratory of Archaeology, Indiana University, Bloomington, IN 47408, USA

[4]   Florida State University, Tallahassee, FL 32306, USA

While theories of diaspora have become multiple and varied, the central tenets remain the same: population dispersion, reference to (or nostalgia for (Buchanan 2020)) a homeland, and maintenance of identities that are at variance with those of the "host" population (Brubaker 2006; Cipolla 2017; Clifford 1994; Cohen 1997; Lilley 2006; Safran 1991). The contributions to this special issue engage with diaspora to understand Mississippian population movements and explore components of Cahokian identity created, preserved, and maintained outside of the American Bottom "homeland" through archaeological case studies that demonstrate the ways in which population movements foment social change. Research representing multiple sites, time periods, and cultures spanning the Mississippian world highlighted the intersections between materiality, memory, place-making, and person-making to address the centrifugal and centripetal forces tied to this unique and monumental place. These papers engage with diaspora in disparate ways through considerations of movements of people and goods to and from Cahokia, which include conversations about diaspora as entangled with cosmology and ties to a "place-as-idea." Here we provide a brief summary of the papers that follow while highlighting the ways diaspora theory contributes to our understanding of Cahokia's emergence and the translation of Mississippian ideals into the Greater Southeast.

## Diasporic Connections

Ashley and Thunen (2020) examine diaspora through connections among persons, place, and the seeking and exchange of knowledge. Perhaps their greatest contribution to the conversation on Cahokia Diaspora is their recognition that people travel long distances not solely to trade or to migrate but also to seek knowledge unique to that disparate place and to perhaps share their own with the people they encounter. Their article examines the possibility of long-distance travelers from Cahokia bringing with them materials steeped in esoteric knowledge to St. Johns people in Florida, but what this article does best is create a vivid imaginary of how these Cahokian travelers might have experienced the "edge of the world"—the Atlantic Ocean. When thinking about diaspora, Ashley and Thunen remind us that diaspora is not a fixed place, but experience entangled with the exchange of knowledge.

Mehta and Connaway (2020) explore potential southern ties with Cahokia in the Yazoo Basin through the lens of a trade diaspora. This concept is drawn from historical references to enclaves of specialized merchant groups who maintain a distinct identity separate from a "host" society. The motivations in a trade diaspora are based on exchange, though Mehta and Connaway suggest for the Carson site specifically, trade may have been a bi-product of a more complex movement of people returning to an ancestral homeland or a "heritage diaspora."

The political-economic view of Mehta and Connaway juxtaposes with Emerson et al.'s (2020) relational perspective on the movement of people, landscape, and "homeland." They highlight the variability of motivations for why people move across a landscape as well as the diversity of processes through which materials and things wind up in regions outside Cahokia. In tackling the concept of diaspora, Emerson and colleagues argue that we need to better understand the complexities of a "homeland" and an originating population in order to understand those motivations and processes of movement.

Buchanan's (2020) contribution to this issue challenges the utility of a "checklist" approach to identifying diasporic populations in the past (and arguably the present); instead, she highlights the concept of nostalgia in processes of population movement. Specifically considering the out-migration of Cahokians during a period of regional violence during the thirteenth to fourteenth centuries, Buchanan describes the phenomenological experience of relocation as a means of mediating past-present-future relations through nostalgic materialities.

Similarly, Wilson et al. (2020) critique the lack of explication that the various typologies of diaspora offer, arguing that the concept of diaspora alone will likely not produce any new explanatory models for Cahokia without a deeper consideration of "different modes of living" and changes in such over time. Using the Central Illinois River Valley (CIRV) as a case study, they offer a diachronic view of population movements between the American Bottom and the CIRV. By decentering Cahokia in the discussion of migrations and movements, they demonstrate long-term persistence of local traditions alongside Cahokian Mississippian and hybrid practices. This persistence highlights the importance of agency and individual choice in making and foregrounding local ties versus distant social connections.

Complementary to Emerson et al. (2020), Baltus and Baires (2020) focus on Cahokia as a Place of Origin and a referential "homeland" where Cahokia's impact across the greater southeast can be traced through the movements of people and their ties to "home." From this perspective, Baltus and Baires consider the implications of this Central Place or Place of Origin in the context of abandonment to examine the choices people make when they leave. What practices are "carried away" and what practices are abandoned altogether, and how does this process of dissolution, then, create Cahokia as a Place of Origin? Baltus and Baires argue that similarity in material goods alone does not make a diaspora and if assumed as such can lead to the attachment of static cultural meanings to people and materials. Instead, they argue for a self-reflexive process of analysis to consider diaspora as a plurality of persons (human and otherwise) where local histories may be the most appropriate lens through which to examine the subtle cultural references to Cahokia as a Place of Origin.

Watts Malouchos' (2020) contribution likewise applies a broadly inclusive definition of diaspora, focusing on the movement of people and an idea of "homeland," while offering a sound critique of the third criteria: maintenance of social boundaries. Demonstrating the problematic nature of a "static" identity that such boundary maintenance suggests, Watts Malouchos considers Cahokian connections in the Ohio River Valley near the site of Angel Mounds. More so than physical objects like stone tools and pottery, Watts Malouchos shows how landscape and architecture reference and physically reinforce ties to Cahokia through people's experience of living and moving within that landscape. These references may connect Angel with Cahokia as a physical homeland for some, or perhaps as a cosmological origin point, while at the same time facilitating the negotiation of local identities.

## Conclusion

Critiques leveled against diaspora theory include the overly broad proliferation of diaspora as descriptive lens (Brubaker 2005), defining criteria of diaspora as little more than a list of traits, and a lack of problematizing how boundaries and identity become reified through the lens of diaspora (see Cipolla 2017). This group of papers is diverse, but each reinforces the idea that we must be wary of trait lists and instead examine the archeological record through a consideration of processes and interactions where materials are one piece of the proverbial puzzle. What unites each of the papers in this issue are the author's struggles with diaspora—how to define it, use it, and make it meaningful in a pre-modern context. While the basic premise of what a diaspora "is" is shared (e.g., communities living outside a recognized homeland), each case study focuses on this concept differently, through examinations of creation of place, material exchange, movement of people, and political or religious connections between communities. This collection demonstrates that a strict focus on diaspora was perhaps too simplistic to encapsulate the diversity of social processes that resulted in Cahokian objects, persons, and practices dispersed throughout the midcontinent and southeast.

Rather than considering diaspora as a specific blanket theory to understand the appearance of Cahokian objects and practices outside of the American Bottom, we suggest the diasporic lens is more broadly useful as a means of engaging the process of homeland creation and imagining. By focusing on this aspect of the diaspora "criteria"—the idea of an ancestral homeland—we can problematize and reconsider the diversity notable in the dispersal of bodies (human and otherwise) outside of the American Bottom. This creation of a homeland to which identities are attached need not require a physical origination, but rather a construction of an imagined origin point of a people united by a centering Place. Through this Origin Place creation, Cahokia had reverberations across the midcontinent, archaeologically visible as unique objects and practices which reference Cahokia in various ways—architectural alignments that cite Cahokian cosmography (Watts Malouchos 2020), ear ornaments that mimic those of a narrative hero, figural carvings, and embossed copper plates (Pauketat 2004). Given the origin of Cahokia in movement and the convergence of human and material bodies, perhaps the circulation of these bodies—along with the human bodies with whom they traveled—are a continuation of the processes by which Cahokia emerged.

Additionally, we question whether we should expect continued "boundary maintenance" between former Cahokians and their new communities in all instances. At parts of Cahokia, rapid transformations to house style and homogenization of pottery assemblages indicate adoption of a local Cahokian identity. Simultaneously, additional evidence at sites peripheral to Cahokia suggests some participants did not "lose" their material identities but rather continued their traditional settlement practices and foodways until they dispersed from the region (Alt 2002; 2006). This does not mean they were unchanged from their time near Cahokia, but perhaps those transformations they take away with them will not be visible to us in the ways we expect (pottery, house style). The negotiation of identity and practice is complicated and locally variable, and we should expect the same variability outside of Cahokia.

As a final note, we wish to acknowledge the debt this work owes to Charles McNutt and Ryan Parish, and their Mid-South Archaeological Conference in 2016, which focused on Cahokian connections and influence across the Mississippian world. With their blessings, we pursued research and publication of these papers as an additional investigation explicitly within the frameworks of diaspora theory. McNutt and Parish's edited volume from the Mid-South meetings, *Cahokia in Context: Hegemony and Diaspora* (McNutt and Parish 2020), exists as an ancestor and cousin to these papers, and as a whole, both consider the myriads of ways in which corn farmers in the Midwest produced a sphere of influence spanning from Wisconsin to Louisiana, and from Oklahoma to Florida. These sets of papers will not be the final consideration of these topics as science is never settled and we hope that future excavations and research shine a brighter light on how humans migrate and why they carry with them what they choose to carry.

We hope the broader anthropological implications of these works help to frame processes of migration and identity during an era of deeply contentious American geopolitics. Mass human migrations as a result of war have characterized the second decade of the twenty-first century, and we can only expect more migrant and refugee crises as sea levels continue to climb an additional meter to meter and a half by AD 2100 (IPCC 2019). With 40% of the world's population living within 100 km of coastal zones, we must expect significant social challenges as mass human migrations seek relief from rising oceans, rapid-onset and destructive storms, and slow-onset disasters like drought and famine. In light of these migrations, issues of diaspora, identity, and culture conflict will remain salient in the public eye. We hope that they, the general public, lawmakers, and scholars across various disciplines, will look to archaeology and the social sciences for insights into how human societies have grappled with the challenges of accepting outsiders, welcoming refugees, and navigating unequal power relationships across contested borders. These papers, like those in the McNutt and Parish volume, grapple with understanding migration, power, and identity, and diaspora as a concept more broadly, and we hope they can serve as lessons, lenses, or heuristics through which we can better understand the present as well as future social issues.

## References

Alt, S.M. (2006) The Power of Diversity: The Roles of Migration and Hybridity in Culture Change. In *Leadership and Polity in Mississippian Society*, edited by B.M. Butler and P.D. Welch, pp. 289–308. Center for Archaeological Investigations Occasional Paper No. 33. Southern Illinois University Carbondale.

Alt, S.M. (2018) *Cahokia's Complexities: Ceremonies and politics of the first Mississippian farmers.* Tuscaloosa: The University of Alabama Press.

Alt, S. M. (2002). Identities, traditions and diversity in Cahokia's uplands. *Midcontinental Journal of Archaeology, 27,* 217–236.

Ashley, K. and R.L. Thunen (2020). St. Johns river fisher-hunter-gatherers: Florida's connection to Cahokia. *Journal of Archaeological Method and Theory,* 27(1).

Baltus, M.R. and S.E. Baires (2020) Defining diaspora: a view from the Cahokia homeland. *Journal of Archaeological Method and Theory,* 27(1).

Brubaker, R. (2005). The 'diaspora' diaspora. *Ethnic and Racial Studies, 28*(1), 1–19.

Buchanan, M. E. (2020). Diasporic longings? Cahokia, common field, and nostalgic orientations. *Journal of Archaeological Method and Theory, 27*(1), 1–18. https://doi.org/10.1007/s10816-019-09431-z.

Cipolla, C. N. (2017). Native American diaspora and ethnogenesis. **Oxford Online**.

Clifford, J. (1994). Diasporas. *Cultural Anthropology, 9*(3), 302–338.

Cohen, R. (1997). *Global diasporas: an introduction.* London: UCL Press.

Emerson, T. E., and K. M. Hedman (2016) The dangers of diversity: the consolidation and dissolution of Cahokia, native North America's first urban polity. In *Beyond collapse: archaeological perspectives on resilience, revitalization, and transformation in complex societies*, edited by Ronald K. Faulseit, pp. 147-175. Center for Archaeological Investigations, Occasional Paper No. 42. Southern Illinois University Press, Carbondale.

Emerson, T.E., K.M. Hedman, T.K. Brennan, A.M. Betzenhauser, S.M. Alt, and T.R. Pauketat (2020). Interrogating diaspora and movement in the greater Cahokian world. *Journal of Archaeological Method and Theory*, 27(1).

IPCC (2019) Summary for policymakers. In: IPCC Special report on the ocean and cryosphere in a changing climate [H.O. Pörtner, D.C. Roberts, V. Masson-Delmotte, P. Zhai, M. Tignor, E. Poloczanska, K. Mintenbeck, M. Nicolai, A. Okem, J. Petzold, B. Rama, N. Weyer (eds.)]. **In press**.

Lilley, I. (2006). Archaeology, diaspora and decolonization. *Journal of Social Archaeology, 6*(1), 28–47.

McNutt, C. H., & Parish, R. M. (2020). *Cahokia in context: hegemony and diaspora*. Gainesville: University Press of Florida.

Mehta, J. M., & Connaway, J. M. (2020). Mississippian culture and Cahokian identities as considered through household archaeology at Carson, a monumental center in North Mississippi. *Journal of Archaeological Method and Theory, 27*(1).

Millhouse, P. (2012) The John Chapman site and creolization on the northern frontier of the Mississippian world. Ph.D. Dissertation, Department of Anthropology, University of Illinois at Urbana-Champaign.

Pauketat, T. R. (2004). *Ancient Cahokia and the Mississippians*. New York: Cambridge University Press.

Safran, W. (1991). Diasporas in modern societies: myths of homeland and return. *Diaspora, 1*, 83–99.

Slater, P. A., Hedman, K. M., & Emerson, T. E. (2014). Immigrants at the Mississippian polity of Cahokia: strontium isotope evidence for population movement. *Journal of Archaeological Science, 44*, 117–127.

Watts Malouchos, E. L. (2020). Angel ethnogenesis and the Cahokian diaspora. *Journal of Archaeological Method and Theory, 27*(1).

Wilson, G. D., Bardolph, D. N., Esarey, D., & Wilson, J. J. (2020). Early Mississippian diasporas of the north American midcontinent. *Journal of Archaeological Method and Theory, 27*(1).

**Publisher's Note** Springer Nature remains neutral with regard to jurisdictional claims in published maps and institutional affiliations.

Journal of Archaeological Method and Theory (2020) 27:7–27
https://doi.org/10.1007/s10816-019-09439-5

# St. Johns River Fisher-Hunter-Gatherers: Florida's Connection to Cahokia

Keith Ashley[1] · Robert L. Thunen[1]

Published online: 2 January 2020
© Springer Science+Business Media, LLC, part of Springer Nature 2020

## Abstract

No area along the far edges of the Mississippian world is as remote from Cahokia as northeastern Florida. But objects of possible Cahokian derivation, though limited in number, made their way to this distant locale The most compelling material evidence in Florida for any kind of connection to Cahokia comes from the Mill Cove Complex and Mt. Royal along the St. Johns River of the northern peninsula. Situated about 100 km from one another, these two fisher-hunter-gatherer communities were recipients of copper and stone artifacts that likely originated in the American Bottom, some 1200 km away. The overall geographical distribution of Cahokian styles and artifacts enmeshed varied internal and external processes and flows that encompassed exploration, migration, diaspora, trade, and politics. While no evidence exists for a Cahokian outpost or diaspora as far south as Florida, the presence of American Bottom artifacts along the St. Johns River could have involved more than the stock answer of simple down-the-line-exchange. This essay explores issues of long-distance travel, direct contact, knowledge seeking, object biographies, and diplomacy among peoples from these geographically disparate locales.

**Keywords** Cahokia · Long-distance interactions · Knowledge seeking · Mississippian · Exotic objects

The question we pose is simple: how did fisher-hunter-gatherers along the St. Johns River, Florida come to possess rare exotic items of the Early Mississippian world, specifically those that came from the American Bottom and likely manufactured at Cahokia, some 1200 km away? An unequivocal answer is not so simple, owing to "problems of equifinality" that currently attend any interpretation of the spatial distribution of these artifacts (Blitz 2010:20; Pauketat 2004:119). Taking a broad-scale

---

Chapter 2 was originally published as Ashley, K. & Thunen, R. L. Journal of Archaeological Method and Theory (2020) 27:7–27. https://doi.org/10.1007/s10816-019-09439-5.

✉ Keith Ashley
  kashley@unf.edu

[1]  Department of Sociology, Anthropology, and Social Work, University of North Florida, 1 UNF Drive, Jacksonville, Florida 32224, USA

perspective, we depart from a typical down-the-line trade model for the movement of exotic materials to propose an alternative interpretation that considers long-distance journeys, knowledge seeking, diplomacy, object biographies, and direct contact between Cahokians and peoples of northeastern Florida. In this essay, we do not speak directly to the notion of a Cahokian diaspora but rather address the nature of possible social relations between Cahokians and groups living on the extreme southeastern periphery of the Early Mississippian world (Fig. 1). Portable objects of probable Cahokian origin recovered from the Mill Cove Complex and Mt. Royal along the St. Johns River, Florida point to social interactions between these geographically disparate regions of eastern North America during Cahokia's founding century (*ca.* A.D. 1050–1150). The exceedingly rare, prized-quality, and isolated occurrence of Cahokian-derived artifacts in northeastern Florida suggest attainment through direct encounters. Distance should not prevent us from considering face-to-face relations between Cahokians and Floridians, particularly in light of early sixteenth-century Spanish accounts that reference long-distance travels by certain Mississippians traders and guides (Ethridge 2017).

## Long-distance Journeys and the Power of Objects

People, objects, ideas, and practices move across the landscape in myriad ways. Diaspora, migration, intermarriage, and exchange are but a few of the important mechanisms that account for a society's broader fields of connectivity. The outward geographical expansion of Cahokian influence involved all these processes, as possible emigrants, dissidents, traders, spirit guides, and community functionaries navigated new frontiers and negotiated diverse relations with allies, enemies, and strangers in varied domestic and ritual contexts (Emerson and Lewis 1991; Green 1997; Pauketat 2004:119–144; Wilson et al. 2017). Attending these movements across space were distinctive physical objects (or knowledge of how to make those objects), some perhaps originally intended to communicate active affiliation or some sort of social, political, or religious connection to Cahokia. Those materials and objects, crafted in the American Bottom, underwent their own metaphorical diaspora as they traveled far afield creating webs of social, geographical, and temporal relationships, yet in the process maintained a genealogical connection to Cahokia.

The most evident material markers of Cahokian interaction consist of a series of well-crafted items possibly made at Cahokia that minimally include copper Long-Nosed God maskettes (earpieces), Ramey Incised pots, and flintclay figurines; the list further could be expanded to include Cahokia style arrowheads and chunkey stones (Pauketat 2004:121). Cahokia's expansive reach is materialized in the broad geographical dissemination of these pieces of Cahokia across portions of midwestern and southeastern North America (Fig. 2). Most of these symbolically charged tokens occur on sites that collectively span nearly the entire Mississippi River and some tributaries, although a few occur far from the American Bottom along the St. Johns River, Florida. Our take on Cahokia's increased connectivity with significantly distant peoples and lands is informed by Mary Helms's (1988, 1992) outstanding comparative work on the political and cosmological dimensions of geographical distance, based on widespread ethnographic and ethnohistoric evidence.

 Springer

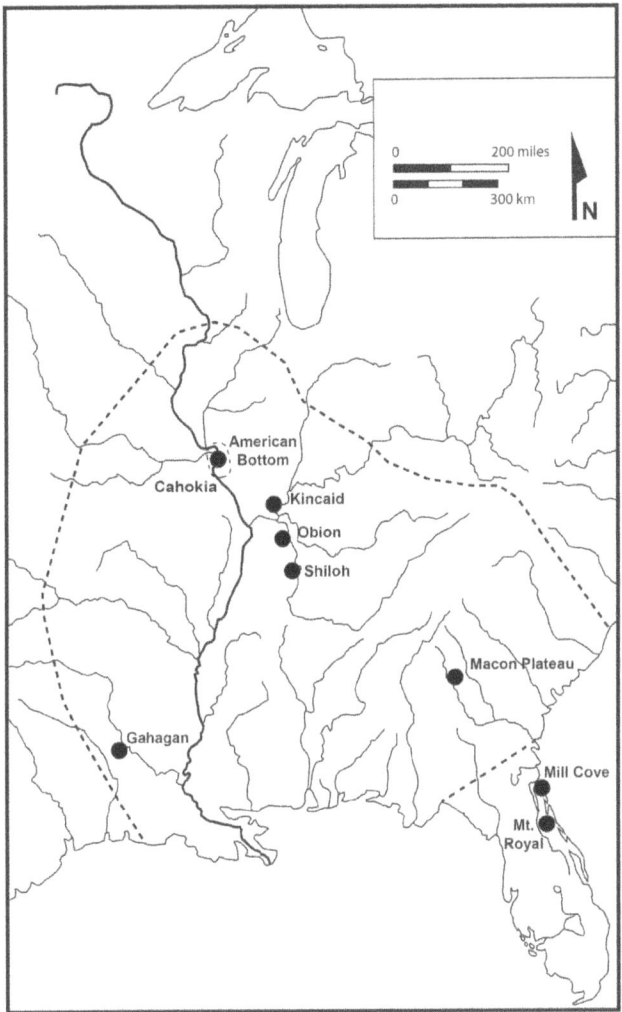

**Fig. 1** Select Early Mississippian sites

The physical world is culturally framed, as groups assign meaning and identity to its layout, features, juxtapositions, and forces. A common distinction contrasts the chaotic, outside world with the normal, everyday ordered world of home and shared community, although specificity and geographic details vary among cultures (Helms 1988:22, 114). Foreign places exist beyond the boundaries of home, inhabited by others whose lives differ greatly from that of the homeland. Helms (1988:4) argues that often in traditional societies geographical distance is equated with spiritual distance, meaning horizontal space and physical distance can be cast in cosmologically or supernaturally referenced terms. In effect, cosmology is imprinted on the physical landscape such that with increased geographical distance comes heightened cosmological, sacred, and supernatural connotations (Helms 1988:114). Faraway places, and the people and things from those places, are thus bestowed with significant symbolic meaning. Geographies are not static, however, and spatial distance can be collapsed through

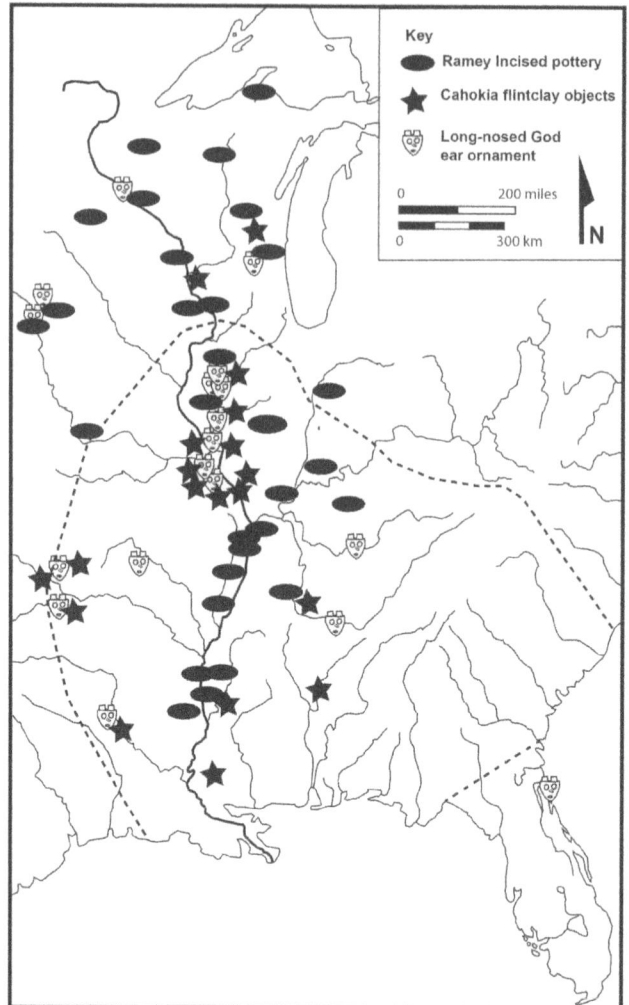

**Fig. 2** Distribution of possible Cahokia-derived artifacts (adapted from Pauketat 2004:Fig. 6.1)

cosmological understandings and social, political, and economic connections that extend into remote lands.

Motivations for venturing into the great beyond are wide-ranging, and journeys were undertaken for individual, social, religious, or political purposes (Helms 1988:66–67). Moreover, a single trip may serve multiple aims. Realization of mystical knowledge or power is a common general objective, and political, ideological, and cognitive reasons typically assume priority over purely economic interests such as trade. Geographically distant and virtually inaccessible lands are often preferred destinations of knowledge seekers, who draw connections to foreign places as a means of directly experiencing complex and layered cosmic realms. The demonstrated ability to encounter first-hand and develop an understanding of the extraordinary wonders and forces of the universe often grants long-distance travelers social reverence, ideological power, and privileged status. From the moment they depart until their successful return from a long-distance journey, some travelers may undergo a liminal or "middle passage" experience similar to that of trance-induced shamans, during which time they must endure physical, psychological, and spiritual challenges of an unfamiliar world (Helms 1988:81).

Raw materials and finished products obtained from afar assume the inalienable qualities bestowed onto distant places associated with other cosmic realms, often operating as tangible manifestations of intangible esoteric knowledge and powers. Measures affecting an object's degree of potency include source, difficulty of acquisition, rarity, and unique physical attributes (Helms 1988:114). Because of their sacredness, exotic materials tend to be reserved for use in exceptional tasks or by elite individuals or specialists. In traditional societies, objects originating from faraway and traveling a great distance tend to be portable and durable as well as "high in value and low in bulk," due to difficulties of transport (Helms 1988:118). Thus, it should come as no surprise that one of the most "frequently exchanged types of long-distance goods is esoteric knowledge" (Helms 1988:118).

For Helms (1988:99), these distant raw materials are marked by "the inalienable qualities associated with their unusual places or sources of origin." The tangibility of raw materials is what Bradley (2000:88) refers to as pieces of place, each of which carries a citation of the place with itself. This concept further can be extended to an object's production and movement, as it gathers more citations through time. As an object moves across the physical landscape, it interacts with various peoples and becomes entangled in social relationships, taking on a personhood of its own (Thomas 1999:72–73). In effect, things have social lives and develop histories or biographies during their life cycle (Kopytoff 1986). These object biographies encompass an amalgam of different people, places, and social relationships.

While Helm's work largely ignores the role of agency and biography in the lives of these powerful objects, recent studies of materiality emphasize the reciprocally constitutive relationships between people and things. While people manufacture objects, objects also help create people as social beings by engendering relationships that shape people's thoughts, actions, experiences, and memories (Meskell 2004; Miller 2005). The Mississippian archaeological record highlights a complex and far-reaching interconnectivity among myriad peoples and places, as certain raw materials and objects traveled great distances. During their itineraries, these circulating items articulated between and across divergent cultural territories, practices, and histories, where they reinforced, mediated, and altered social relationships and assumed a form of social existence (Lazzari 2005:129). By embodying these social, spatial, and temporal relations, such objects hold the capacity to create and reinforce social memories by referencing their past makers and users through citational fields (Jones 2001:339).

In eastern North America, certain raw materials such as copper, mica, galena, and quartz filtered through indigenous awareness were perceived as bits and pieces of the cosmos, simultaneously representing heaven and earth (Bloch 2018:789; Pauketat 2013:165–166). As these fragments of land or "earthly apparitions" of celestial bodies changed hands and moved across the landscape through various interaction networks, so did the supernatural powers and animating properties kept within them (Bloch 2018:789; Pauketat 2013; Zedeño 2008). Fundamental to North American Indian ontologies is the capacity for certain things to have power and agency, enabling them "to animate or otherwise modify surrounding people and things by virtue of their biography" (Zedeño 2008:375).

     Springer

## Starting with Cahokia

The human experience is multiscalar, and in the pre-Columbian Southeast, this is exemplified during the Mississippian period (A.D. 1000–1500), as webs of social interaction intertwined to link faraway peoples and places separated by as much as 1600 km (*e.g.*, Brown et al. 1990). Such long-distance connections, however, were not restricted to the five centuries prior to the European invasion, as evidenced by Late Archaic (3000–1000 B.C.) and Middle Woodland Hopewell (A.D. 100–500) spheres of interaction (Cobb 1991:205–209; Johnson 1994:100). In addition, narrative descriptions and Indian-authored maps of the sixteenth and seventeenth centuries reveal intricate indigenous knowledge of peoples, trails, and events over vast expanses of North America (Ethridge 2017; Lafferty 1994:179; Peregrine and Lekson 2012:64–65; Waselkov 1989). With this said, Cahokia was not needed for the existence of far-flung interaction networks, but the actual trajectory that southeastern pre-Columbian history followed after the eleventh century would have differed greatly had Cahokia never emerged when and where it did.

A new social and political order materialized rapidly at Cahokia during the mid-eleventh century, as a scattering of villages transformed into something urban and cosmopolitan (Alt 2010; Kelly and Brown 2014: Pauketat 2004, 2009). At its peak, the Greater Cahokia area consisted of three major mound centers—Cahokia, East St. Louis, and St. Louis—that collectively straddled the Missouri and Illinois sides of the Mississippi River near modern-day St. Louis. Cahokia reached its zenith within 100 years of its founding but was nothing more than a fading memory by the mid-fourteenth century. The Cahokian phenomenon was a complex set of historically contingent processes of culture making, social transformation, and community diversification associated with new technological innovations, population influxes, trade, agriculturally based ideologies, and religion (Pauketat 2013). Although large-scale immigrations characterized Cahokia's early history, in time, some people moved away in different directions and resettled at varying distances from the great civic centers (Alt 2002; Buchanan 2020; Connaway et al. 2020; Mehta and Connaway 2020; Pauketat and Alt 2003). Some researchers suggest the establishment of Cahokia-inspired trade or mission outposts well to the north in Iowa, Wisconsin, and Minnesota (*e.g.*, Pauketat 2004:124–142; Pauketat et al. 2015; Wilson et al. 2017). Cahokia simultaneously propelled and attracted the movements of people, objects, and other non-human things.

Relocated communities of Cahokians, who maintained their distinctive cultural identity in a foreign land, might constitute a diaspora (Baltus and Baires 2020; Brubaker 2005:5–6). But what about a far-off location well beyond the limits of this diaspora, such as northeastern Florida, which lacks a continuous waterway link to Cahokia? Here, two settlements along the St. Johns River have yielded a handful of presumed Cahokian artifacts of stone and copper, and their presence looks conspicuously out of place on a modern distribution map depicting prized craft items referenced as Cahokia's calling cards (see Fig. 2) (Pauketat 2004:122). Moreover, no evidence of a migrant community, enclave, or even household with domestic artifacts or architectural evidence pointing to any kind of distinguishing Cahokian identity has been recorded within hundreds of kilometers of northeastern Florida. In fact, the closest Early Mississippian (A.D. 1000–1200) mound center is Macon Plateau along the Ocmulgee River in central Georgia. The Lake Jackson site, located to the west in the Florida panhandle, did not burst onto the macroregional scene until the fourteenth century, as Cahokia's geographical influence waned (Jones 1982; Marrinan 2012; Payne 1994).

## St. Johns Tradition of Florida (A.D. 900–1250)

The St. Johns tradition of northeastern Florida is a sequence of regional cultures that existed for two millennia prior to European arrival (Goggin 1952; Milanich 1994). The tradition achieved its broadest geographical extent during early Mississippian times (or locally St. Johns II, AD 900–1250), as it spanned the entire length of the St. Johns River and adjacent Atlantic coast. For this period, domestic refuse indicates a subsistence economy centered mostly on local wild resources, namely fish and shellfish. Maize was not grown along the St. Johns at this time. Current settlement models suggest multi-household communities, marked by extensive middens and an on-site sand mound that served as a community cemetery. Three early St. Johns II earthworks—Grant, Shields, and Mt. Royal—stand out from all others along the river in terms of sheer size, frequency of human burials, and amount and diversity of exotic stone, mineral, and metal (Milanich 1994:269–270; Moore 1894a, b, 1895). Portable objects of both geographic and temporal distances took on sacred value in St. Johns life, as they were rendered imperative to St. Johns ritual and social reproduction (Ashley and Rolland 2014). Participation in exchange networks enabled and fueled contacts with nearby neighbors and distant mound centers and settlements of the Early Mississippian world.

Two St. Johns sites—Mill Cove Complex and Mt. Royal—exhibit more material evidence of engagement with Mississippians than any others in Florida during the tenth through twelfth centuries, positioning them on the forefront of early Mississippian interactions (see various chapters in Ashley and White 2012). In fact, mortuary and ritual contexts at these two civic-ceremonial centers provide the only unequivocal evidence of Florida connections to Cahokia (Ashley 2012:114). The Mill Cove Complex, consisting of the Shields and Grant mounds, is now hypothesized to have been established by a mix of locals and migrants from the south, who coalesced to erect the two mortuary monuments (750 m apart) on relict dune bluffs near the river mouth (Ashley 2020). Mt. Royal emerged organically 100 km upriver (south), immediately north of Lake George. The political economy of these fisher-hunter-gatherers has been characterized as communal, but one in which power and sacred knowledge differentials existed between interest groups (Ashley 2002:168–172; 2012:116–124). No one leader held absolute control over others, but periodic social gatherings and rituals hosted by Mill Cove and Mt. Royal integrated local communities, attracted distant guests, and reinforced the centers' regional preeminence.

Social tensions, played out locally but influenced to some extent by the changing geopolitical landscape of the greater Southeast, precipitated demographic changes throughout the river valley by the late thirteenth century (Ashley 2012:124–25). Mound building ceased at Mt. Royal and Mill Cove, and the latter, at least, seems to have been vacated by St. Johns peoples. The timing of these events is seemingly coincident with the abandonment of Macon Plateau in Georgia and the decline of Cahokia. As a new sociopolitical milieu emerged across the greater Southeast after A.D. 1300, the Apalachicola-Chattahoochee river system of the Florida panhandle became the primary conduit of communication through which people, materials, and information flowed between Florida and major centers of the Mississippian world that now included Moundville and Etowah. The Lake Jackson site in the Florida panhandle rose to prominence at this time.

## "Cahokian" Artifacts at Mill Cove Complex and Mt. Royal

A detailed inventory of all the foreign material taken from the Mt. Royal, Grant, and Shields mounds by C.B. Moore (1894a, 1994b, 1895) in the 1890s is beyond the scope of this essay. Suffice it to say, he recovered a wide assortment of durable, nonlocal materials that included pottery, mica, galena, copper, chert, quartz, greenstone, and other igneous rocks. Shields yielded two spatulate celts and Mt. Royal produced three. Only seven such polished stone celts are known for the entire state of Florida. Raw materials and finished products made their way to the St. Johns River from multiple sources at different times and likely through varying mechanisms of interaction, such as exchange, marriage, and direct procurement, during the period A.D. 900–1250.[1]

Moore's collection highlights a short, yet impressive, list of possible specimens from Cahokia, or more broadly the American Bottom, some 1200 km from northeastern Florida.[2] Mt. Royal includes a tri-notched Cahokia point, whereas Grant Mound yielded two iconic Long-Nosed God maskettes/earpieces (Fig. 3), a rare copper-covered biconical earspool, and a stone biface[3] that resembles a Mill Creek spade-type hoe (Elizabeth Watts, personal communication 2017) or perhaps a chisel of Kaolin chert from Illinois (Charles Cobb, personal communication 2017). All three St. Johns mounds produced small, embossed copper plates, totaling more than 30. Except for the now-famous repousse copper plate with a forked-eye design, remarkably similar to one from Spiro (Phillips and Brown 1978:206–207), and another with depressed lenticular motif from Mt. Royal (Moore 1894a:153, Fig. 14), most plates exhibit simple raised dots and/or circular rings that lack the detail and iconography of later plates.[4] While not a direct link, some of these distinctly hammered copper plates bear a strong stylistic similarity to the Cummings-McCarthy headdress plate from the lower Illinois River valley (Sampson and Esarey 1993:463, 468).

The only sourcing of copper from St. Johns River mounds was Goad's (1978) optical emission spectrographic study that included 10 artifacts recovered by C.B.

---

[1] It has recently been argued that one of the mechanisms responsible for the presence of non-local Ocmulgee Cordmarked pottery from south-central Georgia in St. Johns II contexts was intermarriage (Ashley et al. 2015).

[2] Recognition of the similarities between Grant Mound and American Bottom artifacts is not an original observation on our part. Kelly and Cole (1931) first mentioned it more than 80 years ago, and Williams and Goggin (1956) restated it in the 1950s.

[3] The tentative statements made on the origins of this artifact are based on viewing a stock photograph of the object taken by the National Museum of the American Indian. No one cited as personal communication (or the authors) has examined the artifact in person.

[4] Plates of all sizes typically possess a small center hole, and a number of plates have a large circular protuberance. Some sheets include beaded nodes in a circular pattern around the perforated center or beaded nodes in linear lines extending from the embossed center to the four corners of the plate. Another decorative form includes a continuous raised circle around a perforated center. A recurring comment made by Moore (1894a, b, 1895) with regard to his discovery of copper plates is that most were wrapped in either bark or woven vegetal fibers.

**Fig. 3** Long-Nosed God maskette/earpieces from Grant Mound (photograph courtesy of the National Museum of the American Indian and the Smithsonian Institution)

Moore from Grant Mound and 13 from Mt. Royal. Materials sampled included sections of copper plates, earspools, and rolled tubular beads. Trace element data indicated that these 23 items derived from multiple ore deposits in both the Appalachian Mountains and the Lake Superior region (primarily Keweenaw Peninsula and Isle Royale). She sourced seven to four "ore clusters" in the Great Lakes region and 15 to five "ore clusters" in the Southeast. Specifically, eight Mt. Royal and seven Grant artifacts came from Southeast U.S. geological sources, while five Mt. Royal and three Grant artifacts came from deposits in the Great Lakes region (Goad 1978:136–148). One Grant artifact was linked to float copper from central and southern Wisconsin. Although this suggests multiple sources for copper on north Florida sites, it reveals little about where the plates were manufactured. From a broad-scale stylistic perspective, however, the uniqueness of the plate designs along the St. Johns leaves opens the possibility that some were produced locally from copper imported from different locales. Fragments of unmodified sheet copper could have been obtained at regional transaction centers to the north, as suggested by Goad (1978), or through down-the-line networks.

The three burial mounds (Grant, Shields, and Mt. Royal) are not the only evidence of consecrated acts of ritual and mortuary imprinted on the landscape of these two civic-ceremonial centers. Situated in the shadow of the Shields Mound is Kinzey's Knoll (Fig. 4). This ritual or special-event shell midden contains a staggering quantity and unique variety of faunal materials suggestive of feasting, and an extraordinary assortment of both seemingly domestic and ritual items that includes pottery, decorated bone pins, shell beads, and fragments of greenstone, mica, quartz, hematite, and copper (Ashley and Rolland 2014). Stone points consist of earlier curated or scavenged Archaic forms, contemporaneous arrowheads (Pinellas), and two Cahokia side-notched points (Fig. 5). In addition to evidence for the crafting of ritual artifacts, the presence of scattered human bones and deep pits beneath the shell midden evokes the processing of corpses whose disarticulated and bundled parts were eventually buried in nearby Shields Mound. The Kinzey's Knoll shell midden was a "form of living architecture" that actively conveyed an ongoing history of ritual where ancestors were created, and social relationships, identities, and memories were negotiated among the living and non-living at Mill Cove (McNiven 2013:553).

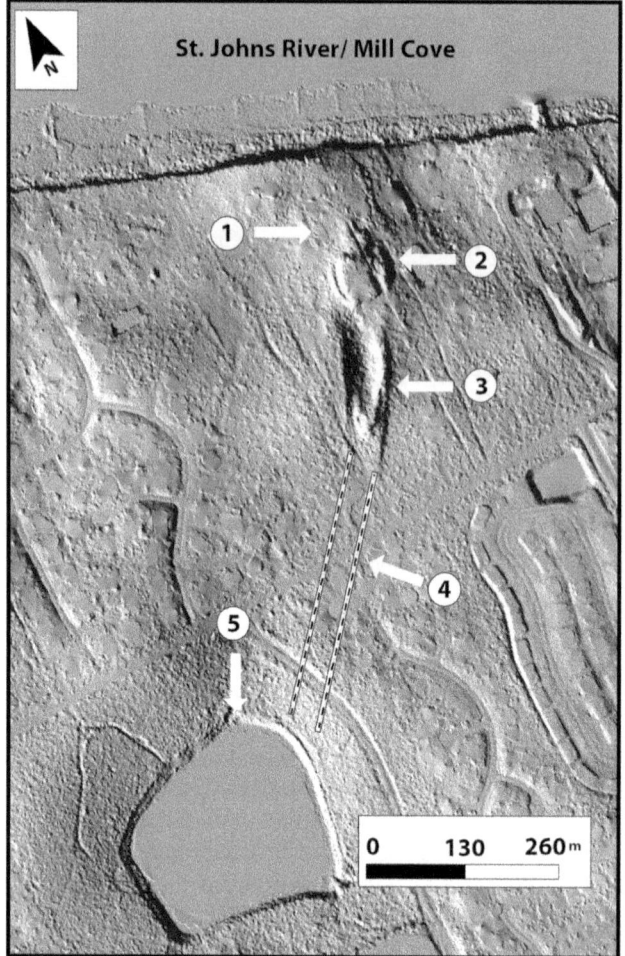

**Fig. 4** Lidar map showing (1) Kinzey's Knoll, (2) Shields burial mound, (3) Shields earthwork, (4) Shields causeway, and (5) artificial pond (enlarged since Moore's time)

Another aspect of Mt. Royal and Shields Mound that is both intriguing and speculative at this time is the possibility that Cahokia may have influenced to some extent new visions of monumentality and site planning at the two St. Johns civic-ceremonial centers. Mt. Royal and Shields each consisted of a set of parallel embankments that formed an "avenue" connecting a large mortuary mound to a pond hundreds of meters away[5] (see Fig. 4; for a depiction of Mt. Royal, see Morgan 1999:213). These two mounds are the only mortuary monuments in Florida that included a set of linear earthworks leading directly to a distant pond. The coupling of mounded earth and water carries strong cosmological implications. At both St. Johns sites, the pond is distant from the community and situated on the side of the mound opposite the river, perhaps

---

[5] According to Moore (1894a:18; 1895:454, 473), Grant also may have possessed earthen embankments leading from the mound, but due to intensive plowing, they disappeared into the surrounding terrain a short distance from the mound. No pond or lake, however, was in the path of the possible embankments at Grant.

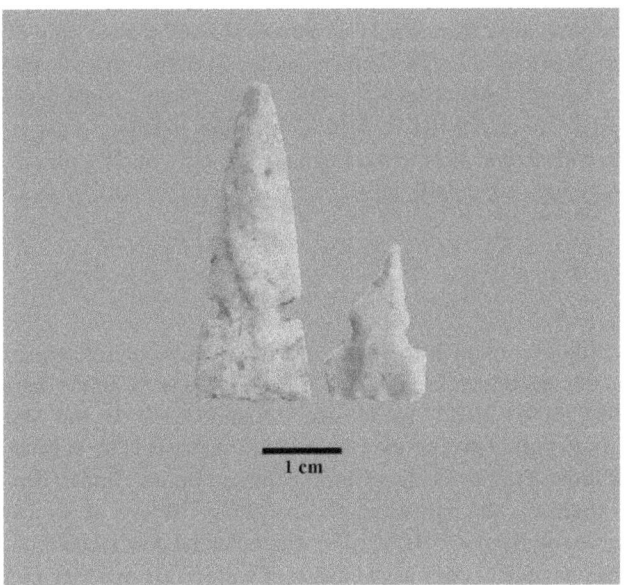

**Fig. 5** Two Cahokia side notched points from Kinzey's Knoll, Mill Cove Complex

representing a spiritual entrance or portal to the watery Under World anchored to Mill Cove's dead by an embankment-lined avenue. Because historic cultivation and development have razed the earthen ridges at Mt. Royal and a large section of those at Shields, we must rely on Moore's descriptions until a geophysical survey of the areas can be performed. Although the embankments at these St. Johns mounds differ from Cahokia's Rattlesnake Causeway in construction details (Baires 2014), each incorporated a raised linear earthwork and water features tied directly to a mounded burial facility.[6]

## Dating St. Johns Contact with Cahokia

Ritual and domestic contexts at the Mill Cove Complex are dated radiometrically to A.D. 900–1250. As for the two Cahokia points, the two-sigma overlap of six calibrated radiometric assays on oyster shells from Kinzey's Knoll date the midden to A.D. 1060–1130 (Ashley 2002:164). At present, a single AMS assay of A.D. 1010–1050 (1 sigma; A.D. 990–1160 2-sigma) is all we have for Mt. Royal. For the Long-Nosed God maskettes, we currently must rely on cross dating in which consensus attributes their production generally to early Mississippian times (Brown et al. 1990:264; Kelly 1991, 2012; Pauketat 2004 114–115; Williams and Goggin 1956). Sampson and Esarey (1993:463-64) also place the biconical earspools from Grant in the A.D. 1000–1200

---

[6] As a reviewer pointed out, embankments are found at earlier Woodland period sites in Florida, such as Crystal River, River Styx, and Fort Center. In fact, Goggin (1952:55) looked to south Florida as a source of influence, noting that the paired ridges on the two St. Johns II sites bear resemblances to those of the Lake Okeechobee area. Fort Center, located deep in the everglades of south Florida, is a ritual landscape that consists of circular and linear earthworks, ditches, and a charnel pond and mound complex (Thompson and Pluckhahn 2011). However, none of the lengthy embankments there directly link a burial mound and a pond.

                                     Springer

timeframe. The previously mentioned Cummings-McCarthy plate from Illinois, with its embossing that resembles the style found along the St. Johns, is assigned loosely to the tenth century, although researchers admit that "sufficient contextual data" from Illinois is lacking to precisely date it (Kelly 2012:300). Taken together, it appears that the St. Johns-Cahokia connection dates to the Lohman and early Stirling phases of Cahokia's founding century (*ca.* A.D. 1050–1150).

## Discussion

Residents of Mill Cove and Mt. Royal were consumers of foreign goods and raw materials that concluded their long travels and use lives in St. Johns mortuary or ritual contexts (Ashley 2002, 2012; Ashley and Rolland 2014). In the past, researchers typically assumed that these exotic items made their way to northeastern Florida through either down-the-line or direct trade between mound (nodal) centers, although these two mechanisms are not mutually exclusive (Brown et al. 1990; Milanich 1994:269; Payne and Scarry 1998:42–48). The outcome was a chain of various-sized spatial links that eventually connected a place of artifact/raw material origin to its locus of final deposition. As a result, there was no direct contact between peoples at the opposite ends. In our case, Floridians and Cahokians never encountered one another; there were always intermediaries. But as Carr's (2006) research on Middle Woodland Hopewellian societies underscores, exotic items are obtained by a variety of means in addition to exchange, such as vision/power questing, pilgrimage, journey to a place of learning, and intermarriage. In effect, myriad social practices and actions at the microscale are responsible for macroscale Mississippian distributions and manifestations.

Distance should not be a precluding factor when considering direct relations between Cahokians and Floridians. Recent stable isotope studies have demonstrated that throughout pre-Columbian times, individuals who spent their early years in locations far from Florida were laid to rest in Florida mounds. For instance, along the middle St. Johns River, two individuals (Burials 13 and 100/101) from the Middle Archaic Harris Creek site were interpreted, based on oxygen isotopic values, as immigrants who originated in nonlocal areas, "perhaps as far north as Tennessee or northern Virginia" (Quinn et al. 2008:2354). To the west in north-central Florida, Burial S426 in Mound B at McKeithen exhibited an oxygen isotope value suggesting she lived in a different region of the Southeast before migrating to McKeithen (Turner et al. 2005:134). In fact, this sole mound interment stood out for her foreign origin, distinctive diet, and prominent burial status. Finally, Burial 12 from a Woodland-period Swift Creek mound at Mayport, 8 km east of the Mill Cove Complex at the mouth of the St. Johns River, exhibited a strontium isotope signature interpreted as "Appalachian-like" by the researchers, meaning, at the very least, "this person did not live in Florida during his/her formative years" (Neill Wallis, personal communication 2017). Researchers now also are beginning to entertain the possibility that distant Hopewellian peoples visited Crystal River along Florida's Gulf coast during the Middle Woodland period (Pluckhahn and Thompson 2018:97).

The extremely low-volume, high-quality, and remote location of Cahokian-derived artifacts in northeastern Florida suggest acquisition through direct means (Ashley

2012:114; Ashley and Rolland 2014:275; Kelly 2012:309). Following this line of reasoning, Pauketat (2004:121) poses the possibility that Cahokians may have left "calling cards" in distant locations they visited to extract exotic raw materials, trade, missionize, or enact diplomacy (see Fig. 2). Among the preserved items proposed as referents are Cahokia style arrowheads and Long-Nosed God maskettes, both of which occur exclusively in St. Johns II contexts in Florida. Although not mentioned as a calling card, the copper-foiled wooden biconical earspools are rare and only known for the Powell Mound (Mound 86) along the western edge of Cahokia, the nearby Booker T. Washington site in the American Bottom, and Spiro in Oklahoma (Brown 1976:297–299; Sampson and Esarey 1993:458). None of these items has been documented for sites in the adjacent state of Georgia, and only a single maskette of shell has been recovered in far northwestern Alabama, some 900 km from northeastern Florida.

Long-Nosed God maskettes or ear ornaments, made of copper, shell, or bone, are known for 20 sites in North America (Kelly 1991:73–74; Williams and Goggin 1956). Of the 15 known copper specimens, complete pairs come from seven sites. The geographical distribution of these sites is interesting, with two originating from the American Bottom and the others coming from five sites positioned on the margins of the Mississippian world (Fig. 6): at Aztalan in Wisconsin to the north, Spiro and Harlan to the west, Gahagan to the south, and Grant Mound to the southeast. Although the only pair from the Greater Cahokia area hails from the St. Louis Mound groups, its location in relation to the other sites suggests Greater Cahokia was the production center (Hall 1997:153; Pauketat 2009:145; Sampson and Esarey 1993:473). That these prized items occur only at sites situated a great distance from their presumed place of origin speaks to their intended use in long-distance interactions. Certain early Cahokians appear to have left their home at the center of the world and embarked on journeys to the ends of the earth, perhaps to explore, seek knowledge, build alliances, obtain powerful objects, spread the word of Cahokia, or any combinations thereof.

The St. Johns River (Florida) is significantly distant from Cahokia, and unlike most sites outside the American Bottom with distinctive Cahokia-made artifacts, the area is not accessible by canoe travel alone; such a trip would have required portaging *via* land trails through portions of the Georgia-Alabama-Tennessee border region. Little (1987:66) estimates that a round trip journey from Cahokia to northeastern Florida would have taken about 118 days. The Atlantic coast would have been far less accessible and much more difficult to reach than the Gulf of Mexico, which is directly linked to Cahokia *via* the Mississippi River. Such an arduous undertaking to the Atlantic Ocean likely required great fortitude to navigate a physically, socially, and linguistically challenging trek through foreign territories also marked with perceived supernatural perils associated with geographically distant and unknown lands. Overcoming these many obstacles would have been a tremendous show of ability, greatly enhancing one's home reputation. Ethnographically, those successfully returning from long-distance sojourns are awarded varying degrees of ritual grace, social respect, and political prestige (Helms 1988:56). Cahokian elites would have possessed the resources and incentives to enact such connections over vast distances. Visiting different Mississippian mound centers along a route from Cahokia to the sea may have presented a traveler with a network of contacts to boast of, upon a triumphant arrival back home. Esoteric knowledge, life experience, and exotic materials would have been gained by journeying to the revered Atlantic Ocean.

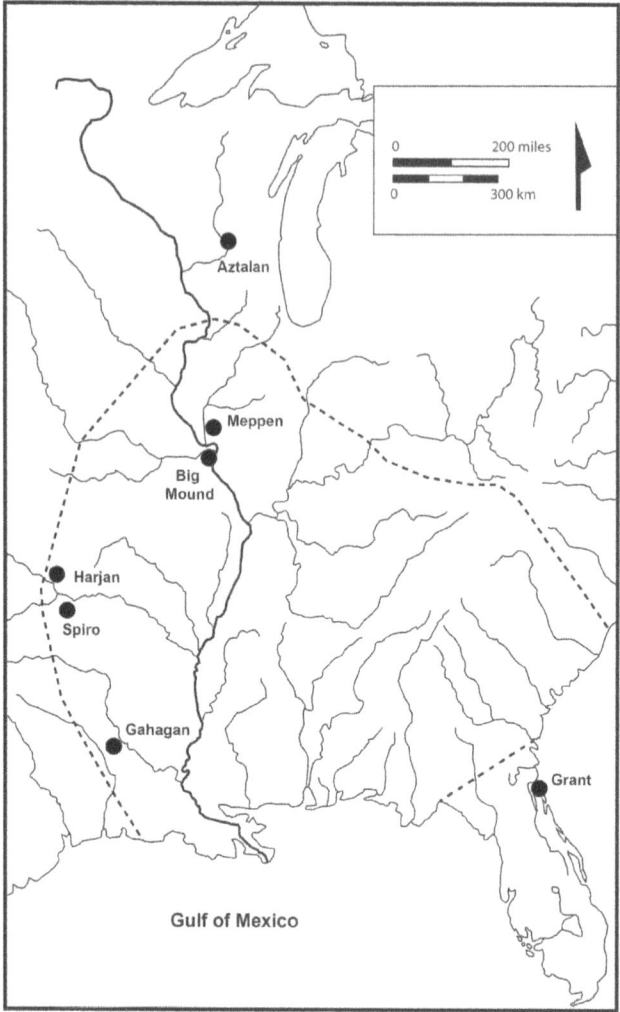

Aztalan

Meppen

Big
Mound

Harjan

Spiro

Gahagan

Grant

Gulf of Mexico

0 _____ 200 miles
0 _____ 300 km

**Fig. 6** Distribution of pairs of Long-Nosed God Masks in copper

Macon Plateau is the only primary Early Mississippian civic-ceremonial center with direct access to the Atlantic Ocean. Located in central Georgia, this multi-mound settlement has long been considered an archaeological anomaly, leading some to consider it a community founded by Mississippian migrants (Williams 1994) and others to propose "perhaps its pioneers were even Cahokian immigrants" (Cobb and King 2015:124). A canoe trip of only a few days would have taken visitors from Macon Plateau to the Atlantic Ocean by way of the Ocmulgee and Altamaha rivers. A would-be priest, shaman, long-distance specialist, or prospective leader may have undertaken the long journey to the ocean as a vision quest in preparation for his/her life calling (see Pauketat 2009:90 for a similar scenario for north of Cahokia). A direct encounter with the expansive salt waters would have evoked a range of sensory and emotional experiences, as they walked the sandy, shell-strewn beaches to the sound of crashing waves. Moreover, at differing times, they would have been eyewitnesses to the gradual emergence of the sun and moon out of the endless waters. An Atlantic coast sunrise presents a different panorama than that of the Gulf of Mexico, rendering it a unique ocean experience at the literal eastern edge of This World. One would expect an extended stay near the ocean shore, allowing a knowledge-seeking wayfarer(s) the opportunity to view the moon in all of its monthly phases.

At present, no coastal sites at or near the mouth of the Altamaha River in Georgia reveal evidence of interactions with greatly distant Early Mississippian realms such as Cahokia. In fact, the only support for this along the eastern seaboard comes from the Mill Cove Complex. For some reason, Mill Cove was able to secure more prized pieces of exotica than any other Atlantic tidewater community during the tenth through twelfth centuries (Ashley 2012:112–115). Knowledge of Mill Cove to residents of Macon Plateau is conceivable based on a deep history of interaction between hunter-gatherers of the lower Ocmulgee River region and northeastern Florida (Ashley et al. 2015:304). The Ocmulgee territory lies immediately south of Macon Plateau along a direct waterway route, eventually linking Macon Plateau to Mill Cove. The cordmarked pottery made by Early Mississippian-period Ocmulgee foragers occurs in large numbers, as imports and local copies, at Mill Cove and other coeval St. Johns sites, including Mt. Royal (Ashley et al. 2015; Rolland 2005). Mill Cove is only a week or so travel by canoe from Macon Plateau, and an additional few days would have taken a journeyer to Mt. Royal. There, they would have encountered a massive widening of the St. Johns River that was described in awe by naturalist William Bartram in 1791 as "the little ocean of Lake George" (Van Doren 1955:103). At 24 km in length and 10 km in width, its daunting presence may very well have appeared to mark the world's southern edge.

We know from sixteenth-century documents that interactions with outsiders often required diplomacy and gift giving (Smith and Hally 1992). Drawing inspiration from the historic Pawnee Calumet Ceremony, Hall (1991:31; 1997:151) proposes that the conveying of Long-Nosed God maskettes was part of an adoption ritual that cemented fictive kinship relationships between Cahokian leaders and political outsiders. Pauketat (2009:145) goes further and identifies them as "badges or gifts handed out to people who would have forever after been affiliated with Cahokia." Moreover, in ethnographically documented encounters such as this, "ideology is likely involved" (Helms 1988:82). Cahokian travelers thus may have used this time to proselytize and spread the word of Cahokia at local social gatherings, extolling its virtues and greatness through the ritualized reciting of cosmological and creation narratives that placed Cahokia at the center of the world (Pauketat 2005:205–207). Such retellings would have been visually enhanced with the aid of numinously meaningful and potent trappings such as Long-Nosed God earpieces and other sacred paraphernalia.

In these historical moments, the transfer of social valuables or other items does not reflect the social interaction but (re)creates it (Gosden and Marshall 1999; Miller 2005). Objects are active constituents and fundamental to the construction of durable social relations. Their passing from one to another sets the stage for future interactions between giver and receiver (Mauss 1967). Such gifts take on a biography of their own that connects recipients to the original makers and all those who subsequently possessed them (Gosden and Marshall 1999:173). Moreover, part of their value stems from the geographical and temporal scales and webs of social relations through which they circulate (Spielmann 2002:201). As these materials move, their use, function, and/

or meaning maintain the capacity to transform, as they become part of the historical process. Objects are infused with meaning, but this meaning is not static or fixed. Rather it is situational and undergoes change as people engage each other through objects in particular contexts (Kopytoff 1986:68).

Cahokian wayfarers were likely presented with offerings of a local nature in their interactions with St. Johns peoples, and the act of gift giving would have fostered positive relations and the right of access to endemic raw materials like shell, shark teeth, yaupon holly, and other portable coastal resources that accompanied them on their return to Cahokia (Kelly 2012:305, 309). Those resources, originating directly from the ocean waters of the eastern horizon where the sun ascends each day, undoubtedly carried indexical connotations and extraordinary cosmological significance. Even more precious than tangible objects may have been the privileged stories of the sea locals knew and impressed upon their visitors from afar. Many cultures imbue distant places with distinctive energies or properties bordering on the supernatural, and knowledge gained from far-off realms combined with physical tokens of these places is associated with power (Helms 1992:186). Gaining mastery of esoteric knowledge and the cosmological realm would have been paramount to the success of community leaders and religious specialists at Cahokia and other "knowledge-based" Mississippian polities where "ritual authority" was used to "overcome constraints on political and economic growth" (Cobb 2003:78).

For St. Johns functionaries, the foreign items likely held cosmological powers because of their distant origins, mystical properties, object biographies, and connections to sacred knowledge (Helms 1988, 1992). What is most important about the "adoption" of foreign objects and ideas is not their acceptance, but the manner in which they are redefined culturally and put to local use (Kopytoff 1986:67). Because of their archaeological occurrence in ceremonial and mortuary contexts, these inalienable items conceivably assumed ritual significance for St. Johns peoples as material citations and holders of memories signaling their social affiliation with distant peoples and lands (Ashley and Rolland 2014:275). Engaging these objects in rituals would have elicited "a presence and a history" connecting Mill Cove to the biographies and histories of those objects and places as well as past peoples and social relations inextricably entangled within them (Meskell 2004:45). Some of these powerful objects might have had animating powers, alone or in combination with other objects (Pauketat 2013; Zedeño 2008). For instance, the Long-Nosed God maskettes of copper, once donned within a culturally sanctioned and spiritually charged ceremonial milieu, perhaps "enabled one's relationships to all the causal powers of this world and the next" (Pauketat 2013:7). As such, these goods were not merely mnemonics or calling cards but social agents that played a role in the transformation of St. Johns II societies during early Mississippian times.

Based on available evidence, we cannot rule out the possibility that individuals from northeastern Florida undertook similar quests of their own to visit distant lands such as Cahokia. Perhaps in response to hearing of the physical and ideological wonders of Cahokia, some St. Johns representative(s) made a pilgrimage there to experience it for themselves. Recent studies are now highlighting the generative role of pilgrimages to Cahokia—and its related mound centers or shrines such as Emerald—in the construction of Cahokia (Skousen 2016). Some of the exotic items linked to the American Bottom might have been procured there by locals and brought back to northeastern

Florida, where they served, in part, as powerful reminders of the sacred center and the relationships their visit engendered. A pilgrim may have easily obtained certain objects, such as Cahokia arrowheads and stone hoes, during a journey to the American Bottom, but the copper Long-Nosed God maskettes and biconical earspools were not some sort of mass-produced trinket available to anyone. Acquisition of these mystical objects probably required intimate and powerful negotiations with high-ranking Cahokians, requiring St. Johns peoples to legitimate their identity and prove their worth to Cahokia, particularly if the visitors were unknown to anyone living there. Those returning from Cahokia with such proof of a successful spiritual journey likely brought back sacred knowledge in the form of stories, rituals, and architectural details (Kantner and Vaughn 2012:70).

During early Mississippian times, St. Johns groups actively sought out and incorporated exotica into their ritual and mortuary life. Although specifics are still unclear, the assortment of nonlocal raw materials and finished products at Mill Cove and Mt. Royal appears to have entered northeastern Florida from multiple sources and through various modes of interaction, as social bonds were continuously forged or broken at different times and in different places, with interacting parties negotiating in their own interests. Throughout its movement, each item accumulated its own social entanglements and powers. In addition to materializing relationships with distant and foreign others, some objects, based on their material and metaphorical properties, carried cosmic significance that helped link the living and the supernatural. In effect, these prized items instantiated forces that had no pre-materialized presence.

Although Moore's (1895:456–468, 475–488) account of his mound excavations is incomplete and vague, he often notes that various pieces of exotica were at times deposited together as caches in the mounds at Grant, Shields, and Mt. Royal, suggesting these artifact concentrations might represent the remains of bundles. This is especially true of tobacco pipes, whelk shell cups, and areas of red pigment that Moore notes are frequently associated with "many" objects. In addition, copper plates often were not worn at the time of interment but "wrapped in bark or in vegetable fabric," perhaps to contain their powerful or animating properties. Among many Native American groups, these bundles and their evocative constituents are cast as "object-persons" who embody "both the physical world and the rules and regulations of the cosmic, natural, and social orders" (Zedeño 2008:365). In St. Johns ritual and mortuary contexts, such powerful entities may have been called upon to draw connections to past places and other worlds. In the same way, curated artifacts, such as Archaic projectile points, stone beads, and bannerstones along with Woodland-period tobacco pipes, found in these same mounds may have served to summon and enliven ancestor spirits. These potent material things were deposited in mortuary mounds, singularly and in bundles, as "pieces of a cosmological map that together with other artifacts and burials served to contextualize their place in the cosmos" (Lucero 2010:142–43).

## Summary

As Cahokia's size swelled, populations soon moved outward to places near and far. However, none of these diasporic communities ever came close to Florida. Cahokians, however, did establish contacts with peoples in remote areas possessing mystical landmarks and places, powerful forces, and/or raw materials. In this essay, we have taken early steps in an attempt to understand the material linkages between Cahokia and northeastern Florida through the occurrence of Cahokian-derived objects on St. Johns River sites during the Early Mississippian period. Moving beyond the simple notion of trade, we suggest episodes of direct contact between the two regions, as travelers from Cahokia visited Mill Cove and Mt. Royal, or *vice versa*. The frequency, length of visit, and duration of any direct interaction between St. Johns and Cahokian peoples remain unclear. Regardless of who undertook the long-distance journeys, St. Johns groups were part of an array of tenth- and eleventh-century relationships that contributed to the making of Cahokia. At the same time, social interactions with Cahokia, other Mississippian communities, and the objects they made and possessed played a role in reshaping St. Johns II societies. Archaeological investigations at the Mill Cove Complex continues, as we work to refine our temporal resolution, conduct chemical sourcing, and perform geophysical survey to better understand interactions at all scales.

**Acknowledgments**   We would like to thank Jayur Mehta, Sarah Baires, Melissa Baltus, and Liz Watts Malouchos for inviting two Floridians to participate in their 2017 SEAC symposium on Cahokia' Diaspora. Special thanks also to Vicki Rolland, Nancy White, and two anonymous reviewers for their insightful comments on an earlier version of this paper.

# References

Alt, S. M. (2002). Identities, traditions, and diversity in Cahokia's uplands. *Midcontinental Journal of Archaeology, 27*, 217–235.

Alt, S. (2010). Complexity in action (s): retelling the Cahokia story. In S. Alt (Ed.), *Ancient complexities: new perspectives in pre-Columbian North America* (pp. 119–137). Salt Lake City: Foundations of Archaeological Inquiry Series. University of Utah Press.

Ashley, K. (2002). On the periphery of the early Mississippian world: within and beyond northeastern Florida. *Southeastern Archaeology, 21*, 162–177.

Ashley, K. (2012). Early St. Johns II interaction, exchange, and politics: a view from northeastern Florida. In K. Ashley & N. M. White (Eds.), *Late prehistoric Florida: archaeology at the edge of the Mississippian world* (pp. 100–125). Gainesville: University Press of Florida.

Ashley, K. (2020). Moving to where the river meets the sea: origins of the Mill Cove Complex. In E. Watts-Malouchos & A. Betzenhauser (Eds.), *Reconsidering Mississippian households and communities (in press)*. Tuscaloosa: University of Alabama Press.

Ashley, K., & Rolland, V. L. (2014). Ritual at the Mill Cove Complex: realms beyond the river. In N. J. Wallis & A. R. Randall (Eds.), *New histories of pre-Columbian Florida* (pp. 262–282). Gainesville: University Press of Florida.

Ashley, K., Wallis, N., Wallis, J., & Glascock, M. D. (2015). Forager interactions on the edge of the early Mississippian world: neutron activation analysis of Ocmulgee and St. Johns pottery. *American Antiquity, 80*, 290–311.

Ashley, K & White, N.M. (2012). Late prehistoric Florida: archaeology at the edge of the Mississippian world (Eds.). Gainesville: University Press of Florida.

Baires, S. E. (2014). Cahokia's rattlesnake causeway. *Midcontinental Journal of Archaeology, 39*, 145–162.

Baltus, M., & Baires, S. (2020). Defining diaspora: a view from the Cahokia homeland. *Journal of Archaeological Method and Theory* this issue.

Blitz, J. H. (2010). New perspectives in Mississippian archaeology. *Journal of Archaeological Research, 18*, 1–39.

Bloch, L. (2018). Tales of Esnesv: indigenous oral traditions about trader-diplomats in ancient southeastern North America. *American Anthropologist, 120*, 781–793.

Brown, J.A. (1976). *Spiro studies: the artifacts*. Vol. 4, Second part of the third annual report of Caddoan archaeology. Spiro focus research, Norman.

Brown, J. A., Kerber, R. A., & Winters, H. D. (1990). Trade and the evolution of exchange relations at the beginning of the Mississippian period. In B. Smith (Ed.), *The Mississippian emergence* (pp. 251–274). Washington, D.C.: Smithsonian Institution Press.

Bradley, R. (2000). *An archaeology of natural places*. London: Routledge.

Brubaker, R. (2005). The 'diaspora' diaspora. *Ethnic and Racial Studies, 28,* 1–19.

Buchanan, M. (2020). Common field: a Cahokian diaspora to southeast Missouri? *Journal of Archaeological Method and Theory* this issue.

Carr, C. (2006). Rethinking interregional Hopewellian "interaction". In C. Carr & D. T. Case (Eds.), *Gathering Hopewell: society, ritual, and ritual interaction* (pp. 575–623). New York: Springer.

Cobb, C. R. (1991). Social reproduction and the longue durée in the prehistory of the midcontinental United States. In P. W. Preucel (Ed.), *Processual and postprocessual archaeologies* (pp. 168–182). Carbondale: Occasional Paper No. 10, Center for Archaeological Investigations, Southern Illinois University.

Cobb, C.R. (2003). Mississippian chiefdoms: how complex? *Annual Review of Anthropology, 32,* 63-84.

Cobb, C. R., & King, A. (2015). The rise and demise of Mississippian capitals in the Southeast. In T. R. Pauketat & S. M. Alt (Eds.), *Medieval Mississippians: the Cahokian world* (pp. 119–125). Santa Fe: SAR Press.

Connaway, J. M., Parish, R. M., & Johnson, J. K. (2020). Carson, Cahokia, and lithic raw material. *Journal of Archaeological Method and Theory* this issue.

Emerson, T. E., & Lewis, R. B. (1991). Cahokia and the hinterlands: middle Mississippian cultures of the Midwest (Eds.). Urbana: University of Illinois Press.

Ethridge, R. (2017). Navigating the Mississippian world: infrastructure in the sixteenth-century Native South. In G. A. Waslekov & M. T. Smith (Eds.), *Forging southeastern identities: social archaeology, ethnohistory, and folklore of the Mississippian to early historic south* (pp. 62–84). Tuscaloosa: University of Alabama Press.

Goad, S. I. (1978). Exchange networks in the prehistoric southeastern United States. Athens: Unpublished Ph.D. dissertation, Department of Anthropology, University of Georgia.

Goggin, J. M. (1952). *Space and time perspective in northern St. Johns archaeology, Florida* (p. 47). New Haven: Yale University Publications in Anthropology.

Gosden, C., & Marshall, Y. (1999). The cultural biography of objects. *World Archaeology, 31,* 169–178.

Green, W. (1997). Middle Mississippian peoples. *The Wisconsin Archeologist, 78,* 202–223.

Hall, R. L. (1991). Cahokia identity and interaction models of Cahokia Mississippian. In T. E. Emerson & R. B. Lewis (Eds.), *Cahokia and the hinterlands: middle Mississippian cultures of the Midwest* (pp. 3–34). Urbana: University of Illinois Press.

Hall, R. L. (1997). *An archaeology of the soul: North American Indian belief and ritual*. Urbana: University of Illinois Press.

Helms, M. W. (1988). *Ulysses' sail: an ethnographic odyssey of power, knowledge, and geographical distance*. Princeton: Princeton University Press.

Helms, M. W. (1992). Political lords and political ideology in southeastern chiefdoms: comments and observations. In A. W. Barker & T. R. Pauketat (Eds.), *Lords of the southeast: social inequality and the native elites of southeastern North America* (pp. 186–194). Archaeological Papers of the American Association 3.

Johnson, J. K. (1994). Prehistoric exchange in the southeast. In T. Baugh & J. Ericson (Eds.), *Prehistoric exchange systems in North America* (pp. 99–125). New York: Plenum.

Jones, A. M. (2001). Drawn from memory: the archaeology of aesthetics and the aesthetics of archaeology in earlier Bronze Age Britain and the present. *World Archaeology, 33,* 334–356.

Jones, B.C. (1982). Southern cult manifestations at the Lake Jackson site, Leon County, Florida. *Midcontinental Journal of Archaeology, 7,* 3-44.

Kantner, J., & Vaughn, K. J. (2012). Pilgrimage as costly signal: religiously motivated cooperation in Chaco and Nasca. *Journal of Anthropological Archaeology, 31,* 66–82.

Kelly, J. E. (1991). Cahokia and its role as a gateway center in interregional exchange. In T. E. Emerson & R. B. Lewis (Eds.), *Cahokia and the hinterlands: middle Mississippian cultures of the Midwest* (pp. 61–82). Urbana: University of Illinois Press.

Kelly, J. E. (2012). The Mississippi period in Florida: a view from the Mississippian world of Cahokia. In K. Ashley & N. M. White (Eds.), *Late prehistoric Florida: archaeology at the edge of the Mississippian world* (pp. 296–310). Gainesville: University Press of Florida.

 Springer

Kelly, J. E., & Brown, J. A. (2014). Cahokia: the processes and principles of the creation of an early Mississippian city. In A. T. Creekmore & K. D. Fisher (Eds.), *Making ancient cities: space and place in early urban societies* (pp. 292–376). New York: Cambridge University Press.

Kelly, A., & Cole, F. C. (1931). Rediscovering Illinois. In *Blue book of the state of Illinois 1931-1932* (pp. 328–344). Springfield: State of Illinois.

Kopytoff, I. (1986). The cultural biography of things: commoditization as process. In A. Appadurai (Ed.), *The social life of things: commodities in cultural perspective* (pp. 64–91). Cambridge: Cambridge University Press.

Lafferty, R. H. (1994). Prehistoric exchange in the lower Mississippi valley. In T. Baugh & J. Ericson (Eds.), *Prehistoric exchange systems in North America* (pp. 177–213). New York: Plenum.

Lazzari, M. (2005). The texture of things: objects, people, and landscape in northwest Argentina (first millennium A.D.). In L. Meskell (Ed.), *Archaeologies of materiality* (pp. 126–161). Malden: Blackwell Publishing.

Little, E. A. (1987). Inland waterways in the northeast. *Midcontinental Journal of Archaeology, 12*, 55–68.

Lucero, L. J. (2010). Materialized cosmology among ancient Maya commoners. *Journal of Social Archaeology, 10*, 138–167.

Marrinan, R. A. (2012). Fort Walton culture in the Tallahassee hills. In K. Ashley & N. M. White (Eds.), *Late prehistoric Florida: archaeology at the edge of the Mississippian world* (pp. 186–230). Gainesville: University Press of Florida.

Mauss, M. (1967). *The gift: forms and functions of exchange in archaic societies.* New York: W. W. Norton.

McNiven, I. J. (2013). Ritualized middening practices. *Journal of Archaeological Method and Theory, 20*, 552–587.

Mehta, J., & Connaway, J. (2020). Trade diaspora as considered through household archaeology at Carson. *Journal of Archaeological Method and Theory* this issue.

Meskell, L. (Ed.). (2004). *Object world in Ancient Egypt.* Oxford: Berg.

Milanich, J. T. (1994). *Archaeology of precolumbian Florida.* Gainesville: University of Florida Press.

Miller, D. (2005). Materiality: an introduction. In D. Miller (Ed.), *Materiality* (pp. 1–50). Durham: Duke University Press.

Moore, C. B. (1894a). Certain sand mounds of the St. Johns River, Florida. Part I. *Journal of the Academy of Natural Sciences of Philadelphia, 10*, 5–103.

Moore, C. B. (1894b). Certain sand mounds of the St. Johns River, Florida. Part II. *Journal of the Academy of Natural Sciences of Philadelphia, 10*, 129–246.

Moore, C. B. (1895). Certain sand mounds of Duval County, Florida. *Journal of the Academy of Natural Sciences of Philadelphia, 10*, 448–502.

Morgan, W. N. (1999). *Precolumbian architecture in eastern North America.* Gainesville: University of Florida Press.

Pauketat, T. R. (2004). *Ancient Cahokia and the Mississippians.* Cambridge: Cambridge University Press.

Pauketat, T. R. (2005). The forgotten history of the Mississippians. In T. R. Pauketat & D. D. Loren (Eds.), *North American archaeology* (pp. 187–212). Oxford: Blackwell.

Pauketat, T. R. (2009). *Cahokia: ancient America's great city on the Mississippi.* New York: Penguin Books.

Pauketat, T. R. (2013). *An archaeology of the cosmos: rethinking agency and religion in ancient America.* London: Routledge.

Pauketat, T. R., & Alt, S. M. (2003). Mounds, memory, and contested Mississippian history. In R. Van Dyke & S. Alcock (Eds.), *Archaeologies of memory* (pp. 151–179). Oxford: Blackwell Press.

Pauketat, T. R., Boszhardt, R. F., & Benden, D. M. (2015). Trempealeau entanglements: an ancient colony's causes and effects. *American Antiquity, 80*, 260–289.

Payne, C. (1994). Mississippian capitals: an archaeological investigation of Precolumbian political structure. Gainesville: Ph.D. dissertation, Department of Anthropology, University of Florida.

Payne, C., & Scarry, J. F. (1998). Town structure at the edge of the Mississippian world. In R. B. Lewis & C. Stout (Eds.), *Mississippian towns and sacred spaces* (pp. 22–48). Tuscaloosa: University of Alabama Press.

Peregrine, P. N., & Lekson, S. H. (2012). The North American oikoumene. In T. R. Pauketat (Ed.), *The Oxford handbook of north American archaeology* (pp. 64–72). Oxford: Oxford University Press.

Phillips, P., & Brown, J. E. (1978). *Pre-Columbian shell engravings from Spiro.* Cambridge: Peabody Museum Press.

Pluckhahn, T. J., & Thompson, V. D. (2018). *New histories of village life at Crystal River.* Gainesville: University of Florida Press.

Quinn, R. L., Tucker, B. D., & Krigbaum, J. (2008). Diet and mobility in middle Archaic Florida: stable isotopic and faunal evidence from Harris Creek archaeological site (8V024), Tick Island. *Journal of Archaeological Science, 5*, 2346–2356.

Rolland, V. R. (2005). An investigation of St. Johns and Ocmulgee series pottery recovered from the Shields site (8DU12). *The Florida Anthropologist, 58*, 211–238.

Sampson, K. W., & Esarey, D. (1993). A survey of elaborate Mississippian copper artifacts from Illinois. *Illinois Archaeology, 5*, 452–480.

Skousen, B. J. (2016). Pilgrimage and the construction of Cahokia: a view from the Emerald site. Urbana: Ph.D. dissertation, Department of Anthropology, University of Illinois at Urbana-Champaign.

Smith, M. T., & Hally, D. J. (1992). Chiefly behavior: evidence from sixteenth century Spanish accounts. In A. W. Barker & T. R. Pauketat (Eds.), *Lords of the southeast: social inequality and the native elites of southeastern North America* (pp. 99–110). Archaeological Papers of the American Association 3.

Spielmann, K. A. (2002). Feasting, craft production, and ritual mode of production in small-scale societies. *American Anthropologist, 104*, 195–207.

Thomas, J. (1999). An economy of substances in earlier Neolithic Britain. In J. E. Robb (Ed.), *Material symbols culture and economy in prehistory, Center for Archaeological Investigations Occasional Paper 26* (pp. 70–89). Carbondale: Southern Illinois University.

Thompson, V. D., & Pluckhahn, T. J. (2011). Monumentalization and ritual landscapes at Fort Center in the Lake Okeechobee basin of south Florida. *Journal of Anthropological Archaeology, 31*, 49–65.

Turner, B. L., Kingston, J. D., & Milanich, J. T. (2005). Isotopic evidence of immigration linked to status during the Weeden Island and Suwannee Valley periods in north Florida. *Southeastern Archaeology, 24*, 121–136.

Van Doren, M. (1955). *The Travels of William Bartram (1791)*. New York: Dover Press.

Waselkov, G. A. (1989). Indian maps of the colonial Southeast. In P. H. Wood, G. A. Waselkov, & M. T. Hatley (Eds.), *Powhatan's mantle: Indians in the colonial Southeast* (pp. 292–343). Lincoln: University of Nebraska Press.

Williams, M. (1994). The origins of the Macon Plateau site. In D. J. Hally (Ed.), *Ocmulgee archaeology 1936–1986* (pp. 130–137). Athens: University of Georgia Press.

Williams, S., & Goggin, J. M. (1956). The long nosed god mask in eastern United States. *The Missouri Archaeologist, 18*, 1–72.

Wilson, G. D., Delaney, C. M., & Millhouse, P. G. (2017). The mississippianization of the Illinois and Apple river valleys. In G. D. Wilson (Ed.), *Mississippian Beginnings* (pp. 97–129). Gainesville: University of Florida Press.

Zedeño, M. N. (2008). Bundled worlds: the roles and interactions of complex objects from the North American Plains. *Journal of Archaeological Method and Theory, 15*, 262–278.

**Publisher's Note**     Springer Nature remains neutral with regard to jurisdictional claims in published maps and institutional affiliations.

Journal of Archaeological Method and Theory (2020) 27:28–53
https://doi.org/10.1007/s10816-019-09432-y

# Mississippian Culture and Cahokian Identities as Considered Through Household Archaeology at Carson, a Monumental Center in North Mississippi

Jayur Madhusudan Mehta[1] · John M. Connaway[2]

Published online: 11 December 2019
© Springer Science+Business Media, LLC, part of Springer Nature 2019

## Abstract

The Carson site in northwest Mississippi is a monumental Mississippian center with evidence of large and small earthen mounds, an extensive palisaded village, and a bundle-burial mortuary complex. Over 70 houses have been uncovered from over a decade of salvage excavations at the site; these households bear evidence of local populations in the form of ceramics and stone tools, often belonging to the Parchman phase. In addition, numerous household structures that bear resemblance to Mississippian buildings from Cahokia and the American Bottom and that date to the Lohmann, Stirling, and Moorehead phases have also been discovered. The presence of these non-local structures and their material culture has provoked continued discussion on the nature of interactions between these two important centers. Herein, we offer a discussion on the nature of trade, diaspora, and Mississippian culture at Carson based on the analysis of material culture and architecture bearing Cahokian influences.

**Keywords** Diaspora · Cahokia · Carson · Household archaeology · Identity · Migration

## Introduction

Agricultural, monument building societies have long been studied in the Lower Mississippi Valley (LMV), the Central Mississippi Valley (CMV), and the American Bottom (AB). Starting at the beginning of the second millennium AD and from Wisconsin to Louisiana, almost the entire Mississippi River Valley (MRV) was populated by village-dwelling, agricultural and foraging societies that constructed earthen and shell mounds, practiced long-distance trade, and shared an iconographic system

Chapter 3 was originally published as Mehta, J. M. & Connaway, J. M. Journal of Archaeological Method and Theory (2020) 27:28–53. https://doi.org/10.1007/s10816-019-09432-y.

✉ Jayur Madhusudan Mehta
    jmehta@fsu.edu

[1]  Department of Anthropology, Florida State University, Tallahassee, FL 32310, USA

[2]  Independent Scholar, Helena, AR 72342, USA

(Brain 1989; McNutt 1996; Morse and Morse 1990; Reilly and Garber 2007; Smith 1990). At the center of this network was Cahokia, and its influence spread far and wide (*i.e.*, Kelly 1991a; Pauketat *et al.* 2015). This article, part of the larger consideration in this special issue of JAMT, focuses on the long documented yet still unclear relationships between Cahokia and southern Mississippian polities in the LMV (Fig. 1). In this article, we focus on the Carson site, a mile-long Mississippian center with over 80 small house mounds and 6 large monumental earthworks, including an earthen berm enclosing a village (Johnson 1987; Mehta *et al.* 2017a; Thomas 1894; Fig. 2).

Fleeting traces of Cahokian-style pottery and noteworthy quantities of white, Burlington chert at Carson have been used to signify trade with Mississippian groups in the American Bottom (Johnson 1987; Mehta *et al.* 2017b). Until recently, we did not know if these material goods represented down-the-line trade or the presence of Cahokians at

**Fig. 1** The locations of archaeological sites discussed in the text are shown above

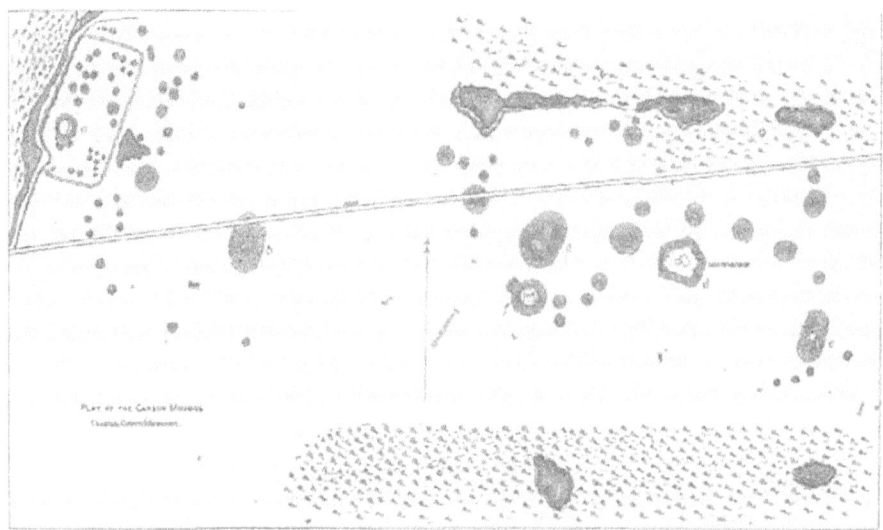

**Fig. 2** Map of the Carson mounds site from the late nineteenth century survey led by William Henry Holmes and Cyrus Thomas (Thomas 1894, p. 11). Mounds A–F are labeled and are the larger mounds at the site. Over 80 unnamed mounds are also shown, many of which were likely smaller house mounds

Carson[1]. SR-isotope analyses of human remains from Carson's mortuary complex would provide the necessary dataset to clarify whether individuals from the American Bottom were directly present in the Yazoo Basin, as might have been the case at localities to the north, like at Aztalan (Slater *et al.* 2014); until such time, material culture and household architecture are the best available proxies for defining the Cahokian presence at Carson.

Jeffrey P. Brain (11, 12) concluded, based on Cahokian material found at Winterville, a large Mississippian site 180 km to the south of Carson via the Mississippi River, and at Lake George, a Coles Creek and Plaquemine/Mississippian center a bit further to the south, that "strong, organized contact from the Cahokia climax of the Stirling and/or Moorehead phases intruded deeply into the Coles Creek world [the LMV]" (Brain 1989, p. 117). While the nature of this "strong, organized contact" has yet to be fully parsed, provocative new household data from the Carson site do demonstrate the following:

1. The presence of multiple American Bottom-style pithouses
2. Their concentration around a centralized pit feature (Pit #434), and
3. Limited material-culture assemblages within the pithouses that include Powell Plain and Cahokia red-filmed sherds (Collins 1990; Holley 1989) and Burlington chert microlithic debitage and tools (Koldehoff and Brennan 2010).

Given these findings, we can finally return to Jeffrey Brain's inquiry into the motivations driving Cahokian influence in the Yazoo Basin. Through the study of material

---

[1] There are approximately 725 river kilometers between Cahokia and Carson; modern canoe expeditions can make this voyage in as little as eleven days, but generally average around twenty-five miles per day, making a twenty-plus day voyage more feasible (Layne Logue and John Ruskey, personal communication 2017).

culture and comparison to case studies of interaction and migration more broadly, we formulate several potential explanations for the mechanisms driving Cahokians downriver that are certainly tied to trade, but also to concepts of political affiliation, to culture making and remaking, and to the homeland of mound and plaza ceremonialism (following Knight's assertion of Cahokias "southeastern character"; Knight 1997). Herein, we first review studies of migration, identity, and culture making in the archaeological record, and then outline Mississippian histories in the Yazoo Basin. Subsequently, we present recent findings on the connections between Carson and Cahokia, including household architecture and ceramics, and then provide a discussion explaining Cahokian material culture at Carson and on practices of cultural affiliation and differentiation as evident through the archaeological record.

## Challenges with Mississippian Culture Making, Diaspora, and Migration

For scholars of intermediate and complex societies, the historical events and processes driving the rise of Cahokia and the dispersal of Cahokian culture across the Eastern Woodlands presents a valuable case study for comparison with the expansion, migration, and diaspora of middle-range and pre-state civilizations across the globe (see Lilley 2007). For regional Mississippian scholars, this study adds to our understanding of Mississippian history, culture contact, and the various culture complexes that existed regionally just before the time of European contact. On a theoretical level, this article engages with concepts of diaspora, and wrestles with the utility of the concept as typically applied to state-level societies (Owen 2005; Stein 2002).

Studies of Mississippian identity variously emphasize widely diverse concepts ranging from migration, to site unit intrusions, to diaspora, and identity, agency, and structuration (Anderson 2017; Baltus and Baires n.d.; McNutt and Parish 2019; Wilson 2017). Consider David Anderson, who writes that "the beginnings of the Mississippian world, we are seeing, are becoming increasingly entangled" (2017, p. 288) and that most scholars seem to agree that the development of Mississippian culture was not a uniform, singular, and/or adaptationist process. Rather, the Eastern Woodlands were populated by many unique and local iterations of agricultural, monument-building, village-dwelling societies, known variously as Plaquemine, Fort Ancient, and/or Oneonta, among others. While these localized cultures flourished, Cahokia and Mississippian society in the American Bottom developed through a series of complicated mechanisms guided by religion, politics, and economy, as well as a history of development in which pilgrimages to Cahokia from "the northern Woodlands, southern valleys, or western Plains—all locations where Cahokia artifacts have been found—may have been profound" (Pauketat 2002, p. 160; see McNutt and Parish 2019 for a recent review). Many studies describe the process of how "Cahokians" made themselves in the American Bottom (Hall 1991, 1997; Holt 2009; Kelly and Brown 2014; Smith 1990; Skousen 2018; Wilson 2017; Wilson and Sullivan 2017). Here, we present a brief review of Cahokian history and how Cahokians carried their newly made identities across the Midwest and Southeastern United States.

Multiple generations of research and interpretation contextualize Cahokian development (Baires 2017; Emerson 1997; Fowler and Hall 1975; Hall 1997; Kelly 1990;

Milner 1998; Pauketat 2002; Pauketat and Alt 2015; Peregrine 1992). Pauketat's "Big Bang in the American Bottom" posits a dramatic resettling of communities from the surrounding uplands and shifts in material culture, architecture, and monumental/ritual practice at around AD 1050 (Alt 2010; Pauketat 2002). The Greater Cahokia region was monumentally transformed through mound building, woodhenge construction, wall trench architecture, and material culture at three major centers—Cahokia, East St. Louis, and St. Louis. This development, the transformation of dispersed Woodland "Late Bluff" or Emergent Mississippian peoples into Cahokians, happened through processes that have been debated over the past 70 years. Among the many stories of how Cahokia came to be, Robert Hall's narrative is perhaps the most evocative, reliant upon ethnohistory, paleoethnobotany, and archaeology (Hall 1997). He argues political relationships and trade networks were maintained through rituals using Long-Nosed God maskettes that mimicked the function of the historically documented calumet ceremony; to facilitate trade, exchange, and interaction, and symbolize elements from World Renewal ritual and the Morning Start. Cahokia arises in the context of the development of floodplain, maize agriculture, and collapses when cold hardy varieties become available. Without a need to redistribute corn, who needs a state to administer it? Bringing communities together in this floodplain context was a hierarchical organization, Cahokia, that could hedge against subsistence and economic distress, while also reifying ritual through Long-nosed God maskettes (Hall 1997, p. 152). In Hall's understanding, the LMV was a critical component in Cahokia's development, writing "the first of those that can be called Mississippian saw interaction to the south and in particular to the lower Mississippi Alluvial Valley" (Hall 1991, p. 33).

Bruce Smith (1990, p. 2) articulates that early models of Cahokia, in which the site was the groundswell of all southeastern complexity, belong to the homology position of Mississippian. In homology, complexity, as evident in maize agriculture, demographic growth, river valley settlement, bow-and-arrow technology, and mound building, emerges out of cultural developments at Cahokia. In this model, the middle and later Mississippian chiefdoms of Winterville, Lake George, Moundville, Etowah, and Lake Jackson, among others, attribute their genesis to site-unit intrusions and Mississippian invasions from the American Bottom. In terms of chronology, Cahokia certainly is the earliest Mississippian settlement, and by its own definition, the Mississippian type-site, and thus, is naturally the first of its kind. However, Cahokia's early emergence does not necessarily mean it is the root and direct lineal ancestor of all late Holocene complexity in the Southeast. In contrast to the homology position, Smith (1990, p. 2) delineates the analogy position of Mississippian, wherein individual late Woodland groups across the Southeast had "quivers of alternative adaptational responses to both internal and external events" which lead to various forms of mound-building, village-oriented, stratified horticultural societies.

The analogy position suggests that many of the similarities seen across Mississippian societies seen across the Southeast are the result of independent and unrelated cultural responses to stimuli (whether ecological, demographic, ideological, or political). This perspective posits no single origin for complexity in the Southeast but implies that most of Mississippian societies were broadly similar, adapting as biological organisms, to specific types and sets of evolutionary pressures. Herein also lies the problem. Societies are not organisms and humans do not always act according to the principles of fitness and survival. Therefore, in its rootedness to diffusion versus

 Springer

independent invention, the analogy position too had its problems, notably, through the absence of history and process (Pauketat 2002, p. 150).

A more modern approach to evaluating Mississippian societies can be found in historical approaches that emphasize the linkages between materialist and idealist archaeologies (Carr and Case 2005; Pauketat 2003, 2008). A historical perspective on Mississippian is event based and oriented toward contingency. Based on a detailed study of demography, structure use-life cycles, and site occupation histories between Cahokia and the adjacent Richland Uplands, Pauketat (78) emphasizes that Mississippian, as culture (little c), is negotiated, contested, and dynamic, and not a monolithic cultural complex nor an adaptive response. He suggests that Mississippian, with its shell-tempering, wall trench architecture, maize agriculture, and platform mounds, only becomes ubiquitous in the highlands adjacent to Cahokia after various pluralistic groups move into the region. The resettlement of farmers into the uplands was a complex and negotiated process, fully embodied by pluralistic groups maintaining polyvalent cultural practices, yet adopting Mississippian lifeways as well. In Pauketat's understanding, Mississippian is not seen as a deterministic, pan-cultural leviathan, or a panglossian best-of-all-worlds, but rather, an interwoven history contingent upon unique developments in the American Bottom and the Yazoo Basin, among other places.

In order to ask anthropological questions about migration and identity at Carson, fundamental questions needed to be answered first: what was the timing of mound development, who were the people who built these mounds, how were they related to Mississippian societies farther north and Plaquemine, non-Mississippian mound-builders, peoples to the south, and what social mechanisms were responsible for organizing large-scale landscape modification at the site? Some of this early work has finally been completed and has demonstrated some degree of contact with the American Bottom (Brain 1978, Williams and Brain 1983; Johnson 1987; Johnson and Connaway 2019; Mehta *et al.* 2017b). Initially, this article and others in the special issue of JAMT sought to engage "diaspora" as a mechanism for explaining Cahokian settlements and material culture scattered across the Eastern Woodlands, in this case, at the Carson site in north Mississippi. An early use of diaspora outside of the Jewish historical tradition was by Cohen (1969), who described Hausa traders in Yoruba cities in Western Africa as comprising an "interregional exchange network composed of spatially dispersed specialized merchant groups which are culturally distinct, organizationally cohesive, and socially independent from their host communities while maintaining a high level of economic and social ties with related communities who define themselves in terms of the same general cultural identity" (Cohen 1969, pp. 266–267). The fundamental utility of diaspora exists as an analogical concept with reference to specific historical traditions, and it has been used in archaeological case studies locally and globally, from the American Southwest (Clark *et al.* 2012; Hill *et al.* 2004; Lyons and Clark 2012; Mills *et al.* 2015) to Mesopotamia (Stein 1999, 2002). However, its use in archaeology is critiqued because of the difficulty in defining forced, voluntary, religious, and/or economic social choices that drive migration (the core of the diaspora model) in archaeological contexts (Butler 2001; Owen 2005; Stone 2015).

Gil Stein adapted Cohen's model to describe an Uruk enclave at Haçınebi, located in modern-day Turkey, over 1000 km from the Uruk-Warka city-state (Stein 1999, 2002). The trade diaspora describes traders-as-agents who choose to establish enclaves in foreign lands to facilitate exchange between distant locales. Stein identifies a full suite

  Springer

of artifacts at Uruk enclaves at Haçınebi that are Uruk-in-style and redundant with locally available goods, as well as characteristic Uruk-style architecture, signifying strong ties to the homeland and not to local populations. Trade diaspora is thus a principally economic mechanism by which identity is maintained outside of the Uruk homeland. However, Stein's example is for a state-level system; what about middle-range societies? Below, we present the American Southwest and the Iroquoian Northeast as two other frameworks to engaging with concepts of diaspora, identity, and migration.

In the American Southwest, relatively small and disperse communities scale up to become what we call Ancestral Pueblo, Hohokam, and Mogollon during the first millennium AD. Many different processes of migration describe how communal identities were formed, maintained, shared, and changed within these three broad culture areas (Mills 2011, p. 347). The migration of groups out of the Kayenta region, part of the Ancestral Pueblo tradition, and into the Mogollon highlands has long been described as a diaspora (Clark 2011; DiPeso 1958) but also critiqued as such (Stone 2015). That they already had a well-developed social identity, as defined on ceramic traditions, and that they maintained these traditions and connections to their homeland was sufficient for many to satisfy the diaspora model. However, Tammy Stone's reanalysis and critique of Kayenta archaeology in the Mogollon area suggests that enclaves of Kayenta immigrants did not sufficiently interact with one another or maintain economic ties to their northern Arizona homelands. In addition, distinctive wares attributed to the Kayenta, Roosevelt Red wares, are too similar to ceramic traditions in the Mogollon area, suggesting they are widespread and common rather than controlled by one group (Crown 1994). These debates around archaeological cases of diaspora highlight challenges of using the model where textual evidence and state-level organization are lacking. Part of the challenge is that processes of identity formation can be described without recourse to the diaspora model at all, like in the Iroquoian North Atlantic.

Within the Iroquoian world of the North Atlantic, Wendat communities around Lake Ontario after AD 1300 began practicing innovative forms of ossuary burial to integrate previously distinct social groups and to create a unified community identity around similar burial practices (Birch and Williamson 2015, p. 147). By making ossuaries near village sites comprised of multiple social groups and communities, proto-Iroquoians were connecting themselves socially and materially to the landscape. Later, in the fifteenth and sixteenth centuries, when larger social units were formed from distinct communities, they brought with them ties to their ancestral homelands and ossuaries, leading to fractious and contentious claims to homelands. "By conceptualizing the historical development of Iroquoian cultural landscapes in this way, we can envision how processes of village relocation, the internment of the dead, and the continued passage through the landscape served to emplace peoples and nations within it" (Birch and Williamson 2015, p. 148). Considering the Cahokia and Carson connections within this framework, and Mississippian archaeology more broadly, we might consider how identity construction worked at Carson and Cahokia at the community level through signifiers like artifact styles, house architecture, mortuary practices, and other subtle practices (Blitz 2010, p. 16).

Thus, is diaspora an appropriate model to elucidate the presence of Cahokian pottery, Burlington chert artifacts, and Cahokian-style pithouse architecture outside of the Cahokian homeland? Did Cahokians travel downriver to sell and/or trade their wares at Carson or did a Carsonian travel upriver, obtain Cahokian goods, and then

return home to sell them? The evidence in some cases would be equivocal. Tammy Stone suggests "active ethnic signaling, connections with the homeland, and interaction between enclaves are the elements that separate diasporic behavior from other kinds of migrations and ethnic interactions" (Stone 2015, p. 21). Brubaker (2005) also indicated three criteria, define more loosely, are necessary for diaspora—dispersion in space, orientation to a homeland, and boundary maintenance. The presence of Cahokians outside of Cahokia is dispersion, and many scholars argue that orientation to homeland may or may not be necessary in diaspora (Anthias 1998; Brubaker 2005; Clifford 1994; Falzon 2003; Safran 1991). Finally, boundary maintenance is "the preservation of a distinctive identity vis-à-vis a host society" (Brubaker 2005, p. 6), and the "diaspora experience... is defined, not by essence of purity; by a conception of 'identity' which lives with and through, not despite, difference; by hybridity" (Hall 1990, p. 235). Tangible goods like Cahokian-style pottery and Burlington and/or Mill Creek chert, as well as intangibles like ideologies, beliefs, and rituals, certainly moved up and down the MRV—the challenge is in parsing migration versus diaspora, and while it is certainly evident that Cahokian influence was felt in north Mississippi, it is unclear if Stone's bar for diaspora can be met (Brubaker's criteria are easier to satisfy, however). The question is which mechanism(s) best explain(s) this phenomenon? Furthermore, is it necessarily reasonable that specific historical examples (Jewish, Uruk, Wendat, etc.) would in any way resemble historical processes in the MRV? These discussions structure our analysis of Cahokian material culture and architecture at Carson.

## Carson in the Northern Yazoo Basin

The Carson site is located in northwestern Mississippi, in the Yazoo Basin, a floodplain of the Mississippi River. The Yazoo is a geographically delimited region, defined by Memphis to the north, Vicksburg to the south, the Mississippi River to the west, and Aeolian bluffs and the Yazoo River to the east. Topographic contours in this floodplain are created through meandering river deposition and erosional processes that leave scrollbars, ridge-and-swale features, backswamps, and levee ridges behind. In this fertile, annually renewed deltaic environment, the Carson site was constructed on a mile-long levee ridge perpendicular to what was then the active channel of the Mississippi River. The site consists of a village, featuring 70 structures (as of today) that were surrounded by a 1 to 2-m embankment and palisade (Fig. 3), 6 large named mounds (A–E; Thomas 1894, pp. 253–255), and approximately 83 small house mounds that have largely been plowed away. Radiocarbon and optically stimulated luminescence dates from Carson date most of the site's occupation to after AD 1200 and well into the sixteenth century, and perhaps seventeenth century. Research at Mound D, the largest monument by volume, suggests that mound construction began perhaps as early as AD 1100 or as late as AD1300 (820 ybp ± 100; 95.4%; Tulane EENS; Mehta *et al.* 2017a), and that mound construction ceased between the mid AD1400s and the early 1600s (Mehta 2019). A Bayesian analysis of stratigraphy, ceramics, and absolute dates from mound D suggests the monument was constructed over a period of 150 years in two to three large construction stages (Mehta 2019, p. 15). While more research is still needed, the authors favor a model that starts mound D at around AD 1250/1300 and ends at around AD 1450/1500.

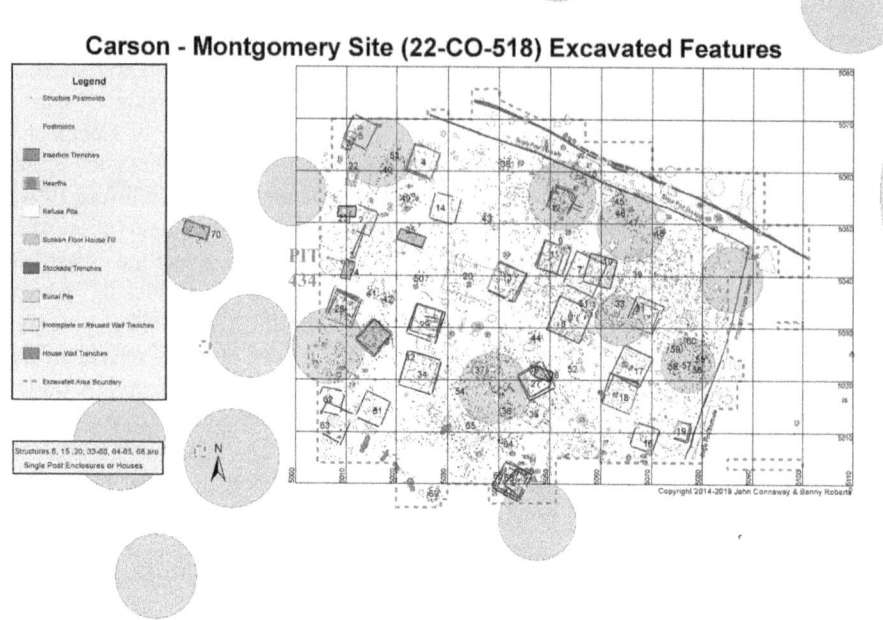

**Fig. 3.** Mound A village at Carson. Gray circles are the footprints of smaller mounds from the 1894 Holmes and Thomas map. Structures are denoted with post alignments, wall trenches, and numbers. Yellow shapes are pits and blue shapes are mortuary bundle burials. Image by Benny Roberts and John Connaway

A rather large summit structure (42.25 m$^2$) identified on mound D dated to the fifteenth century and was determined to have been used for processing shell; Burlington chert microlithic tools and small chisels on local lithics were also identified, pointing to some degree of crafting activities (Mehta *et al.* 2016). Radiocarbon dates from square houses and burials in the mound A village range from the thirteenth to sixteenth centuries. Furthermore, numerous Late Mississippian ceramics have been identified, including Owens Punctated, Avenue Polychrome, and Winterville Incised (Lansdell 2009), as well as later rim modes (House 1993; Lansdell 2009; Mainfort 2003). Based on age ranges from mound D and the mound A village, it is likely much of the site was contemporaneously in use by the later Mississippi period; nevertheless, our understandings of earlier occupations in the village and the timing of mound construction elsewhere at the site are still quite nascent. At a broad, regional scale, Carson can be assigned to the Parchman I and Parchman II phases (Haley 2014; Mehta 2015; Nelson 2016); however, its role in regional political and cultural dynamics is yet still unclear, as is the regional chronology itself (Brown 2008, p. 380). Following Weinstein's chronology (see Fig. 9), occupations at Carson spanned from the Peabody/Walnut Bend phases and into the Parchman and perhaps Oliver phases. Nelson (2016, p. 276) tantalizingly hints that Carson may have played a role in regional social integration as a necropolis or place for the gathering of the dead; in a landscape of equals (*primus inter pares*; Barker 1993; Kidder 1998), perhaps Carson's role as a gathering place of the dead was influenced by contact with a distant political entity that tilted power over the political landscape toward its direction.

 Springer

The village near mound A (Fig. 3) was once surrounded by an embankment and palisade. This village contains the archaeological remains of numerous houses, pits, postmolds, and bundle-burials, as well as one large earthen mound and many smaller house-mounds. Mound A is 4.2 m in height, and approximately 68 m × 52 m at its base. Sediment coring and downhole magnetic susceptibility studies of mound sediment suggest that mound A was built in as little as two large construction stages (Mehta *et al.* 2012, p. 8; Mehta 2015, p. 132). A modern home was built on the mound and unfortunately has impacted the integrity of the mound and destroyed any evidence of summit structures. Surveyors with the Bureau of American Ethnology described concentrations of burned clay bearing impressions of cane and timber near the mound and in the surrounding area, which indicate that many indigenous wattle-and-daub structures were once built in the surrounding area (Thomas 1894, p. 253). From a material culture perspective, identifying a non-local presence can only be accomplished by first understanding the local material culture signature. Fortunately, over a decade of excavations and surface collections in the mound A village have uncovered a diverse array of local architectural styles and ceramics, making the identification of non-local materials more feasible.

Six structure types are found in the mound A village: (1) square houses with wall trenches [$n = 18$, most common at 51%], (2) square single-set post houses [$n = 5$, 14%], (3) rectangular single-set post houses [$n = 1$, 3%], (4) circular single-set post houses [$n = 3$, 9%], (5) platform houses [$n = 2$, 6%], and (6) pithouses [$n = 6$, 17%] (McLeod 2015, pp. 48–50). In addition to structures, 66 burial pits were also identified within the mound A village area. Local architectural styles are types 1–5. Type 6 is the semi-subterranean Lohmann or Stirling phase style pithouse structure typical of the American Bottom. McLeod noted that the most common structure type, the square wall trench house (1), is typically aligned to site grid, while other structure types, like single set post buildings and the pithouses, are not aligned to site grid (McLeod 2015, pp. 48–49). He also noted that pithouses were the likely earliest buildings in the mound A village, given they were the only buildings not to intrude into other buildings (but, rather, are intruded upon by other structures), and that radiocarbon dates from structure 22 and structure 70 predate all of the other architecture in the mound A village (Table 1). A charred wooden post from the southeast corner of structure 22 yielded an age of 820 ± 30 [14]C yr BP (cal. AD 1160–1270; Beta-370515). More recently, a radiocarbon date from a native persimmon seed has been processed from structure 70 and it has yielded an age of 915 ± 15 [14]C yr BP (cal. AD 1041–1163; UCIAMS #202016). Radiocarbon dates from local-style, square structures typically date to the fifteenth century and afterwards (Table 1).

## Carson-Cahokia Connections: Architecture, Pottery, and Lithics

### Pithouse Architecture

Rectangular pithouses have been defined and documented at the Lohmann site (Esarey 1981; Esarey and Pauketat 1992), the East St. Louis Mound center (Kelly *et al.* 2005), the Range site (Hanenberger *et al.* 2003), at the ICT-II tract at Cahokia (Collins 1990), and at numerous Mississippian sites surrounding Cahokia's countryside (Mehrer 1995,

**Table 1** Grey rows represent early Mississippian, Cahokian-influenced occupations. Calibrations performed using OxCal 4.3 using IntCal 13 (Bronck Ramsey 2009)

| Sample | Measured age | Intercept | 2-Sigma range | Context |
|--------|--------------|-----------|---------------|---------|
| 12 | 720 ± 20 BP | Cal AD 1230 | Cal AD 1263–1292 | Organic residue found on pottery in structure 31 |
| 26 | 810 ± 30 BP | Cal AD 1220 | Cal AD 1160–1270 | Burned SE corner post in structure 22 |
| 202016 | 915 ± 15 BP | Cal AD 1098 | Cal AD 1041–1163 | Persimmon seed fragment from structure 70 house floor |
| 3 | 420 ± 50 BP | Cal AD 1502 | Cal AD 1415–1633 | Large burned outer stockade post |
| 4 | 510 ± 30 BP | Cal AD 1410 | Cal AD 1320–1430 | Charred center-post of structure 17 |
| 5 | 360 ± 30 BP | Cal AD 1543 | Cal AD 1450–1635 | Charred post in structure 12 floor |
| 17 | 260 ± 30 BP | Cal AD 1640 | Cal AD 1490–1650 | Charred post in north central stockade row |
| 20 | 350 ± 30 BP | Cal AD 1460 | Cal AD 1440–1630 | Charred post in east inner stockade |
| 22 | 330 ± 30 BP | Cal AD 1500 | Cal AD 1450–1640 | Charred post in structure 8 |
| 30 | 320 ± 30 BP | Cal AD 1564 | Cal AD 1483–1646 | Charred post fragment in floor fill of DR#5. |
| 36 | 420 ± 30 BP | Cal AD 1420 | Cal AD 1410–1450 | Charred post in north inner stockade |

pp. 95–122). Rectangular pithouses are most common during the Lohmann phase and structure diversity increases during the subsequent Stirling and Moorehead phases (Mehrer 1995, pp. 99–100). Typically, Lohmann-style pithouses typically do not have hearths or significant quantities of internal storage features (Collins 1990, pp. 221–224), but rather contain large communal storage pits between households. In terms of dimensions, these types of pithouse are long and skinny, rarely rebuilt, and with deep basins (Collins 1990, p. 224; Hanenberger *et al.* 2003, p. 43; Fig. 9). Over time, buildings get larger and squarer (Mehrer 1995, p. 101).

Interior areas of Lohmann phase buildings range from 5.73 to 15.49 m², averaging at around 10.12 m², with length/width ratios of 1.8 to 2.4 (Hanenberger *et al.* 2003, p. 43). This style of pithouse architecture is also potentially consistent with the Stirling phase; however, Stirling phase structures are more diverse in size and tend to be larger (Mehrer 1995, p. 100). Since structure 22 at Carson post-dates the Lohmann phase and structure 70's radiocarbon distribution could also postdate the Lohmann phase, it is worth considering that even though they certainly look more like Lohmann style structures, they could also date to Cahokia's Stirling, or potentially even Moorehead phase. In general, Stirling phase structures can be identified because they have interior storage pits, tend to be larger, and typically have more squarish dimensions (Hanenberger *et al.* 2003, p. 216).

Six rectangular semi-subterranean structures (pithouses, numbered 22–26, 70; Fig. 4) have been identified in the mound A village at Carson. Five have interior wall trenches in the floor (structures 23, 24, 25, 26, and 70), while the other (22) has a post in each corner, at least three on each side, and two at the north end, with the south end open, suggesting an open-sided, roofed, house. Consistent with Lohmann-style buildings in the American Bottom, none of these pithouses had interior hearths.

The six rectangular pithouses were fairly uniform in size with one exception. Most have length/width ratios ranging from 1.59 to 1.75—structure 25 has a ratio of 2.35. The former ranges are more consistent with Stirling phase pithouses from ICT-II but consistent with Lohmann ratios from the Lohmann site (Esarey and Pauketat 1992, p.

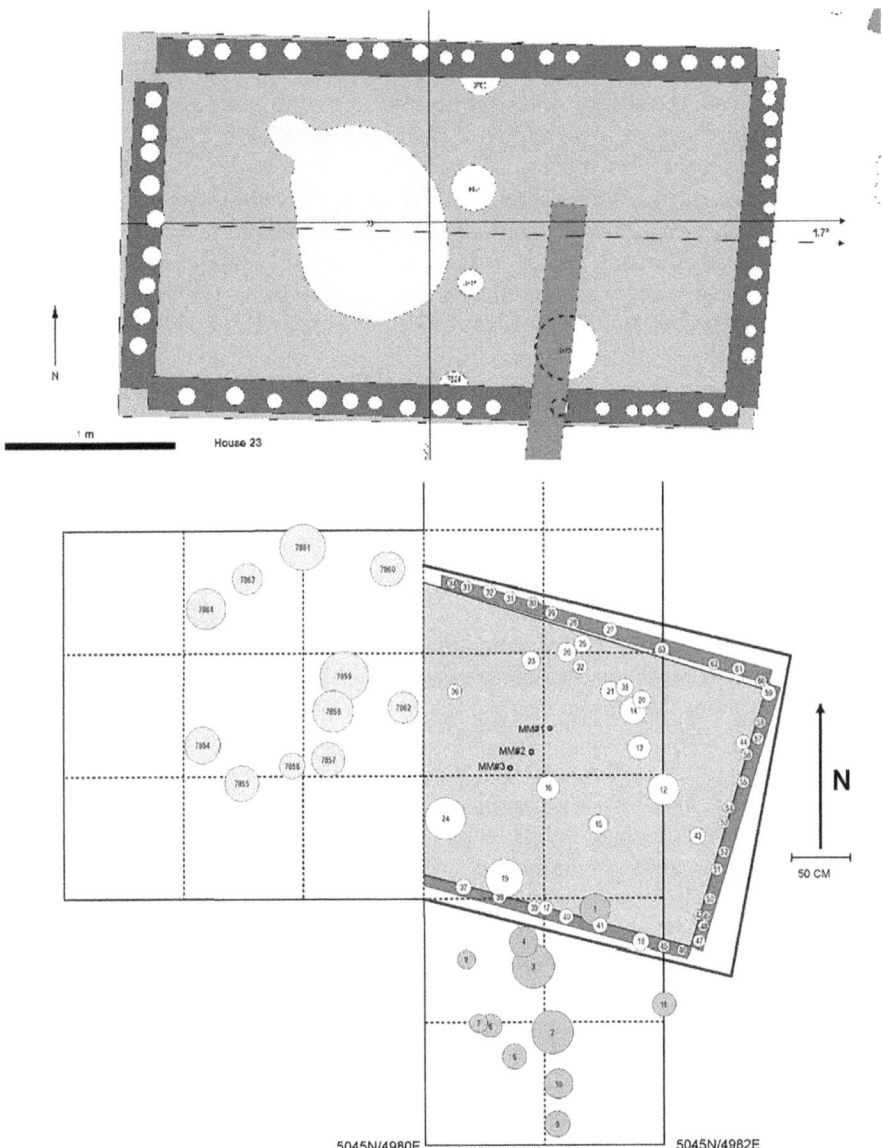

**Fig. 4** Pithouse 23 (upper image) and pithouse 70 (lower image) are shown here. Images drawn by Benny Roberts and John Connaway

42), while structure 25 fits the pattern for Lohmann-style houses at ICT-II (Collins 1990; Hanenberger *et al.* 2003). Most pithouses at Carson were severely truncated due to land-leveling operations that occurred at the site before archaeological mitigation work; most had basins that were 20 cm deep below the plowzone, except for structure 26, which was 52 cm deep, and structure 70 which has a basin that was of similar depth; the structure itself was located a meter below the plowzone. The alignments of these structures vary, some oriented north-south, others more east-west, and not particularly parallel to the "site grid," suggesting again their early construction before the more local-style, square wall trench houses were aligned to site grid and the stockades built (Fig. 9). Structure 25 is the closest to such an alignment toward site grid. At Lohmann phase sites, pithouses tended to be constructed at either parallel or perpendicular orientations to the site landform, and they tend to be close to one another in feature/structure clusters with shared storage pits (Hanenberger et al. 2003).

Pithouse contents included the usual locally available citronelle gravel flakes and a few Mississippi Plain sherds, much of which came from surrounding area or middens used to fill the pithouses after they ceased to be used. However, pithouse floors contained significant[2] quantities of white Burlington flakes, some larger Burlington chert and citronelle cobbles, and typically little to no local ceramics. Of note were contents of structure 23 which included a large jar rim of red-slipped Cahokian pottery (Fig. 5), turned upside down near the center of the house and sherds of this jar scattered around it, as if the jar had been placed on the floor and then the body portion broken and scattered purposely, perhaps as part of a ceremonial rite (Grinsell 1961). This was part of four different pottery concentrations on the structure 23 pithouse floor. Other tools recovered from structure 23 were a polished celt fragment, a white Burlington wedge, a broken Burlington biface, 15 Burlington perforators, and 4 perforators made of local chert.

Cahokian pithouse architecture at Carson stands in stark contrast to square, wall trench, and single-set post architecture in the rest of the mound A village (McLeod and Connaway 2014; McLeod 2015). Most of these structures have been identified based on the remains of posts and wall trenches and they have been truncated due to land-leveling operations. While radiocarbon dates from pithouses date to the eleventh, twelfth, and/or early thirteenth centuries, square wall trench structures date to the fifteenth century and later. Square wall trench structures of the local variety contain commonly found, local Mississippian pottery that typically is assigned to the Parchman phase; ceramic types include Barton Incised and Mississippi Plain pottery. Reviewing from the earlier discussion of the mound A village, 19 square wall trench structures and 4 single-set post square structures are present in the village. Three circular single-set circular structures are present and two square, Wilsford-style platform structures are present (Connaway 1984). The square structures are all mostly aligned to the "site grid" and post-date the Cahokian pithouses by several hundred years. Sometime later in the sixteenth and possibly seventeenth centuries (McLeod 2015, p. 77), the village was transformed into a cemetery and/or mortuary space (Baires 2017).

What did Carson look like during the time of "Cahokian influence" perhaps quite unpopulated or newly settled. We do not have local-style structures that date from AD 1100 to 1300—instead, we have Cahokian-style pithouses and no evidence of a palisade/stockade (which dates to much later in the Mississippi period; Table 1). Mound D was built after AD 1100 and most likely after AD 1200, reaching its final shape approximately 150 years later (Mehta 2019). Therefore, Cahokians at Carson may have watched mound D erected and perhaps even sponsored its construction. Otherwise, the village, its mortuary complex, and palisade/stockade, were non-existent. Insofar as we know, Carson may not have existed at all when Cahokians first arrived.

---

[2] It should be noted that terms like "usual" and "significant" are qualitative qualifiers describing amounts of material and the style of material culture; the senior author of this paper uses these terms in the absence quantifiable data (left for later students to analyze), and rather, is choosing to emphasize qualitative terms based on almost ten years of excavation at Carson and fifty years of excavation experience in the Mississippi Delta.

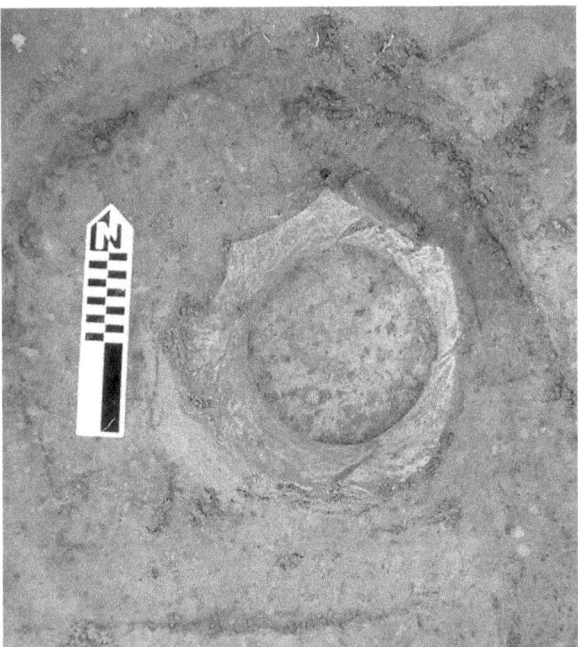

**Fig. 5** Red filmed, Cahokian vessel from pithouse structure 23. Photograph by John Connaway

## Pithouse Clusters

With the exception of structure 70, pithouses 22–26 were all located within the same general area, in what could potentially be defined as a structure or feature cluster (Hanenberger *et al.* 2003, p. 30), or potentially even an ethnic enclave (Spence 2005; Fig. 6). In many cases and at multiple Lohmann phase sites in the American Bottom, pithouses tended to be found in clusters with shared storage pits (Collins 1990; Esarey 1981; Esarey and Pauketat 1992; Hanenberger *et al.* 2003; Kelly *et al.* 2005). At Carson, Cahokian-style pithouses are found in a cluster in the NW section of the village with a large storage pit (pit 434) in the immediate vicinity. It is our assertion that the Carson pithouses mimic Lohmann feature clusters found in the American Bottom and that the similarities are another signifier of the extent to which Cahokian influence was felt at Carson. These pithouses were found at the same stratigraphic level below the plowzone and were potentially part of the same feature cluster. Additionally, the contents of pit 434 do not reflect local Yazoo Basin-style Mississippian wares, but rather, Cahokian-style wares like Powell Plain (Fig. 7). Sherds from the pit are predominantly shell-tempered jar forms typical in Lohmann, Stirling, and Moorehead phase contexts.

## Cahokian-Style Pottery

Archaeological research at the East St. Louis site, Range, ICT-II, and the Lohmann site has been used to define typical Lohmann and Stirling ceramic phase assemblages. From East St. Louis, Kelly *et al.* (2005) suggest that Powell Plain and Cahokia Red-filmed jars with thickened lip margins are definitive for the Lohmann phase. Holley

**Fig. 6** Lower image shows the mound A village at Carson. Gray circles represent the remains of small house mounds transcribed from the 1894 BAE survey map. The red square encloses an enclave of Cahokian-style pithouses; Upper image detail shows an enclave of pithouses (Strs. 22–25) near a large storage pit (#434) that contained significant quantities of Cahokian-style artifacts. Black circle are postmolds, yellow polygons are pits, and blue polygons are bundle burials. Image by Benny Roberts and John Connaway

(11) suggests that common features of Lohmann pottery are dark, slipped surfaces, and black, smudged Powell Plain shell-tempered pots, typically in jar forms with extruded rims. From the Lohmann site itself, Esarey and Pauketat have claimed that 66% of Lohmann assemblages are jars and that 60% are shell-tempered. In the absence of a

**Fig. 7** Sample assemblage of Powell plain rim sherds from pit 434, the large centrally located pit in the pithouse enclave at the mound A village at Carson. Image by John Connaway.

formal and quantitative analyses of Cahokian ceramics from Carson, it is possible to definitively state the following: (1) typical Lohmann or Stirling phase style pottery, including Powell Plain, is found exclusively at Carson in the Cahokian-style pithouses and pit 434; (2) much of the Cahokian pottery are jar forms; (3) black, smudged Powell Plain is especially common; and (4) mixed, local, and non-local Mississippian assemblages do not occur at Carson; rather, local ceramic types tend to be delimited to later contexts and square structures. Cahokian-style ceramics like Powell Plain and Cahokia Red-filmed seem to be limited Cahokian contexts potentially dating to Lohmann, Stirling, and possibly Moorehead phases (Figs. 8 and 9).

Given the limited architectural diversity of the pithouses, their limited material culture assemblage (with goods exotic to the Yazoo Basin but not to Cahokia itself), and their centralized arrangement around a storage pit (#434), there is sufficient evidence to claim these structures were built by individuals from the American Bottom or significantly emulating American Bottom traditions. Radiocarbon dates from structures 22 and 70 do not readily allow a Lohmann phase designation, but rather Stirling or Moorehead. It is feasible that at the end of the Lohmann phase (or during the Stirling and/or Moorehead phases), migrants traveled downriver and colonized the banks of the Mississippi River, catalyzing events leading to the rise of Carson. Additional chronology-driven and ceramic analysis work is needed.

## Discussion: Implications of Material Culture and Architecture

In terms of its Cahokian connections, Carson is not unique in the Yazoo Basin; both Winterville and Lake George, two large Mississippian centers, as well as Griffin, Haynes Bluff, Shell Bluff, and Duck Lake, smaller mound centers, have also produced

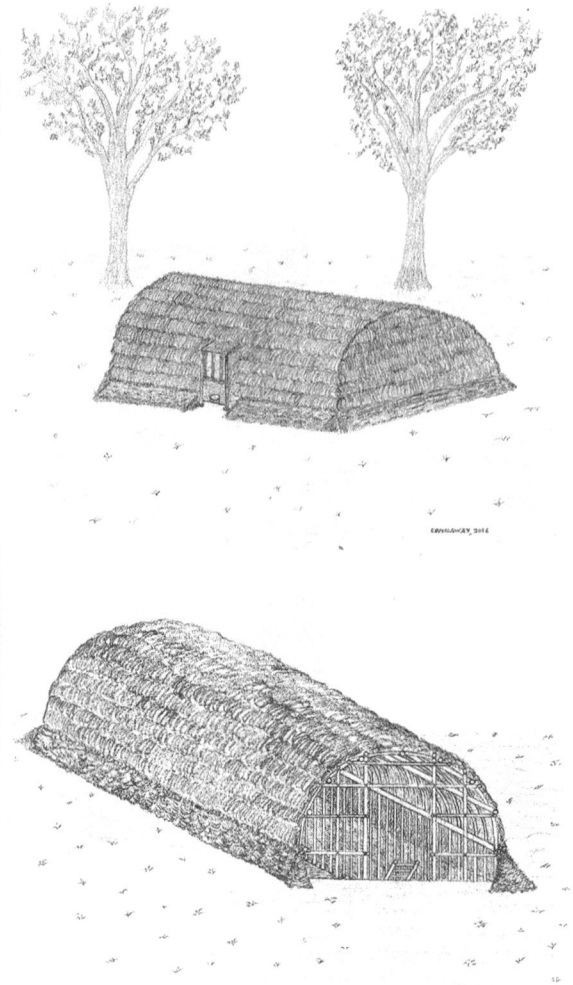

**Fig. 8** Two views of Carson pithouses, modeled after archaeological data from the mound A village. Drawn by the senior author, John Connaway

Cahokian diagnostics, that Jeffrey Brain assigns to the Moorehead phase (Brain 1991, p. 98). However, outside of these sites located on principal streams, the Yazoo Basin is largely devoid of Cahokian diagnostics (Brain 1991, pp. 98–99). Evidence for Cahokian interaction at these sites comes exclusively from Powell Plain and Ramey Incised ceramics and only Carson has produced definitive architectural evidence in the form of rectangular pithouses and significant quantities of Burlington chert.

Moving outside of the Yazoo Basin, well-known case studies of Cahokian interaction include Aztalan and its foreigner-dominant mortuary precinct (Goldstein 1991; Hall 1991, p. 13; Stoltman 1991, p. 350); strontium isotope studies have demonstrated that individuals interred in mound and/or special contexts at Aztalan could have been from Cahokia, although they could also have come from other parts of the Midwest with similar strontium composition in the bedrock (Price *et al.* 2007, p. 536). While it is still unclear if Aztalan was colonized by Cahokia, burial practices are interpreted to

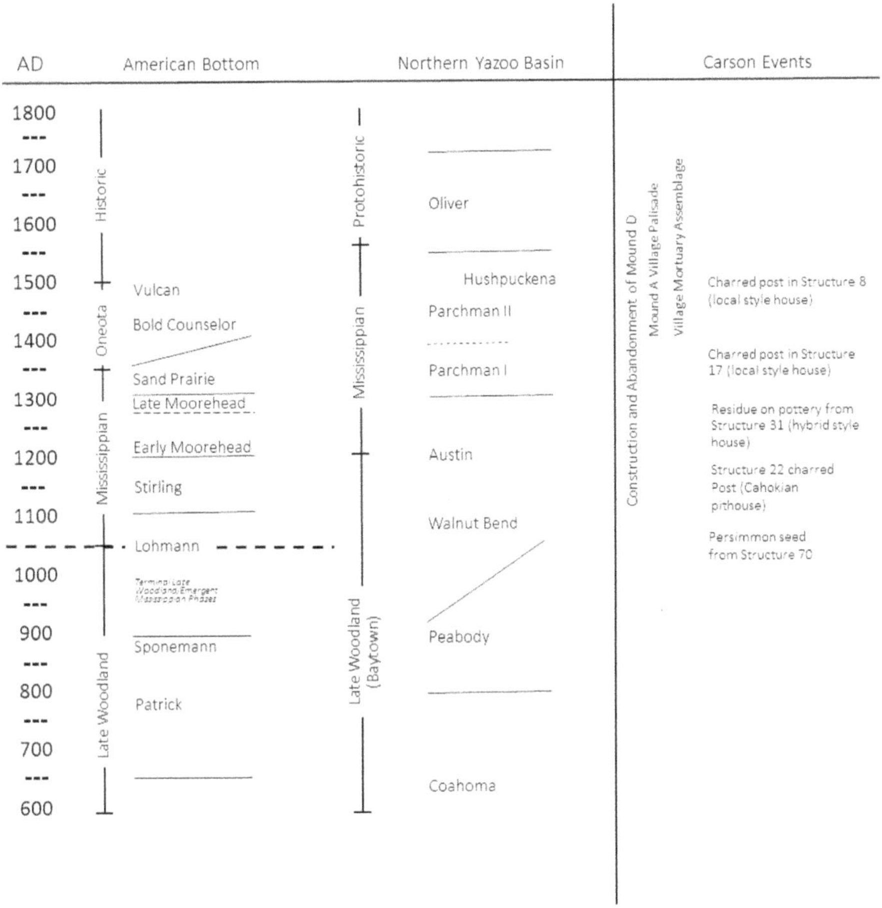
AD
American Bottom
Northern Yazoo Basin
Carson Events
1800
1700
1600
1500
1400
1300
1200
1100
1000
900
800
700
600
Historic
Oneota
Mississippian
Late Woodland
Vulcan
Bold Counselor
Sand Prairie
Late Moorehead
Early Moorehead
Stirling
Lohmann
Sponemann
Patrick
Protohistoric
Mississippian
Late Woodland (Baytown)
Oliver
Hushpuckena
Parchman II
Parchman I
Austin
Walnut Bend
Peabody
Coahoma
Construction and Abandonment of Mound D
Mound A Village Palisade
Village Mortuary Assemblage
Charred post in Structure 8 (local style house)
Charred post in Structure 17 (local style house)
Residue on pottery from Structure 31 (hybrid style house)
Structure 22 charred Post (Cahokian pithouse)
Persimmon seed from Structure 70

**Fig. 9** American bottom versus Northern Yazoo basin chronology (Baires 2017; Fortier *et al.* 2006; Hall 1991, 2006; Mehta 2015; Nelson 2016; Weinstein 2004: Figure 4.1; see also Brain 1989, Phillips 1970 for alternate interpretations of Northern Yazoo Basin chronology)

have privileged foreigners (Hedman *et al.* 2018, p. 203; Price *et al.* 2007, p. 535). Therefore, even if Cahokian's were not directly present, the influence of foreigners was certainly significant. In addition, while Late Woodland pottery sets from Aztalan differ from those at Cahokia, they are similar to Late Woodland ceramics from other parts of Illinois, like at the Collins site in the nearby Wabash Valley (Hall 1991, p. 13). The Collins site culture was transformed into Mississippian culture through interactions with Cahokia after the Late Woodland period. At the Little Bluff site in Trempealeau, Wisconsin, stylistic analyses of ceramics suggest that Cahokians traveled upriver to remake a bluff summit with a black-capped monument for potentially cosmic and ideological purposes (Pauketat *et al.* 2015; Pauketat *et al.* 2017). Similar stylistic studies of ceramics at the Trempealeau site itself indicate that Cahokians established an enclave or outpost to "impress upon the local people the power, prestige, and ideology of the American Bottom elites" (Green and Rodell 1994, p. 353). However, it should be noted that no strontium isotope studies of human mortuary remains were

conducted at Little Bluff and/or Trempealeau, and thus any claim of a direct Cahokian presence can only be made through indirect evidence.

In the Mississippian world, Cahokia was itself an outlier or outsider, located closer to Midwestern prairies and Caddoan and Siouan speakers, as opposed to the Musko-gean speakers of the Southeastern United States (Hall 2006, p. 188). Much as proto-Cahokians and Cahokians traveled widely, outsiders too came into the American Bottom to witness the mythic landscapes of Greater Cahokia region, including the mounded cities in St. Louis and East St. Louis, as well as Cahokia. After these cities defragmented and their populations sought greener pastures elsewhere, they became what we call Osage, Omaha, and Ponca today, groups related to the Kansa and Quapaw, the latter of which can be found in the CMV (Hall 2006, p. 192). The dispersal of these communities included the dispersal of Cahokian ideals as well, including the power of the mythic and monumental landscape, both born in the LMV and transformed in the AB. The salient points here are that (1) visitors to Greater Cahokia and/or people who emigrated from there carried memories of monumental and mythic landscapes with them, which they remade elsewhere; and (2) that as we learn more about interactions between the AB and the rest of the Eastern Woodlands, archaeologists are beginning to understand with greater clarity the linkages between the two (Hall 2006, p. 193). Diapora as a singular mechanism need not be the only interpretive framework of value here, and to that point, some scholars have proposed using five different contact scenarios as models for understanding interaction and cultural exchange.

James Stoltman has summarized peripheral interactions with Cahokia around the Eastern Woodlands and defined five different contact situations entailing admixture, unit-intrusions, hybridization, and stylistic copying (Stoltman 1991, pp. 350–351). He writes, "it seems likely that a number of hinterland communities founded around immigrant populations… [like at Aztalan] are best perceived as active and willing participants in a Cahokia-centered exchange system" (Stoltman 1991, p. 352). At Cahokia itself, Kristen Hedman and colleagues have demonstrated using strontium-isotope analysis the role of immigrants from the greater Central and Lower Mississippi Valley in building Cahokia itself, both during and after Cahokia's Big Bang; most notably, Slater *et al.* find that immigrants into the American Bottom came from many different places of origin, rather than one singular region (Slater *et al.* 2014, p. 125; see also Hall 1991). In support of this conclusion, consider the presence of grog-tempered, fine-ware pottery at Cahokia and the ICT-II tract, pottery that likely came with immigrants from the LMV who were arriving into the American Bottom to be remade or to remake themselves into Cahokians (Holley 1989, p. 65; Kelly 1991b; Williams and Brain 1983, p. 317). Consider, as well, Jim Knight's comparison of developmental sequences at Moundville and Cahokia; platform-mound ceremonialism and "the ap-pearance of mound and plaza complexes in the American Bottom is an homage of the power of southern ideas in Cahokia's transformation" (Knight 1997, p. 231; see also Peregrine and Lekson 2012).

These perspectives demonstrate the complexity of historical processes in the Eastern Woodlands and the challenges inherent in identifying and classifying interactions and practices of affiliation and differentiation in the prehistoric record. Cohen and Stein posit features of trade diasporas that include (1) spatial differentiation, (2) distinct cultural practices unique from host communities, (3) interregional trade, and (4) lasting connections to the homeland. Can the evidence presented herein be used to argue for a *trade diaspora* at Carson *per se*? Pithouses in the mound A village are spatially delimited from the rest of the village; however, they are much earlier than the later structures. If contemporaneous local populations were living in the mound A village while Cahokians were living there, they certainly were not living near them. However, the evidence as it exists currently indicates that the Cahokian pithouses were first, and then the later Mississippian village with its local traditions was built later and after the fourteenth century. Therefore, we cannot state that spatial differentiation has been achieved as in a trade diaspora. Rather, it may be possible that these early pithouses represent a founding event, colonization event, and/or a site unit intrusion (*sensu* Willey *et al.* 1955).

Furthermore, Cahokians at Carson maintained their own cultural practices by building rectangular structures similar to Lohmann, Stirling, and/or Moorehead-style pithouses, with features like the absence of internal hearths and storage pits that are consistent with sites to the north. The only potential hybrid is structure 31, which has a semi-subterranean basin, like the rectangular pithouses, but a ceramic assemblage resembling local, Yazoo Basin-style Mississippian wares. Given sherds indicative of a Cahokian presence are limited to pithouses and associated pits, we do not think Cahokian-style pottery can be interpreted as a trade item. If it were traded, it should be available more broadly throughout the site, or limited to specific elite contexts, since it would be rarer. In this case, Powell Plain and Cahokia Red-filmed is found only in rectangular pithouses or in a centralized pit near the rectangular houses. However, Burlington chert is found far more extensively around the site and in later fifteenth and sixteenth century contexts as well, so perhaps Burlington chert can be understood as an interregional trade item, just not directly attributable to any one agent or political entity. It has been demonstrated that surface-collected Burlington chert from Carson was sourced from many different places and that only about 10% of it was sourced from Crescent Quarry (Mehta *et al.* 2017b). This means that Burlington chert, a resource once controlled by Cahokia (Koldehoff and Brennan 2010), was used downriver at Carson and that it was brought there by many different traders acting independently. Consequently, pottery and lithic resources do not help satisfy the trade diaspora label.

Let us consider if there were there lasting connections to the homeland. Could the 10% Burlington chert identified at Carson represent a connection to homeland? Unfortunately, this is difficult to answer with the present data. The eleventh, twelfth, and thirteenth centuries at Carson are still dramatically unclear. It is clear that a Cahokian presence is manifested on the landscape after AD 1041 and that may have lasted until AD 1270, but many of the details in between have not yet been clarified. Were Cahokians traveling up- and down-river during this 200-year window while their homeland was ascendant and ultimately, in decline? At this stage, we do not know. Consequently, we find ourselves in a position where Cohen and Stein's trade diaspora model does not quite work. What about less definite forms of diaspora, such as what Stone and/or Brubaker posit?

Tammy Stone's claim is that diaspora is defined by the following: (1) active ethnic signaling, (2) connections with the homeland, and (3) interactions between enclaves (Stone 2015, p. 21). Above, we noted that connections to homeland are difficult to define presently, given the nature of the data we have available. Similarly, we cannot know how the residents of these different pithouses were interacting with another without additional, detailed chronology building using radiocarbon dating. Certainly, building Cahokian-style houses outside of the homeland is a form of ethnic signaling and it persisted for some time; however, since the rest of the Carson village is much later than the Cahokian pithouses, we cannot know if there was anyone around to see this signaling. Brubaker's criteria for diaspora are defined more loosely—dispersion in space, orientation to a homeland, and boundary maintenance. The presence of Cahokians outside of Cahokia is dispersion, and many scholars argue that orientation to homeland may or may not be necessary in diaspora (Anthias 1998; Brubaker 2005; Clifford 1994; Falzon 2003; Safran 1991). If so, it may not necessarily be important if the Cahokians at Carson were traveling up and down river back to their homeland.

Finally, boundary maintenance is "the preservation of a distinctive identity vis-à-vis a host society" (Brubaker 2005, p. 6). Cahokian-style pottery, Burlington and Mill Creek chert, as well as Cahokian architecture definitely signal a Cahokian influence, but it does not appear that much of a local population was present, especially since the square, local-style houses all date to much later in the Mississippi period. We do not think Stein's trade diaspora model fits here and we do not think Stone's bar for diaspora can be met in this case. Brubaker's criteria are easier to satisfy, however, and while we might be able to tentatively classify these pithouses, pottery, and lithics as representative of a Cahokian diaspora, we are still unclear on the social mechanisms driving the emigration of Cahokians downriver. Is this a colonization event? Perhaps so, especially since the Cahokian materials are much earlier than the local material culture.

Future analysis needs to be focused on chronology, morphological structure and ceramic analysis, and lithic sourcing studies, in order to add flesh to the bones of this fascinating and inchoate narrative of Cahokian diaspora in the LMV and at Carson.

## Conclusion

The nature of the Cahokian diaspora at Carson is still up for debate, as is the use of the term "diaspora" in and of itself. Nevertheless, evidence for connections to the Cahokian homeland is present in the form of architecture, pottery, and Burlington and Mill Creek chert. Thus, how might we describe Cahokian motivations driving expansion across the MRV and the construction of an enclave or neighborhood at what over time becomes the Carson site? Earlier, we introduced Jeffrey P. Brain's ideas about Cahokians traveling downriver to establish Mississippian and Plaquemine monumental centers in the LMV (Brain 1989, pp. 117–122, 131–132). While in-situ sociopolitical developments likely also played a significant role in the transition from Coles Creek to Plaquemine and Mississippian cultures (Griffin 1993, p. 5; Kidder 2007, pp. 199–205), recent scholarship and new archaeological findings are adding to the story of how we understand the monumental cities of the LMV and their relationship to the emergence of complex, agricultural societies in the American Bottom (see McNutt and Parish 2019).

The Cahokian-style pithouses at Carson were built in a neighborhood before the mound A village and mortuary complex was ever constructed. We do not know when mound A was built but the earliest mound D could have been built was after AD 1100, and thus, the Cahokian pithouses are either contemporary with mound D or potentially even predate mound D; we have no other chronology on the other mounds at Carson. What might this early Cahokian presence at the landform that the monumental Carson site was built on signify? As Pauketat has suggested elsewhere in this special issue, and

reflecting back upon Jim Knight's critique of mound-plaza ceremonialism in the American Bottom (Knight 1997), as well as the long-standing tradition of mound building in the lower Mississippi River Valley (Peregrine and Lekson 2012, p. 68), especially in Mississippi and Louisiana (Arco *et al.* 2006; Saunders *et al.* 2005), perhaps we might consider that Cahokians at Carson were returning back home to the homeland of monumental architecture. Consider this—Cahokians (themselves once immigrants who coalesced in the American Bottom; Hall 1997, pp. 151–153) are re-emigrating back to the stronghold and birthplace of earthen mound monumentality, renewing their associations with older monumental landscapes dating back to the Middle Archaic (~3500 BC), and perhaps catalyzing contemporaneous monumental earthworks at Carson. Much like at Little Bluff, Aztalan, and Trempealeau, and perhaps in ways that Pauketat (personal communication, 2017) has suggested more broadly, Cahokians traveled far and wide to engage in activities relevant to their ideology and cosmos. Mound building is such an activity, a building of the world; at Carson, they brought with them Cahokian flotsam, and established an enigmatic monumental center that lasted through to the fifteenth and perhaps sixteenth centuries.

Future analyses will systematically measure attributes and features of Cahokian pottery at Carson, comparing findings to features and attributes of local, Mississippian pottery at Carson. Ideally, these approaches will help refine our understanding of the Cahokian presence at Carson, and what motivations comprised the Cahokian diaspora in the LMV. It is evident that citizens familiar with the American Bottom way of life left their homeland to start anew somewhere else. We hope through analytical approaches to ceramic styles, forms, and pastes, as well as bone chemistry, to enhance our understanding of these historical events a bit further.

**Acknowledgments** Greg Wilson started me down this road and catalyzed this paper inadvertently at SEAC several years ago. I might have quit if not for your encouragement, so thank you! Sarah Baires, Melissa Baltus, and Liz Watts have been incredible collaborators. Tim Pauketat, thank you for the guidance. The following all deserve recognition—Rachel Stout Evans, Chris Rodning, Marcello Canuto, Grant McCall, Jason Nesbitt, all of the students who worked on the Carson Mounds Archaeological Project (CMAP), Ben Davis, Molly Cloutier, Haley Holt Mehta, and Jesse Holt. Charles McNutt and Ryan Parish for allowing us to follow their example. The Mississippi Department of Archives and History, the New Orleans Center for the Gulf South, and Rick Marksbury and the Tulane Summer School helped support this work. Thanks to the Center for Applied Isotope Studies at the University of Georgia, the NSF Arizona lab, and the UIUC Radiocarbon Dating Laboratory for processing my radiocarbon dates. Jessica Crawford and the Archaeological Conservancy are the best. Thanks to Jay K. Johnson as well.

# References

Alt, S. M. (2010). Complexity in Action(s): Retelling the Cahokia Story. In S. Alt (Ed.), *Ancient Complexities: New Perspectives in Precolumbian North America* (pp. 119–137). Salt Lake City: Foundations of Archaeological Inquiry Series. University of Utah Press.

Anderson, D. G. (2017). Mississippian beginnings: multiple perspectives on migration, monumentality, and religion in the prehistoric Eastern United States. In G. D. Wilson (Ed.), *Mississippian Beginnings* (pp. 293–321). Gainesville: University of Florida Press.

Anthias, F. (1998). Evaluating "diaspora": Beyond ethnicity. *Sociology, 32*(3), 557–580.

Arco, L. J., Adelsberger, K. A., Hung, L.-y., & Kidder, T. R. (2006). Alluvial geoarchaeology of a middle archaic mound complex in the lower Mississippi Valley, U.S.A. *Geoarchaeology, 21*, 591–614.

Baires, S. (2017). *Land of Water, City of the Dead: Religion and Cahokia's Emergence*. Tuscaloosa: University of Alabama Press.

Baltus, M., & Baires S. (n.d.). Defining diaspora: a view from the Cahokia homeland. *Journal of Archaeological Method and Theory*, in press.

Barker, A. (1993). *Settled on complexity: defining and debating social complexity in the lower Mississippi Valley*. Paper presented at the fifty-eighth annual meeting of the Society for American Archaeology, St. Louis, Missouri.

Birch, J., & Williamson, R. F. (2015). Navigating ancestral landscapes in the Northern Iroquoian World. *Journal of Anthropological Archaeology, 39*, 139–150.

Blitz, J. H. (2010). New perspectives in Mississippian Archaeology. *Journal of Archaeological Research, 18*, 1–39.

Brain, J. P. (1978). Late Prehistoric settlement patterning in the Yazoo Basin and Natchez Bluffs Regions of the Lower Mississippi Valley. In M. Settlement (Ed.), *Patterns, edited by Bruce Smith* (pp. 331–368). New York: Academic Press.

Brain, J. P. (1989). *Winterville: Late Prehistoric Culture Contact in the Lower Mississippi Valley*. Lower Mississippi Survey of Harvard University. Submitted to Mississippi Department of Archives and History, Archaeological Report No. 23. Jackson, Mississippi.

Brain, J. P. (1991). Cahokia from the Southern Periphery. In New Perspectives on Cahokia: Views from the Periphery. In J. B. Stoltman (Ed.), *Monographs in World Archaeology 2* (pp. 93–100). Madison: Prehistory Press.

Bronk Ramsey, C. (2009). Bayesian analysis of radiocarbon dates. Radiocarbon, 51(1), 337–360.

Brown, I. W. (2008). Culture contact along the I-69 corridor: protohistoric and historic use of the northern Yazoo Basin, Mississippi. In J. Rafferty & E. Peacock (Eds.), *Times River: Archaeological Syntheses from the Lower Mississippi River Alluvial Valley* (pp. 357–394). Tuscaloosa: The University of Alabama Press.

Brubaker, R. (2005). The 'diaspora' diaspora. *Ethnic and Racial Studies, 28*(1), 1–19.

Butler, K. D. (2001). Defining diaspora, refining a discourse. *Diaspora: A Journal of Transnational Studies, 10*(2), 189–219.

Carr, C., & Case D. T. (Eds) (2005). *Gathering Hopewell, society, ritual, and ritual interaction*. Springer.

Clark, J. J. (2011). Disappearance and diaspora: contrasting two migrations in the southern U.S. Southwest. In G. S. Cabana & J. J. Clark (Eds.), *Rethinking Anthropological Perspectives on Migration* (pp. 84–110). Gainesville: University Press of Florida.

Clark, J. J., Hill, J. B., Lyons, P. D., & Lengyel, S. N. (2012). Of migrants and mounds. In Mounds and Migrants: Late Prehistoric Archaeology of the Lower San Pedro River Valley, Arizona. In J. J. Clark & P. D. Lyons (Eds.), *Anthropological Papers No. 45* (pp. 345–405). Tucson: Archaeology Southwest.

Clifford, J. (1994). Diasporas. *Cultural Anthropology, 9*(3), 302–338.

Cohen, A. (1969). *Custom and politics in urban Africa: a study of Hausa Migrants in Yoruba Towns*. Berkeley: University of California Press.

Collins, J. M. (1990). *The archaeology of the Cahokia Mounds ICT-II Tract: site structure. Illinois Cultural Resources Study No. 10*. Springfield: Illinois Historic Preservation Agency.

Connaway, J. M. (1984). *The Wilsford site (22CO516), Coahoma County, Mississippi: a late Mississippi period settlement in the Northern Yazoo Basin of Mississippi. Archaeological Report No. 14*. Jackson: Mississippi Department of Archives and History.

Crown, P. (1994). *Ceramics and ideology: Salado polychrome pottery*. Albuquerque: University of New Mexico Press.

DiPeso, C. C. (1958). *The Reeve ruin of Southeastern Arizona*. Dragoon AZ: Amerind Foundation.

Emerson, T. E. (1997). *Cahokia and the Archaeology of Power*. Tuscaloosa: University of Alabama Press.

Esarey, D. S. (1981). *Final report on FAI-270 and Illinois Route 460 Related Excavations at The Lohmann Site (11-S-49), St. Clair County, Illinois. Archaeological Research Laboratory, Reports of Investigations Number 3*. Macomb: Western Illinois University.

Esarey, D. S., & Pauketat, T. (1992). The Lohmann site: an early Mississippian center in the American Bottom. In C. J. Bareis & J. A. Walthall (Eds.), *American Bottom Archaeology FAI-270 Site Reports, Volume 25*. Urbana: University of Illinois Press.

Falzon, M.-A. (2003). "Bombay, our cultural heart": rethinking the relation between homeland and diaspora. *Ethnic and Racial Studies, 26*(4), 662–683.

Fortier, Andrew C., Emerson, Thomas E., McElrath, Dale L. (2006). Calibrating and Reassessing American Bottom Culture History. Southeastern Archaeology 25:170–211.

Fowler, M. L., & Hall, R. L. (1975). Archaeological phases at Cahokia. In M. Fowler (Ed.), *Perspectives in Cahokia Archaeology* (pp. 1–14). Urbana: Illinois Archaeological Survey Bulletin No. 10.

Goldstein, L. (1991). The implication of Aztalan's location. In J. B. Stoltman (Ed.), *New Perspectives on Cahokia: views from the periphery. Monographs in World Archaeology 2* (pp. 209–227). Madison: Prehistory Press.

Green, W., & Rodell, R. L. (1994). The Mississippian presence and Cahokia interaction at Trempealeau, Wisconsin. *American Antiquity, 59*(2), 334–359.

Griffin, J. B. (1993). Cahokian interaction with contemporary Southeastern and Eastern Societies. *Midcontinental Journal of Archaeology, 18*(1), 3–17.

Grinsell, L. V. (1961). The breaking of objects as a funerary rite. *Folklore, 72*(3), 475–491.

Haley, B. S. (2014). The big picture at Hollywood: geophysical and archaeological investigations at a Mississippian Mound Centre. *Archaeological Prospection, 21*(1), 39–47.

Hall, S. (1990). Cultural identity and diaspora. In J. Rutherford (Ed.), *identity: community, culture, difference* (pp. 222–237). London: Lawrence & Wishart.

Hall, R. (1991). Cahokia identity and interaction models of Cahokia Mississippian. In T. E. Emerson & R. Barry Lewis (Eds.), *Cahokia and the Hinterlands* (pp. 3–34). Urbana and Chicago: University of Illinois Press.

Hall, R. (1997). *An Archaeology of the Soul*. Urbana and Chicago: University of Illinois Press.

Hall, R. (2006). Exploring the Mississippian Big Bang at Cahokia. In J. Quilter & M. Miller (Eds.), *A Pre-Columbian World. Dumbarton Oaks Research Library and Collection* (pp. 187–229). Cambridge: Harvard University Press.

Hanenberger, N., Milner, G. C., Pullins, S. C., Paine, R., Kelly, L., Parker, K. E. (2003). *The range site 3: Mississippian and Oneota occupations*. Illinois Transportation Archaeological Research Program Report No. 17, Department of Anthropology, University of Illinois at Urbana-Champaign.

Hedman, K. M., Slater, P. A., Fort, M. A., Emerson, T. E., & Lambert, J. M. (2018). Expanding the strontium isoscape for the American midcontinent: Identifying potential places of origin for Cahokian and Pre-Columbian migrants. *Journal of Archaeological Science: Reports, 22*, 202–213.

Hill, J. B., Clark, J. J., Doelle, W. H., & Lyons, P. D. (2004). Prehistoric demography in the Southwest: migration, coalescence, and Hohokam population decline. *American Archaeology, 69*(4), 689–716.

Holley, G. R. (1989). *The archaeology of the Cahokia mounds ICT-II: ceramics. Illinois Cultural Resources Study No. 11*. Springfield: Illinois Historic Preservation Agency.

Holt, J. Z. (2009). Rethinking the Ramey state: was Cahokia the center of a theater state? *American Antiquity, 74*, 231–254.

House, J. H. (1993). Dating the kent phase. *Southeastern Archaeology, 12*(1), 21–32.

Johnson, J. K. (1987). Cahokia core technology in Mississipp: the view from the South. In J. K. Johnson & C. A. Morrow (Eds.), *The Organization of Core Technology* (pp. 187–206). Boulder and London: Westview Press.

Johnson, J. K., & Connaway, J. M. (2019). Carson and Cahokia. In C. H. McNutt & R. M. Parish (Eds.), *Cahokia in Context: Hegemony and Diaspora*. Gainesville: University Press of Florida.

Kelly, J. E. (1990). The emergence of Mississippian culture in the American bottom. In B. D. Smith (Ed.), *The Mississippian Emergence* (pp. 113–152). Washington, D.C.: Smithsonian Institution Press.

Kelly, J. E. (1991a). Cahokia and its Role as a Gateway Center in Interregional Exchange. In T. E. Emerson & R. Barry Lewis (Eds.), *Cahokia and the Hinterlands: Middle Mississippian of the Midwest* (pp. 61–80). Urbana and Chicago: University of Illinois Press.

Kelly, J. E. (1991b). The evidence for prehistoric exchange and its implications for the development of Cahokia. In J. B. Stoltman (Ed.), *New Perspectives on Cahokia: Views from the Periphery. Monographs in World Archaeology 2* (pp. 65–92). Madison: Prehistory Press.

Kelly, J. E., & Brown, J. A. (2014). Cahokia: the processes and principles of the creation of an early Mississippian City. In A. T. Creekmoore III & K. D. Fisher (Eds.), *Making Ancient Cities: Space and Place in Early Urban Societies* (pp. 292–336). New York: Cambridge University Press.

Kelly, J. E., Parker, K. E., & Kelly, L. S. (2005). Lohmann phase feature 418. In T. R. Pauketat (Eds.), *The Archaeology of the East St. Louis Mound Center*, pp. 57–112. Transportation Archaeological Research Reports 21, Department of Anthropology, University of Illinois Urbana-Champaign.

Kidder, T. R. (1998). Mississippi period mound groups and communities in the lower Mississippi Valley. In R. B. Lewis & C. Stout (Eds.), *Mississippian Towns and Sacred Spaces: Searching for an Architectural Grammar* (pp. 123–150). Tuscaloosa: University of Alabama Press.

Kidder, T. R. (2007). Contemplating Plaquemine culture. In M. A. Rees & P. C. Livingood (Eds.), *Plaquemine Archaeology* (pp. 196–205). Tuscaloosa: University of Alabama Press.

Knight, V. J. (1997). Some developmental parallels between Cahokia and Moundville. In T. R. Pauketat & T. E. Emerson (Eds.), *Cahokia, Domination and Ideology in the Mississippian World* (pp. 229–247). Lincoln: University of Nebraska Press.

Koldehoff, B., & Brennan, T. (2010). Exploring Mississippian polity interaction and craft specialization with Ozark chipped-stone resources. *The Missouri Archaeologist, 71*, 131–164.

Lansdell, B. (2009). *A chronological assessment of the Carson mound group, Stovall, Mississippi.* Unpublished Masters thesis, Department of Anthropology and Sociology, University of Mississippi, Oxford.

Lilley, I. (2007). Diaspora and identity in archaeology: moving beyond the black Atlantic. In L. Meskell & R. W. Preucel (Eds.), *A companion to social archaeology* (pp. 287–312). Malden: Blackwell.

Lyons, P. D., & Clark, J. J. (2012) A community of practice in diaspora: the rise and demise of Roosevelt Red ware. In L. S. Cordell and J. Habicht-Mauche (Eds.), *Potters and Communities of Practice: Glaze Paint and Polychrome Pottery in the American Southwest AD 1250-1700* (pp. 19–33). Anthropological Paper No. 75. University of Arizona Press, Tucson.

Mainfort Jr., R. C. (2003). Late period ceramic rim attribute variation in the Central Mississippi Valley. *Southeastern Archaeology, 22*(1), 33–46.

McLeod, T. (2015). *Developing an architectural sequence for a portion of the mound A enclosure at the Carson mound group, Coahoma County,* Mississippi. Master's Thesis, Department of Anthropology, University of Mississippi, Oxford.

McLeod, T., & Connaway, J. M. (2014). *Developing an architectural sequence for a portion of the mound A Enclosure at the Carson mound group, Coahoma County, Mississippi.* Paper presented at the Southeastern Archaeological Conference, November 13-15, 2014, Greenville, SC.

McNutt, C. H. (1996). The upper Yazoo Basin in Northwest Mississippi. In C. H. McNutt (Ed.), *Prehistory of the Central Mississippi Valley* (pp. 155–185). Tuscaloosa: University of Alabama Press.

McNutt, C. H., & Parish, R. M. (Eds.). (2019). *Cahokia in context: hegemony and diaspora.* Gainesville: University of Florida Press.

Mehrer, M. W. (1995). *Cahokia's Countryside: household archaeology, settlement patterns, and SOCIAL Power.* DeKalb: Northern Illinois University Press.

Mehta, J. M. (2015). *Native American monuments and landscape in the lower Mississippi Valley.* Unpublished PhD Dissertation, Department of Anthropology, Tulane University, New Orleans.

Mehta, J. M. (2019). Mound building and summit architecture at the Carson site, a Mississippian mound center in the southeastern Unites States. *North American Archaeologist.* https://doi.org/10.1177/0197693119863975.

Mehta, J. M., Lowe, K. M., Stout-Evans, R., & Connaway, J. (2012). *Moving earth and building monuments at the Carson mounds site, Coahoma County.* Journal of Anthropology: Mississippi. https://doi.org/10.1155/2012/192923.

Mehta, J., Abbott, D., & Pevny, C. D. (2016). Mississippian craft production in the Yazoo basin: thin-section analysis of a Mississippian structure floor on the summit of mound D at the Carson site. *Journal of Archaeological Science: Reports, 5*, 471–484.

Mehta, J., Stout-Evans, R., & Shen, Z. (2017a). Mississippian monumentality in the Yazoo basin: recent investigations at the Carson site (22CO505), northwestern Mississippi. *Southeastern Archaeology, 36*(1), 14–33.

Mehta, J., McCall, G., Marks, T., & Enloe, J. (2017b). Geochemical source evaluation of archaeological chert from the Carson mounds site in Northwestern Mississippi using Portable X-ray Fluorescence (pXRF). *Journal of Archaeological Science: Reports, 11*, 381–389.

Mills, B. J. (2011). Themes and models for understanding migration in the Southwest. In M. C. Nelson & C. Strawhacker (Eds.), *Movement, Connectivity, and Landscape Change in the Ancient Southwest* (pp. 345–359). Boulder: University Press of Colorado.

Mills, B. J., Peeples, M. A., Randall Haas Jr., W., Borck, L., Clark, J. J., & Roberts, J. M. (2015). Multiscalar perspectives on social networks in the late Prehispanic Southwest. *American Antiquity, 80*(1), 3–24.

Milner, G. R. (1998). *The Cahokia chiefdom: the archaeology of a Mississippian society.* Washington, D.C.: Smithsonian Institution Press.

Morse, D. F., & Morse, P. A. (1990). Emergent Mississippian in the Central Mississippi Valley. In B. D. Smith (Ed.), *The Mississippian Emergence* (pp. 155–173). Washington D.C.: Smithsonian Institution Press.

Nelson, E. (2016). *Community identity in the Late Prehistoric Yazoo basin: the Archaeology of Parchman Place, Coahoma County,* Mississippi. Unpublished PhD Dissertation, Department of Anthropology, University of North Carolina, Chapel Hill.

Owen, B. D. (2005). Distant colonies and explosive collapse: the two stages of the Tiwanaku Diaspora in the Osmore Drainage. *Latin American Antiquity, 16*, 45–80.

Pauketat, T. R. (2002). A fourth-generation synthesis of Cahokia and Mississippianization. *Midcontinental Journal of Archaeology, 27*(2), 149–170.

Pauketat, T. R. (2003). Farmers with agency: resettlement, Mississippianization and historical processes. *American Antiquity, 68*, 39–66.

Pauketat, T. R. (2008). Founders' cults and the archaeology of Wa-kan-da. In B. Mills & W. H. Walker (Eds.), *Memory Work: Archaeologies of Material Practices* (pp. 61–79). Santa Fe: School for Advanced Research Press.

Pauketat, T. R., & Alt, S. M. (2015). Medieval life in America's heartland. In T. R. Pauketat & S. M. Alt (Eds.), *Medieval Mississippians: The Cahokian World* (pp. 1–12). Santa Fe: School for Advanced Research Press.

Pauketat, T., Boszhardt, R. F., & Benden, D. M. (2015). Trempealeau entanglements: an ancient colony's causes and effects. *American Antiquity, 80*, 260–289.

Pauketat, T., Boszhardt, R. F., & Kolb, M. (2017). Trempealeau's little bluff: an early Cahokian terraformed landmark in the upper Mississippi Valley. *Midcontinental Journal of Archaeology, 42*(2), 168–199.

Peregrine, P. N. (1992). *Mississippian evolution: a world-system perspective*. Madison: Prehistory Press.

Peregrine, P. N., & Lekson, S. H. (2012). The North American Oikoumene. In T. Pauketat (Ed.), *The Oxford Handbook of North American Archaeology* (pp. 64–72). Oxford: Oxford University Press.

Price, T. D., Burton, J. H., & Stoltman, J. B. (2007). Place of origin of prehistoric inhabitants of Aztalan, Jefferson Co., Wisconsin. *American Antiquity, 72*(3), 524–538.

Reilly, F. K., & Garber, J. F. (Eds.). (2007). *Ancient objects and sacred realms: interpretations of Mississippian Iconography*. Austin: University of Texas Press.

Safran, W. (1991). Diasporas in modern societies: myths of homeland and return. *Diaspora, 1*(1), 83–99.

Saunders, J. W., Mandel, R. D., Sampson, C. G., Allen, C. M., Allen, E. T., Bush, D. A., Feathers, J. K., Gremillion, K. J., Hallmark, C. T., Jackson, H. E., Johnson, J. K., Jones, R., Saucier, R. T., Stringer, G. L., & Vidrine, M. F. (2005). Watson Brake, A Middle Archaic Mound Complex in Northeast Louisiana. *American Antiquity, 70*(4), 631–668.

Skousen, B. J. (2018). Rethinking archaeologies of pilgrimage. *Journal of Social Archaeology, 18*(3), 261–283.

Slater, P. A., Hedman, K. M., & Emerson, T. E. (2014). Immigrants at the Mississippian Polity of Cahokia: strontium isotope evidence for population movement. *Journal of Archaeological Science, 44*, 117–127.

Smith, B. D. (1990). Introduction, research on the origins of Mississippian chiefdoms in Eastern North America. In *The Mississippian Emergence* (pp. 1–8). Washington D.C.: Smithsonian Institution Press.

Spence, M. (2005). A Zapotec diaspora network in classic-period Central Mexico. In G. Stein (Ed.), *The Archaeology of Colonial Encounters* (pp. 173–205). Sante Fe: School of American Research Press.

Stein, G. (1999). *Rethinking world-systems, diasporas, colonies, and interaction in Uruk Mesopotamia*. Tucson: The University of Arizona Press.

Stein, G. (2002). *From passive periphery to active agents: emerging perspectives in the Archaeology of Interregional Interaction*. Archaeology Division, Distinguished Lecture at the AAA Annual Meeting, Philadelphia.

Stoltman, J. B. (1991) Cahokia as seen from the periphery. In J. B. Stoltman (Eds.), *New Perspectives on Cahokia: Views from the Periphery* (pp. 349–0254). Monographs in World Archaeology 2. Prehistory Press, Madison, Wisconsin.

Stone, T. (2015). *Migration and ethnicity in middle-range societies, a view from the Southwest*. Salt Lake City: The University of Utah Press.

Thomas, C. (1894). *Report on the mound explorations of the Bureau of Ethnology for the Years 1890-1891*. 12th Annual Report to the Bureau of American Ethnology, Smithsonian Institution, Washington D.C.

Weintein, Richard A 2004 Aboriginal Cultural Sequence within the I-69 Corridor. Manuscript on file with the Mississippi Department of Archives and History, Jackson, Mississippi.

Willey, G. R., DePeso, C. C., Ritchie, W. A., Rouse, I., Rowe, J. H., & Lathrap, D. W. (1955). An archaeological classification of culture contact situations. *Memoirs of the Society for American Archaeology, 11*, 1–30.

Williams, S., & Brain, J. P. (1983). *Excavations at the Lake George Site, Yazoo County, Mississippi 1958–1960. Papers of the Peabody Museum of Archaeology and Ethnology* (Vol. 74). Cambridge: Harvard University.

Wilson, G. D. (Ed.). (2017). *Mississippian beginnings*. Gainesville: University of Florida Press.

Wilson, G. D., & Sullivan, L. P. (2017). Mississippian beginnings, from emergence to beginnings. In G. D. Wilson (Ed.), *Mississippian Beginnings* (pp. 1–28). Gainesville: University of Florida Press.

**Publisher's Note**    Springer Nature remains neutral with regard to jurisdictional claims in published maps and institutional affiliations.

Journal of Archaeological Method and Theory (2020) 27:54–71
https://doi.org/10.1007/s10816-019-09436-8

# Interrogating Diaspora and Movement in the Greater Cahokian World

Thomas E. Emerson[1] · Kristin M. Hedman[1] · Tamira K. Brennan[2] ·
Alleen M. Betzenhauser[1] · Susan M. Alt[3] · Timothy R. Pauketat[1]

Published online: 22 November 2019
© Springer Science+Business Media, LLC, part of Springer Nature 2019

## Abstract

Archaeological and isotopic evidence from Greater Cahokia and several prominent outlier sites argues against simple diaspora models either for the rise or fall of this pre-Columbian urban phenomenon. Besides indications that a culturally diverse population was associated with the city throughout its history, we argue that a spiritual vitality undergirded its origins such that many movements of people would have been two-way affairs. Some Cahokians who ultimately left the city may have been members of foreign lineages in the beginning.

**Keywords** Cahokia · Diaspora · Immigration · Mississippian · Bundle · Isotopes

Over the last 15 years, the view of pre-Columbian Cahokia as (1) a city (2) with pluralistic foundations (3) that had profound impacts on the history of the Mississippi Valley has moved to the foreground in North American archaeology (following Alt 2002, 2006; Emerson 2002; Emerson and Hedman 2016; Pauketat 1998, 2007). As a result, many of the historical and processual questions that archaeologists of the Midwest, trans-Mississippi South, Great Plains, and Southeast ask continue to change (e.g., Emerson 2018a; Pauketat 2002). Most notable has been the diminution of questions that begin and end with societies as units of analysis. These have been or are being replaced by questions that seek to understand change as it happens within variably scaled webs of relationships.

Chapter 4 was originally published as Emerson, T. E., Hedman, K. M., Brennan, T. K., Betzenhauser., A. M., Alt, S. M. & Pauketat, T. R. Journal of Archaeological Method and Theory (2020) 27:54–71. https://doi.org/10.1007/s10816-019-09436-8.

✉ Thomas E. Emerson
teee@illinois.edu

[1] Illinois State Archaeological Survey, University of Illinois, 209 Nuclear Physics Building, 23 East Stadium Drive, Champaign, IL 61820, USA

[2] Center for Archaeological Investigations, Anthropology, Southern Illinois University, Faner Hall, MC-4502, Carbondale, IL 62901, USA

[3] Department of Anthropology, Indiana University, 701 E. Kirkwood Ave, SB 13, Bloomington, IN 47405, USA

Recent large-scale archaeological investigations in the Greater Cahokia region, reviewed here, allow us to advance such an approach. As a result, we are now able to consider two related questions surrounding Cahokian urbanism and Mississippian history. First, did departing Cahokians form a diaspora in the pre-Columbian past? Second, depending on one's answer to the first, how are we to understand the movements of people and things in and out of the Greater Cahokia region? With regard to the former, we argue that Cahokia was not a homeland in a classic diasporic sense. That said, we offer alternatives that redirect our answer to the second question, positing that Cahokians actively centered themselves vis-à-vis both the regional landscape and the distant places/powers, from Carson and Lake Providence in the lower Mississippi Valley to Trempealeau in the upper Mississippi Valley (see Mehta and Connaway, this volume; Pauketat et al. 2015b; Weinstein 2005). These alternatives will entail distinguishing early Cahokian colonial sites, pilgrimage complexes, and expatriate settlements from later post-Cahokian settlements and then differentiating the reasons that Cahokians or their things might have ended up in distant lands (Emerson and Lewis 1991; Stoltman 1991; see other diaspora articles, this volume).

After briefly introducing diaspora theory, we turn to review the latest archaeological evidence of Cahokian urbanism and its expansive qualities. We use that review to suggest that a major source for Cahokia-inspired historical change in the Mississippi Valley and beyond was the movement, alignment, and emplacement of political-religious forces and the things that conveyed those forces into and through the Greater Cahokia region and beyond. We conclude that some but not all Cahokian movements, alignments, and emplacements involved significant human population relocations. Where they did, we caution against models that uncritically treat American Indian people as passive culture bearers who might transfer a full complement of cultural knowledge and cosmic order from here to there.

## Diaspora Revisited

Ian Lilley (2004:287) defines *diaspora theory* as being concerned with "creating and maintaining identity in communities dispersed among other peoples." However, diasporic studies have become fragmented (Anthias 1998; Clifford 1994; Lilley 2004, 2006). Some theorists categorize diasporic societies as unique social forms, the products of postcolonial forces (Hall 1992). Other theorists generalize the social processes to many societies, including those in the deep past (Bender 2001). Safran (1991:83) laments that diasporic labels "seem increasingly to be used as metaphoric designations for . . . expatriates, expellees, political refugees, alien residents, immigrants, and ethnic and racial minorities."

There is no doubt that diaspora, in the modern sense, emerged directly from its roots as a descriptor for the Jewish dispersions that Robin Cohen (2008:1), in his broad treatment of *Global Diasporas*, describes as the classic "victim" diaspora—that is, a people's "central historical experience of victimhood at the hands of a cruel oppressor." In tracing the intellectual and theoretical peregrinations of the idiom, Cohen (Cohen 2008:2–3; see also Clifford 1994) reiterates Safran's observations that current discussions have turned metaphoric, both within the academy and outside it, through the increasingly popular self-identification by groups as being diasporic. Post-1990s anthropologists "sought to de-compose two of the major building blocks . . . delimiting and demarcating the diasporic idea, namely 'homeland' and 'ethnic/religious community'" (Cohen 2008:2–3). In their place, Cohen (2008) offers a new typology of diasporic societies.

While we are in sympathy with Cohen's concern over the diminution of the explanatory power of diaspora, we cannot follow his lead in recognizing a series of societal types (whose identification too often rests on the *intentionality* of the diasporic community [Anthias 1998:561–565]). An alternative position, strongly promoted by Clifford (1994), is to characterize diasporas as conditions that emanate from movement from *place* and from the *localized interactions and social construction* within a host society (see also Anthias 1998:565–568). In a modern context, this is an attribute of globalization.

In ancient contexts, we might identify this process as hybridity or creolization—a fluid process that transcends boundaries, be they social, cultural, ethnic, or territorial (Alt 2006, 2018a). Melissa Baltus and Sarah Baires (this volume) elaborate on this perspective, describing diasporic communities as processes always in a state of redefinition, re-creation, and reimagining. They employ concepts of relational ontology to explore how the interwoven variables of gender, sex, kinship, ethnicity, status, age, subsistence, landscape, and so forth may interact within a "diasporic" framework that is often described in analogical terms such as networks, rhizomes, meshworks, and entanglements occupying a world filled with other-than-human agents. While concepts of relational ontology are useful in visualizing the complexity of human interactions, they are challenging to operationalize in an analytical framework.

Aspects of all of these approaches have potential, depending on the problem at hand. For our present purposes, it seems useful not to conflate diaspora with all sorts of movement processes or to overentangle the concept in a wider relational context. Thus, we follow Safran (1991), who usefully mandates that diaspora events entail (1) the scattering of a population from an original homeland, (2) the existence of isolated enclaves, and (3) the creation of ties with, and nostalgia for, the ancestral lands. Safran's parameters are not only key to identifying diasporic populations but they also emphasize a central shortcoming of much diaspora research—its lack of interest in *the point of origins* and in the context and condition of the original homeland population. While Anthias (1998:558) contends that, conceptually, diaspora too often "deploy(s) a notion of ethnicity which privileges the point of 'origin' in constructing identify and solidarity," the reality is that the contextualization of the homeland populations, who form the essential core of diaspora movements, remain understudied and undertheorized. They are a shadow people who are most often characterized in terms of an essentialized homogeneity that obscures internal variation and entanglements such as ethnicity, age, gender, and status/class—they are all too often created through a diasporic mythology of ancestral unity (*e.g.*, Anthias 1998).

With regard to Cahokia, it seems likely that such ancestral unity never existed. Possibly this is because, like all early cities, Cahokia was a work in progress involving a continual coalescence and dispersal of ethnically and culturally diverse groups (Emerson 2018a). To be sure, Greater Cahokia was a Pan-Indian city comprised of culturally, ethnically, and probably linguistically diverse groups. Cahokia could be equally understood as a diasporic destination as groups left their Woodland homelands in the surrounding regions to participate in the Cahokia phenomena. We have argued in various places that one of the goals of the Cahokian leadership was, in fact, to create a virtual homogeneity through consensual ritual, religion, and social behaviors—to create a new mythic Cahokian "homeland" for its diverse population. Cahokia was essentially

a gathering of strangers, making the implications of the recorded chronological shifts in population and cultural practices even more important for our understanding of the relationship of movements to pre-Columbian history.

## Delineating Greater Cahokia

Such implications hinge on properly characterizing that which happened at Greater Cahokia, beginning in the tenth century AD. These happenings now include recognizing a preurban Terminal Late Woodland period of a century and half, where the introduction of maize and the ingredients needed to nixtalamize it during the ninth century were driving forces in the wide patch of Mississippi River floodplain called the "American Bottom" (Kelly 1980; McElrath et al. 2000; Pauketat 2018a). These centuries saw the first significant coalescence of maize farmers into a restricted number of Terminal Late Woodland villages, some showing evidence of incipient internal status and ritual segmentation. The several examples thus far excavated suggest that these villages' inhabitants numbered in the hundreds (Brennan et al. 2018a; Kelly 1990). The disappearance of these villages at approximately AD 1050 was abrupt, and they were replaced by dense population clusters, including immigrants from surrounding regions, with residents reaching into the thousands.

These first Cahokians built a new world that contained a structured landscape of monumental mounds and plazas that were deeply embedded with astronomical, religious, and sociopolitical referents and a homogenized materiality that incorporated a new religious orthodoxy (Emerson 2018a, 2018b; Pauketat 2018a). It now appears that religion was a key impetus for the foundation of Cahokia, perhaps stemming from a pre-Mississippian pilgrimage program focusing on sacred loci in the American Bottom locality (e.g., Alt 2018a, 2018b; Alt and Pauketat 2018; Pauketat 2013, 2018a; Skousen 2016). On these foundations, three great precincts of a single city were designed and built around AD 1050 (Fig. 1; Emerson 2018b).

### Greater Cahokia's Three Precincts

The least well understood precinct was the St. Louis complex, immediately across the Mississippi River from East St. Louis, its 26 pyramidal mounds and possible residential areas destroyed in the nineteenth century (Marshall 1992). Just to the east, across the Mississippi River channel, was the second largest precinct at East St. Louis, with its 50 earthen pyramids, hundreds of marker posts, and thousands of pole-and-thatch buildings (Brennan 2016, 2018; Fortier 2007; Pauketat 2005). Four-plus kilometers to the northeast sprawled the largest precinct of Cahokia proper, with even more ($N = 120$) flat-topped pyramidal mounds, great plazas, a kilometer-long causeway, marker posts, and buildings (Emerson 2018b; Fowler 1997; Pauketat et al. 2015a).

In the mid-eleventh century, the human population of the Cahokia Precinct surged dramatically over two or three decades, from a starting Terminal Late Woodland population of some 2,000 people (Pauketat and Lopinot 1997). George Milner (1998) estimated the subsequent Lohmann and Stirling phase Cahokia Precinct populations at 3,000–8,000 and 2,800–7,500 people, respectively. Pauketat and Neal Lopinot's (Pauketat and Lopinot 1997) estimates are higher, mostly because they are calibrated

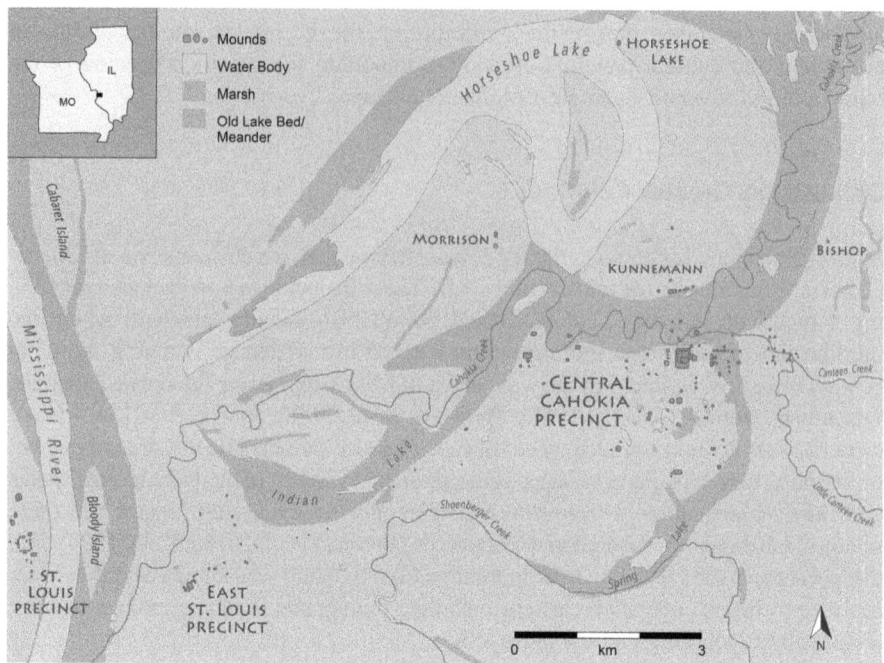

**Fig. 1** Map of the three precincts of Greater Cahokia. (Used by permission of Illinois State Archaeological Survey.)

to the region's newer chronology (Pauketat 2003). Their Lohmann phase population figure falls between 10,200 and 15,300 people, while that of the Stirling phase ranges between 5,300 and 7,200 people. Both Milner's and Pauketat and Lopinot's estimates recognize a sharp population decline at Cahokia after AD 1200, at the beginning of the Moorehead phase. Milner (1998) estimates 2,000 to 2,500, while Pauketat and Lopinot (1997) estimate 3,000–4,500 residents are present during the Moorehead phase.

If the Cahokia Precinct numbers are not sufficiently dramatic, the data from the Illinois State Archaeological Survey (ISAS) excavations of the East St. Louis Precinct should make the case. Based on an excavated sample of 1,501 pole-and-thatch buildings, East St. Louis went from a prominent Terminal Late Woodland village of 300–400 maize farmers to a major Lohmann phase ritual-residential complex populated by 4,900–7,400 people, according to Brennan and colleagues (Brennan 2018; Brennan et al. 2018a). From there, population grew into Stirling phase neighborhoods filled with 7,600–11,500 residents before collapsing to Moorehead phase lows of just several hundred people. In short, ballpark estimates of the city of Greater Cahokia's maximum late eleventh- through twelfth-century human population should range from roughly 10,000 to 20,000 people. These numbers do not include the rural residents who supported, in one way or another, the city's construction and ceremonial events.

## Immigrant Populations

Rural population trends are known to have complemented those of the urban cores, leading to the conclusion that the entire Cahokian experiment could only have

happened with significant immigration into the region (Alt 2006; Pauketat 2003). Based on both artifact assemblages and isotopic studies, one can estimate that a third or more of the new city's residents were outsiders (Hedman et al. 2018; Slater et al. 2014). Some of the archaeological evidence of foreigners derives from the upland Richland Complex east of Cahokia. For example, Alt (2018a) describes over 80 structures, including unusual single-post houses and storage huts grouped around courtyards at the Lohmann phase Halliday site. The village contained an array of local, foreign, or hybrid ceramics, including numerous Varney Red Filmed jars similar to those from southeast Missouri (see Morse and Morse 1983). The significant percentage of these unusual ceramics led Alt (2006, 2008) to postulate that the origin point of many Halliday villagers was the Eastern Lowlands and southern Ozarks of Missouri.

The resulting diversity of this and other suspected rural and central residential areas may have lasted throughout Cahokian history. Evidence of this tentative inference derives from a mortuary analysis by Emerson and Eve Hargrave (Emerson and Hargrave 2000), who demonstrated that burial practices at the thirteenth-century (Moorehead phase) Kane Mound site were distinct from typical Cahokian burial traditions. The mortuary contained idiosyncratic burial goods, extensive use of fire in burial ceremonies, the occasional presence of foreign ceramics, and significant variance in burial orientations. These various attributes suggested close ties to the central and upper Illinois River valley and indicated that the burials were associated with a group who were ethnically distinct from the local Cahokians (Emerson 2012).

Coming on the heels of such evidence has been new bioarchaeological research that demonstrates conclusively that immigrants were present in large numbers in and around Greater Cahokia throughout its history. These new findings are based on analyses of strontium isotopes recovered from the remains of Cahokians who died during the eleventh through thirteenth centuries. Phil Slater et al. (2014) analyzed 87 individuals, including males and females and people of high and low status, from the Greater Cahokia region who were interred during the early through late Mississippian periods. They determined that upwards of a third of all the individuals from all time periods were born to immigrant mothers or were immigrants themselves. Lenna Nash et al. (2018) subsequently examined the strontium from 65 individuals and demonstrated that 15% of the Terminal Late Woodland and Lohmann phase individuals from the East St. Louis Precinct were foreigners.

Dietary isotope studies have also revealed surprising Cahokian diversity. Emerson et al. (2015) have confirmed, through isotope analysis, the macrobotanical studies by Mary Simon (2014) suggesting that maize did not arrive in the American Bottom until AD 900. In that case, carbon isotope analysis of pre-AD 900 Late Woodland–era dogs and people indicates that neither were consuming maize. It was not until circa AD 1000 that maize consumption became dominant in the American Bottom (Emerson and Hedman 2016). Instead, there is evidence of a diversity of dietary practices within early Cahokian populations. To wit, by analyzing early and late developing teeth from single individuals, Slater et al. (2014) were able to recognize people who had not consumed maize as infants but later had a maize diet as adolescents. Also present were individuals who were fed maize as infants but who, as adolescents, relied on a nonmaize diet. In short, there is now evidence to argue that nonmaize horticulturalists or even hunter-gather groups from outside the Greater Cahokia region were being attracted to the city.

⚛ Springer

One may presume that such foreigners became active participants in Cahokian urbanism. Indeed, in the Cahokia Precinct itself, the proportion of foreigners seems to hold constant throughout its early coalescence and later dissolution, suggesting that the city continued to attract outsiders throughout its existence. Apparently, even when some residents were departing, others were arriving.

Such data call into question one of the underlying core assumptions of diaspora theory—that of an original diaspora homeland represent the dispersal of a unified, integrated, ethnically and linguistically homogeneous homeland population. It seems likely that the Greater Cahokia region remained a fluid, diverse, culturally and linguistically heterogeneous population throughout its history, with significant numbers of its participants at any one time being foreigners. Given that, what might have been the immediate impacts and legacy effects of Cahokia on other Native Americans?

Drawing liberally from the last 30 years of scholarship, we might summarize these impacts and effects as follows (Bardolph 2014; Emerson 2007, 2012; Emerson and Lewis 1991; Emerson et al. 2008; Pauketat et al. 2015b; Stoltman 1991, 2000; Vanderwarker et al. 2013; articles this volume).

1. The Cahokian religious and sociopolitical phenomena appear to have been spread by people moving to or visiting distant locations. However, it is a key component in migration theory that migrants classically target locations where they have previously established relationships. It is worth considering that what some identify as diasporic populations may in fact be descendants of earlier immigrants to Cahokia returning to their ancestral lands.

2. We must consider that this dispersion was carried out by diverse factions over two centuries. Different generations of Cahokians might have carried with them very different sets (*i.e.*, bundles) of Cahokian things and knowledge. And they may have left for very different reasons. Cahokia at AD 1050 was a very different place than Cahokia post–AD 1200.

3. There is little evidence that expatriate Cahokian factions or émigrés, at least as known in the upper Mississippi River valley, were politically or socially linked to other former Cahokian groups. Displaced and relocated Cahokian descendants seem to have lacked the broad social coherence and networks of diasporic populations.

4. While some emigrants may have harkened back to Cahokia as a source for traditional power, archaeological evidence suggests such ties were short-lived. If there was a nostalgic longing for the homeland, it left few traces.

5. In the upper Mississippi River valley, where Cahokia-hinterland interaction has been studied for over a half-century, intrusive Cahokian populations (in the central Illinois [see Wilson *et al.*, this volume] and Apple River [Emerson et al. 2008] valleys and in the Red Wing area of Minnesota) rapidly integrated with the local populations. There is little evidence of long-lasting, culturally isolated Cahokian enclaves.

## The Basis of Cahokian Expansion

Nevertheless, these newly created Cahokians were very proactively spreading their sense of the world around, emplacing it here or there via site-unit intrusions in distant lands. We

now think that we have a handle on the impetus for such intrusions, thanks largely to the robust body of architectural and artifact data on hand, some from Greater Cahokia itself. That body of data was already substantial before 2008, given the early highway salvage archaeology at Cahokia, the FAI-270 project, and the work of ISAS (Bareis and Porter 1984; Emerson and Walthall 2007; Fortier et al. 2006; Walthall et al. 1997). However, since 2008, three more projects have taken place, pushing our ability to distinguish who or what was emplaced when, where, and to what effect, vis-à-vis the larger goals of this volume.

Among these, the most impressive has been the aforementioned ISAS investigation of the New Mississippi River Bridge tracts at Cahokia's East St. Louis Precinct between 2008 and 2012 (Emerson et al. 2018). ISAS archaeologists excavated the remains of a leveled and monumentalized landscape, 1,501 pole-and-thatch building constructions and reconstructions, the sherds of nearly 23,000 ceramic pots, and about 9 tons of other debris (Boles 2018; Brennan 2018; Brennan et al. 2018a, 2018b). In addition, we draw on the joint 2012–2016 Indiana University–Illinois University excavations at the Emerald Acropolis, an unusual "shrine complex" of 12 mounds 24 km east of Cahokia (Pauketat et al. 2017a). These, in turn, complement and extend insights that resulted from focused investigations of a distant Cahokian shrine center at Trempealeau, Wisconsin, 900 river-km north of Cahokia, from 2009 to 2011 (Pauketat et al. 2015b; Pauketat et al. 2017b). This latter complex provides a model for our projections of the processes behind the founding of the Carson site, in northwestern Mississippi (see also Mehta and Connaway, this volume).

## Three Critical Patterns

Three critical patterns that pertain to the question of how people were folded into a Cahokian view of the world may now be identified thanks to these three projects. First, there are multiple pieces of evidence complementing extant data from Cahokia and several outlying sites of massive anthropogenic modifications to the landscape dating from the mid-eleventh century (Brennan 2018; Brennan et al. 2016; Kolb 2007, 2011, 2018; Pauketat 2018b; Pauketat et al. 2017a; Pauketat et al. 2017b). More than just building mounds and leveling plazas, Cahokians were reshaping the physical appearance of entire landforms at a scale that can only have been accomplished with a large labor force.

Second, analyzed ceramic data sets confirm that labor had been or was being reorganized at the time. The evidence comes in the form of the dynamic homogenization of pottery during the late eleventh century. That is, we can demonstrate that the localized diversity of pottery making during the Terminal Late Woodland era, before AD 1050, became subordinated within or swamped by the regional production of shell-tempered jars during the subsequent Lohmann phase, AD 1050–1100 (Pauketat 2018a). Whereas before the mid-eleventh century villages made their own distinctive jars, bowls, and utility pots using limestone, grog, shell, or grit tempers, afterward the early East St. Louisans and Cahokians seem to have facilitated the production of a regionally homogeneous shell-tempered domestic jar form (*i.e.*, Powell Plain), and they did this while encouraging the old village potters and their apprentices to manufacture only a select subset of their former repertoire for use in Cahokia's central rituals. In addition, Cahokian religious leaders appear to have sponsored the manufacture and distribution of symbolically charged and iconic Ramey Incised jars across the American Bottom

                                                      Springer

during centralized rites of intensification, including feasting and Black Drink ceremonialism (Pauketat and Emerson 1991). These jars are strongly linked to the Black Drink
rituals that were an integral part of the twelfth-century life renewal-fertility religion that
marked the Cahokian apotheosis (Emerson 2015, 2018c).

The impetus for such a dynamic homogenization is also evident in the third critical
pattern: the specific mix of domestic and nondomestic architecture at East St. Louis. As
opposed to the pre-urban Terminal Late Woodland village there and at Cahokia, post–
AD 1050 domestic zones were now interspersed with the official architecture of
Cahokia (Betzenhauser and Pauketat 2018; Brennan et al. 2018a, 2018b). These
include a standardized set of large council houses or temples, T- and L-shaped medicine
lodges or elite homes, and circular rotundas and steam baths, most built for the first
time using wall trenches (Fig. 2).[1] These Cahokian public or religious buildings make
up 17% of the East St. Louis architectural sample, on average, and are indicative of an
infiltration of official order—likely in the form of several nonkin-based sodalities or
societies—into the everyday lives of people. The result was not a village order, as had
been before 1050, but a newly urban order of neighborhoods and, in outlying farming
districts, "dispersed communities" (Emerson 1997, 2018a, 2018b).

## A Spiritual Vitality

To be clear, the public urban order of which we speak was most assuredly nascent if not
tenuous, based around group-oriented participatory and spiritual experience. The

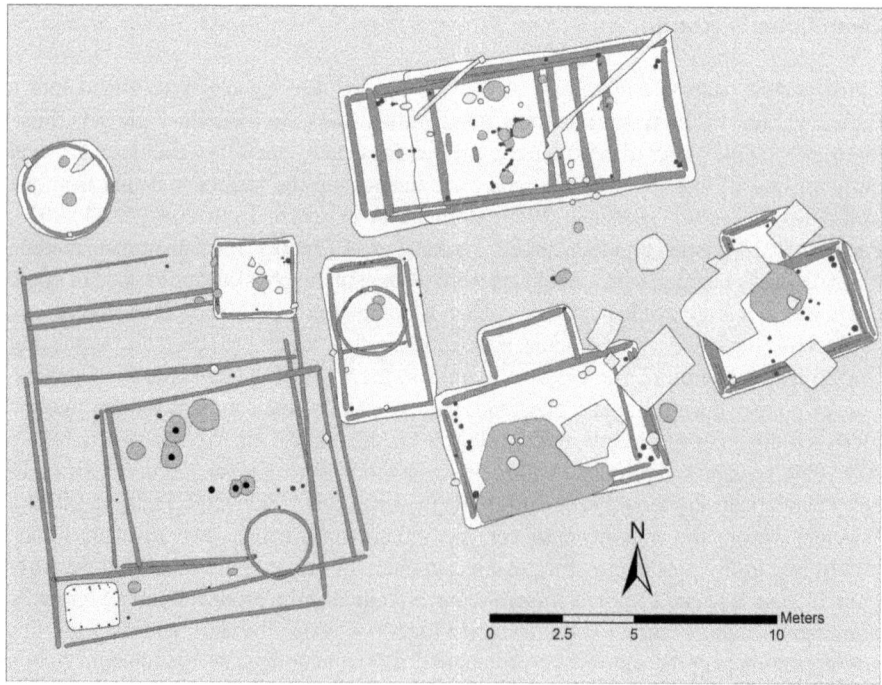

**Fig. 2** Greater Cahokia's special architecture at the East St. Louis Precinct: circular (*upper center-left*), T-
shaped (*right*), and oversized rectangular "council" houses (*lower left*). (Used by permission of Illinois State
Archaeological Survey.)

council houses, for instance, may have been sites of spiritual intervention—prayer houses or meeting rooms for groups of 10 to 20 people (Alt 2018a, 2018b; Alt and Pauketat 2018; Betzenhauser and Pauketat 2018; Pauketat 2013). T- and L-shaped medicine lodges probably housed medicine bundles and their human keepers, both of which would have been necessary for conducting virtually all community ceremonies, much as they were among Plains and Mississippi Valley people historically (Pauketat 2013). The circular Cahokian rotundas and steam baths were almost certainly animate, vision-inducing structures where people might directly engage spiritual energies and be healed of their aches and pains in the process (Alt and Pauketat 2018). Certainly, this is what happened within the circular sweat lodges of Plains Indians, who were neighbors to and descendants of Cahokians.

Each building type might have been associated with Cahokia-centric sodalities, medicine societies, or cult organizations that crosscut families and kin groups, and their simultaneous emplacements at key nodal locations across the region are good lines of evidence that the events of circa 1050 involved a greater political-religious order. Indeed, these buildings would have been instrumental in bringing about that order, as now seems confirmed by evidence in the large-scale excavations of the Emerald Acropolis (Pauketat et al. 2017a).

Dating from the end of the Terminal Late Woodland period, this seemingly vacant ceremonial complex of shrine buildings sat on a 10-m high hill surmounted by small circular mounds in rows at right angles to a large truncated pyramid. All were aligned, in turn, to a maximum north moonrise. Stratified construction fills on the sides of the natural hill indicate that the top was flattened and the slopes modified at about AD 1050, one of the many enormous labor projects of the time. Euro-American pioneers spoke of a "well-worn" Indian avenue that led from Emerald to Cahokia, hinting that this complex was frequented by Cahokians themselves, among others (Skousen 2016). Most importantly, clusters of circular rotundas and steam baths dating from AD 1050 crowded the summit and suggest that large groups of people would visit the acropolis for ritual sweats. Whatever the religious-experiential attractions, clearly Cahokia was not all about eating a corn diet while living in high-density residential neighborhoods. There was a spiritual vitality behind the order.

That same conclusion can be reached by considering the implications of the Trempealeau site in modern-day west-central Wisconsin (Pauketat et al. 2015b). The Cahokian occupations at Trempealeau and its sister site, Fisher Mounds, were established at or just before AD 1050 and abandoned by 1100, judging from both radiocarbon dates and artifacts. Seemingly built by and for Cahokians, the sites occupy two of the more dramatic landforms in the unglaciated Driftless region, both in close proximity to concentrations of Woodland burial mounds and both in view of the river. Wall-trench buildings at the sites produced nearly pure Cahokian artifact assemblages—pots, chert, sandstone abraders, Cahokia points, and more—imported from the American Bottom.

Artifact densities were low, indicating short-term uses, and the platform mound complex at Trempealeau was a one-off construction event consisting of lower soil blocks, an intermediate yellow fill, and an upper black "biochar" cap, as seen in the 2010 excavation trench (Pauketat et al. 2017b). But off-mound wall-trench buildings were reconstructed and their American Bottom supplies replenished, indicating repeated returns to both Fisher and Trempealeau by Cahokians traveling for weeks up the

Illinois River, cutting overland through northwestern Illinois to the Rock River, and then paddling down it and then up the Mississippi River the rest of the way, all while avoiding the winter ice that would block river travel. It would have been an arduous 1,000 km journey of river and overland travel, and they seem to have done it repeatedly. Based on the prevalence of Cahokian finery at the site and its establishment in the midst of a storied and unusual landscape, we suspect that entourages of important Cahokians traveled to the site for purposes of communing with powerful other-than-human forces that resided there.

## Discussion: Urbanizing Processes

Thanks to recent discoveries of Cahokian pithouses and artifact assemblages together at the Carson site, we now argue that Cahokians (including converts who lived in the city for an extended period) traveled almost as far southward—about 750 river km—at about the same time—shortly after AD 1050 (Mehta and Connaway, this volume). There, in northwestern Mississippi, a series of classic Lohmann phase semisubterranean buildings are producing moderate amounts of Cahokian pottery and Cahokia-region Burlington and Mill Creek chert tools. The relatively pure imported assemblages of pots and tools and correctly proportioned early Cahokian post-wall and wall-trench pithouses constitute good evidence of the presence of Cahokians. The high frequencies of Cahokian microtools may imply that a highly specific activity or material was being processed on-site.

That raises the question: If these were Cahokians (broadly defined), as seems likely, why were they so far from the American Bottom shortly after Cahokia's AD 1050 urban conversion? Given the data at hand, it seems unlikely that the Carson occupation was the result of an unhappy faction fleeing Cahokia (as per Emerson 1991). Rather, we may be seeing the remains of a dedicated group of Cahokians, in touch with if not on a mission for the city, or we may be seeing fully Cahokianized people establishing a settlement closer to their original homeland in Mississippi. Lastly, as at Trempealeau, these people might have been part of an entourage of Cahokians making a pilgrimage of sorts to a southern land perceived to possess powers that they needed to accommodate or occupy. After all, historically and ethnographically, this is precisely what leaders and would-be influential people did, as Mary Helms (1988) has shown in her global studies of long-distance travel.

The travels of early Cahokians and Cahokian converts, that is, may have been motivated by a need to lay claim to the wider world (already inscribed by the mounds of earlier eras and already filled with various dispersed spiritual powers) and, in that way, legitimize their new city back in the American Bottom. How better to become the great center on the Mississippi than by sending out emissaries to reconnoiter—Lewis-and-Clark style—or freshly converted former immigrants to occupy the world beyond? This may be why we see such major outreach and landscape modification efforts happening at the beginning of Greater Cahokia, when its urbanity was yet tenuous and in process. That is not to say that there were not additional cohorts of Cahokians or Cahokian shrine installations in foreign lands later in time. In the twelfth and early thirteenth centuries, southeastern candidates for such sites include Lake Providence in Louisiana, Winterville in Mississippi, and the Mound Bottom and Savannah sites in Tennessee (Fig. 3).

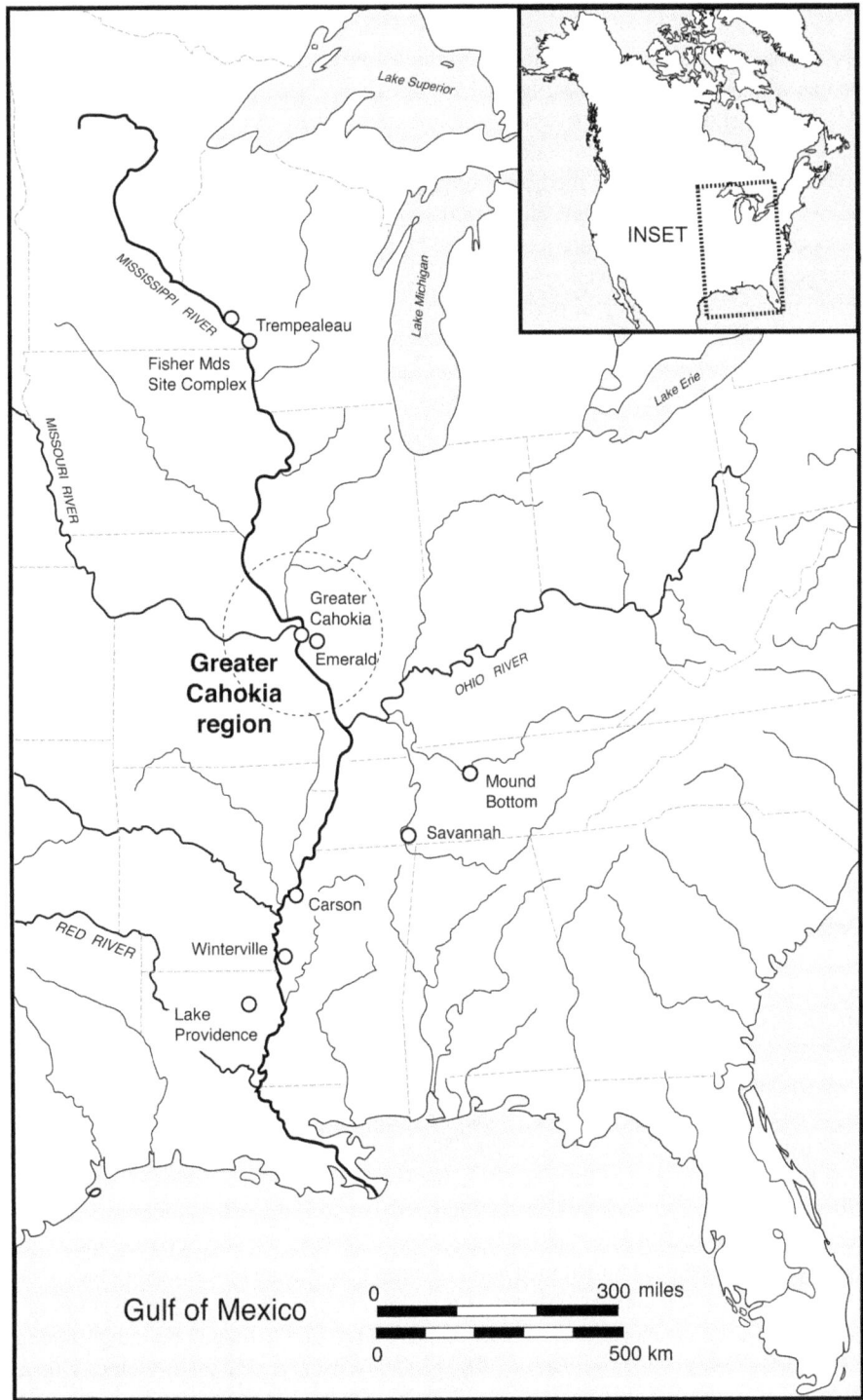

**Fig. 3** Cahokian outlier shrine complexes and settlements noted in the text

🦅 Springer

Such places would make sense relative to what we know from newer excavations around the Greater Cahokia region. In order to attract and motivate the numbers of people who now seem to have migrated to Cahokia in the decades just before and after AD 1050, Cahokia needed to demonstrably embody the powers of the known world. This is the significance of the landscape modifications and the introduction of official architecture, especially the medicine lodges and steam baths, after AD 1050. In so doing, Cahokians were dramatically remodeling the terrain on which human experience was occurring, interjecting into it other-than-human powers that might be demonstrably engaged by people. Excavations at Cahokia, East St. Louis, and Emerald testify in different ways to the integral part played by such crafted landscapes and buildings at the urban foundations of the Greater Cahokia region.

But such urbanizing processes were not, and perhaps never are, merely regional. They were simultaneously interregional. And, as apparent in Wisconsin and possibly at Carson, the people doing the urbanizing were not necessarily interested in contacting, trading with, or proselytizing foreign people. In fact, some of them may have started off as foreigners from the very same region to which they later returned as Cahokians/ converts. All of them may have been more interested in the nonhuman forces and things in and from those distant lands. Historically, the objects and materials from afar incorporated into bundles would then empower the community when opened and incorporated in rituals back home (*e.g.*, Pauketat 2013). Thus, many of the so-called trade items at and around Cahokia might have been acquired and curated objects within bundles. Such bundles could be reproduced and conferred on apprentices who lived in a community long enough to learn the secrets of the bundles before returning home. How many Cahokian objects in foreign lands, Cahokian occupations of foreign lands, or even Cahokian practices, such as sweating in special buildings, may have been the result of foreign dignitaries or apprentices having visited Cahokia for extended periods before returning home?

## Conclusion

When Cahokia did finally break down into its political if not ethnic parts, with observable sloughing off of societal segments happening as early as AD 1150 and continuing late into the AD 1200s, the cultural logic that we have outlined here may not have shifted that much. That is, one of the first things to happen was the outmigration of farmers from the uplands east of Cahokia, people whom we are seemingly unable to track using material culture (Alt 2018a). The second major historical happening comes with the torching of part of the East St. Louis Precinct late in the 1100s (Pauketat et al. 2013). At the same time as this, the circular and T- and L-shaped buildings effectively ceased to be built. Possibly, the last generation of priests, bundle keepers, and ritual leaders—heirs to the continued mediation of other-than-human power among the living Cahokians—also left Greater Cahokia at that time. Perhaps many of them went north, based in part on the appearance of steam baths and T- and L-shaped buildings among the Illinois Valley Mississippians of the 1200s (Wilson *et al.*, this volume; Duane Esarey, personal communication 2017). Their forebearers had already Mississippianized the South to the extent that the bundle-transfer process had allowed, with most remaining at or returning to Cahokia rather than constituting a true diaspora.

Of course, all Cahokians did eventually leave the American Bottom, but there is little theoretical or empirical reason—at least as based in the archaeology of Greater Cahokia, Emerald, and Trempealeau—to believe that they migrated anywhere en masse. How the Cahokians melted into the post-Cahokian landscape remains a central problem of Greater Cahokia, if not migration studies generally. In the American Southwest, for instance, relocations were opportunities for large-scale cultural reinvention (Alt 2006; Bernardini 2005; Lekson 1995, 1999). In some instances, even habits and cultural know-how—which some might incorrectly assume are deep-seated and slow to change—were terminated as part of the migration.

Given what we understand of Cahokia itself, and its interaction with its northern hinterland with which we are most familiar, we would have to conclude that the diaspora model, at least as framed here, fails to match the currently available archaeological evidence. Instead, we suggest envisioning a historical situation where departing expatriates willfully rejected a Cahokian identity when they finally arrived in their new homes.

## End Notes

1. Determining the function of Cahokian buildings has challenged regional scholars for many decades. The interpretation of presumably special-function structures, such as council houses, sweat houses, medicine lodges, and so forth, is best considered interpretive rather than definitive. Most of these buildings are disappointingly devoid of contents that might help determine function. However, the general rarity of special building forms, their locations restricted to places associated with elite or ritual activities, the occasional presence of functionally supportive material assemblages, and a broad correlation with ethnographically and ethnohistorically recorded similar native buildings allow us to recognize their uniqueness. The functions we describe and attribute to them here generally follow the regional scholarly consensus.

**Acknowledgments**    The information on which this article is based was primarily gathered as a part of earlier research on the East St. Louis New Mississippi Bridge Archaeological project funded by the Illinois Department of Transportation and the Emerald Acropolis Project funded by John Templeton Foundation (JTF; grant 51485), by the Religion and Human Affairs program of the Historical Society of Boston, sponsored by the JTF, and by the National Science Foundation (grant 1349157). We thank all of our many colleagues who participated in that research. We also appreciated the comments of three anonymous reviewers that helped sharpen the interpretation presented here.

## Compliance with Ethical Standards

**Conflict of Interest**    The authors declare that they have no conflict of interest.

## References

Alt, S. M. (2002). Identities, traditions, and diversity in Cahokia's uplands. *Midcontinental Journal of Archaeology, 27*, 217–236.

Alt, S. M. (2006). The power of diversity: the roles of migration and hybridity in culture change. In B. M. Butler & P. D. Welch (Eds.), *Leadership and polity in Mississippian society* (pp. 289–308). Carbondale: Center for Archaeological Investigations, Southern Illinois University.

                                     Springer

Alt, S. M. (2008). Unwilling immigrants: culture, change, and the "Other" in Mississippian societies. In C. M. Cameron (Ed.), *Invisible citizens: slavery in ancient pre-state societies* (pp. 205–222). Salt Lake City: University of Utah Press.

Alt, S. M. (2018a). *Cahokia's complexities: ceremonies and politics of the first Mississippian farmers.* Tuscaloosa: University of Alabama Press.

Alt, S. M. (2018b). Putting religion ahead of politics: Cahokian origins as viewed through Emerald's shrines. In B. Koldehoff & T. R. Pauketat (Eds.), *Big data and ancient religion in the North American midcontinent* (pp. 208–231). Tuscaloosa: University of Alabama Press.

Alt, S. M., & Pauketat, T. R. (2018). The elements of Cahokian shrine complexes and the basis of Mississippian religion. In S. Barber & A. Joyce (Eds.), *Religion and politics in the ancient Americas* (pp. 51–74). London: Routledge.

Anthias, F. (1998). Evaluating "diaspora": beyond ethnicity? *Sociology, 32*(3), 557–580.

Bardolph, D. N. (2014). Evaluating Cahokian contact and Mississippian identity politics in the late prehistoric central Illinois River valley. *American Antiquity, 79*(1), 69–89.

Bareis, C. J., & Porter, J. W. (Eds.). (1984). *American Bottom archaeology: a summary of the FAI-270 project contribution to the culture history of the Mississippi River valley.* Urbana: University of Illinois Press.

Bender, B. (2001). Landscapes on the move. *Journal of Social Archaeology, 1*(1), 75–89.

Bernardini, W. (2005). *Hopi oral tradition and the archaeology of identity.* Tucson: University of Arizona Press.

Betzenhauser, A. M., & Pauketat, T. R. (2018). Elements of Cahokian neighborhoods. In D. Pacifico & L. Truex (Eds.), *Neighborhoods in the perspective of anthropological archaeology, 30,*133–147. Washington, DC: Archeological Papers of the American Anthropological Association.

Boles, S. L. (Ed.). (2018). *East St. Louis Precinct lithics.* Urbana–Champaign: Illinois State Archaeological Survey, Prairie Research Institute, University of Illinois.

Brennan, T. K. (Ed.). (2016). *Main Street Mound: a ridgetop monument at the East St. Louis Mound Complex.* Urbana–Champaign: Illinois State Archaeological Survey, Prairie Research Institute, University of Illinois.

Brennan, T. K. (Ed.). (2018). *East St. Louis Precinct Mississippian features.* Urbana–Champaign: Illinois State Archaeological Survey, Prairie Research Institute, University of Illinois.

Brennan, T. K., Kolb, M. F., & Boles, S. L. (2016). Landscape modification. In T. K. Brennan (Ed.), *Main Street Mound: a ridgetop monument at the East St. Louis Mound Complex* (pp. 113–141). Urbana–Champaign: Illinois State Archaeological Survey, Prairie Research Institute, University of Illinois.

Brennan, T. K., Betzenhauser, A. M., Lansdell, M. B., Plocher, L. A., Potter, V. E., & Blodgett, D. F. (2018a). Community organization of the East St. Louis Precinct. In T. E. Emerson, B. H. Koldehoff, & T. K. Brennan (Eds.), *Revealing Greater Cahokia, North America's first native city: rediscovery and large-scale excavations of the East St. Louis Precinct* (pp. 147–202). Urbana–Champaign: Illinois State Archaeological Survey, Prairie Research Institute, University of Illinois.

Brennan, T. K., Lansdell, M. B., & Betzenhauser, A. M. (Eds.). (2018b). *East St. Louis Precinct Mississippian ceramics.* Urbana–Champaign: Illinois State Archaeological Survey, Prairie Research Institute, University of Illinois.

Clifford, J. (1994). Diasporas. *Cultural Anthropology, 9*(3), 302–338.

Cohen, R. (2008). *Global diasporas: an introduction* (2nd ed.). New York: Routledge.

Emerson, T. E. (1991). Some perspectives on Cahokia and the northern Mississippian expansion. In T. E. Emerson & R. B. Lewis (Eds.), *Cahokia and the hinterlands: Middle Mississippian cultures of the Midwest* (pp. 221–236). Urbana: University of Illinois Press.

Emerson, T. E. (1997). *Cahokia and the archaeology of power.* Tuscaloosa: University of Alabama Press.

Emerson, T. E. (2002). An introduction to Cahokia 2002: diversity, complexity, and history. *Midcontinental Journal of Archaeology, 27*(2), 127–148.

Emerson, T. E. (2007). Cahokia and the evidence for late pre-Columbian war in the North American midcontinent. In R. J. Chacon & R. G. Mendoza (Eds.), *North American indigenous warfare and ritual violence* (pp. 129–148). Tucson: University of Arizona Press.

Emerson, T. E. (2012). Cahokia interaction and ethnogenesis in the northern midcontinent. In T. R. Pauketat (Ed.), *The Oxford handbook of North American archaeology* (pp. 398–409). Oxford: Oxford University Press.

Emerson, T. E. (2015). The Earth goddess cult at Cahokia. In T. Pauketat & S. Alt (Eds.), *Medieval Mississippians: the Cahokian world* (pp. 54–60). Santa Fe: School for Advanced Research Press.

Emerson, T. E. (2018a). Greater Cahokia—chiefdom, state, or city? Urbanism in the North American midcontinent, AD 1050–1250. In T. E. Emerson, B. H. Koldehoff, & T. K. Brennan (Eds.), *Revealing Greater Cahokia, North America's first native city: rediscovery and large-scale excavations of the East St.*

*Louis Precinct* (pp. 487–535). Urbana–Champaign: Illinois State Archaeological Survey, Prairie Research Institute, University of Illinois.

Emerson, T. E. (2018b). Creating Greater Cahokia: the cultural context of the East St. Louis Precinct. In T. E. Emerson, B. H. Koldehoff, & T. K. Brennan (Eds.), *Revealing Greater Cahokia, North America's first native city: rediscovery and large-scale excavations of the East St. Louis Precinct* (pp. 25–58). Urbana–Champaign: Illinois State Archaeological Survey, Prairie Research Institute, University of Illinois.

Emerson, T. E. (2018c). The history and prehistory of Black Drink. In T. M. Peres & A. Deter-Wolf (Eds.), *Baking, bourbon, and Black Drink: foodways archaeology in the southeastern United States* (pp. 63–80). Tuscaloosa: University of Alabama Press.

Emerson, T. E., & Hargrave, E. (2000). Strangers in paradise: recognizing ethnic mortuary diversity on the fringes of Cahokia. *Southeastern Archaeology, 19,* 1–23.

Emerson, T. E., & Hedman, K. M. (2016). The dangers of diversity: the consolidation and dissolution of Cahokia, native North America's first urban polity. In R. K. Faulseit (Ed.), *Beyond collapse: archaeological perspectives on resilience, revitalization, and transformation in complex societies.* Carbondale: Southern Illinois University Press.

Emerson, T. E., & Lewis, R. B. (Eds.). (1991). *Cahokia and the hinterlands: middle Mississippian cultures of the Midwest.* Urbana: University of Illinois Press.

Emerson, T. E., & Walthall, J. A. (2007). Archaeological practice in large transportation related corridors: the I-270 archaeological mitigation project. In L. Lozny (Ed.), *Landscapes under pressure: theory and practice of cultural heritage research and preservation* (pp. 163–185). (Rev. paperback ed.). New York: Springer.

Emerson, T. E., Millhouse, P. G., & Schroeder, M. B. (2008). The Lundy site and the Mississippian presence in the Apple River valley. *The Wisconsin Archeologist, 88*(2), 1–123.

Emerson, T. E., Hedman, K. M., Simon, M. L. (2015) Cahokia and Corn: multidisciplinary research on the timing and intensity of maize consumption in the American Bottom. Paper presented at the 72nd Annual Southeastern Archaeological Conference, Nashville, Tennessee.

Emerson, T. E., Koldehoff, B. H., & Brennan, T. K. (Eds.). (2018). *Revealing Greater Cahokia, North America's first native city: rediscovery and large-scale excavations of the East St. Louis Precinct.* Urbana–Champaign: Illinois State Archaeological Survey, Prairie Research Institute, University of Illinois.

Fortier, A. C. (Ed.). (2007). *The archaeology of the East St. Louis Mound Center, Part II: the northside excavations.* Urbana: Illinois Transportation Archaeological Research Program, University of Illinois.

Fortier, A. C., Emerson, T. E., & McElrath, D. L. (2006). Calibrating and reassessing American Bottom culture history. *Southeastern Archaeology, 25*(2), 170–211.

Fowler, M. L. (1997). *The Cahokia atlas: a historical atlas of Cahokia archaeology.* Urbana: Illinois Transportation Archaeological Research Program, University of Illinois.

Hall, S. (1992). The question of cultural identity. In S. Hall, D. Held, & T. McGrew (Eds.), *Modernity and its futures* (pp. 273–325). London: Polity Press.

Hedman, K. M., Slater, P. A., Fort, M. A., Emerson, T. E. & Lambert, J. M. (2018). Expanding the strontium isoscape for the American midcontinent: Identifying potential places of origin for Cahokian and Pre-Columbian migrants. *Journal of Archaeological Science: Reports 22,* 202–213.

Helms, M. W. (1988). *Ulysses' sail: an ethnographic odyssey of power, knowledge, and geographical distance.* Princeton, NJ: Princeton University Press.

Kelly, J. E. (1980). *Formative developments at Cahokia and the adjacent American Bottom: a Merrell Tract perspective.* Madison, WI: Unpublished PhD dissertation, Department of Anthropology, University of Wisconsin.

Kelly, J. E. (1990). Range site community patterns and the Mississippian emergence. In B. Smith (Ed.), *The Mississippian emergence* (pp. 67–112). Washington, DC.: Smithsonian Institution Press.

Kolb, M. F. (2007). Site setting and prehistoric landscaping practice. In A. C. Fortier (Ed.), *The archaeology of the East St. Louis Mound Center, Part II: the northside excavations* (pp. 477–511). Urbana: Illinois Transportation Archaeological Research Program, University of Illinois.

Kolb, M. F. (2011). *Emerald Mound geomorphological report, submitted to the Illinois State Archaeological Survey.* Urbana: University of Illinois.

Kolb, M. F. (2018). Riverine and anthropogenic landscapes of the East St. Louis area. In T. E. Emerson, B. H. Koldehoff, & T. K. Brennan (Eds.), *Revealing Greater Cahokia, North America's first native city: rediscovery and large-scale excavations of the East St. Louis Precinct* (pp. 95–125). Urbana–Champaign: Illinois State Archaeological Survey, Prairie Research Institute, University of Illinois.

Lekson, S. H. (1995). The abandonment of Chaco Canyon, the Mesa Verde migrations, and the reorganization of the Pueblo world. *Journal of Anthropological Archaeology, 14,* 184–202.

Lekson, S. H. (1999). *The Chaco meridian: centers of political power in the ancient Southwest*. Walnut Canyon, CA: AltaMira.

Lilley, I. (2004). Diaspora and identity in archaeology: moving beyond the black Atlantic. In L. M. Meskell & R. W. Preucel (Eds.), *A companion to social archaeology* (pp. 287–312). Oxford: Blackwell.

Lilley, I. (2006). Archaeology, diaspora and decolonization. *Journal of Social Archaeology*. https://doi.org/10.1177/1469605306060560.

Marshall, J. B. (1992). The St. Louis Mound Group: historical accounts and pictorial depictions. *The Missouri Archaeologist, 53*, 43–79.

McElrath, D. L., Emerson, T. E., & Fortier, A. C. (2000). Social evolution or social response? A fresh look at "good gray cultures" after four decades of Midwest research. In T. E. Emerson, D. L. McElrath, & A. C. Fortier (Eds.), *Late Woodland societies: tradition and transformation across the midcontinent* (pp. 3–36). Lincoln: University of Nebraska Press.

Milner, G. R. (1998). *The Cahokia chiefdom: the archaeology of a Mississippian society*. Washington, DC: Smithsonian Institution Press.

Morse, D. F., & Morse, P. A. (1983). *The archaeology of the central Mississippi Valley*. New York: Academic.

Nash, L. M., Hedman, K. M., & Fort, M. A. (2018). The people of East St. Louis. In T. E. Emerson, B. H. Koldehoff, & T. K. Brennan (Eds.), *Revealing Greater Cahokia, North America's first native city: rediscovery and large-scale excavations of the East St. Louis Precinct* (pp. 219–262). Urbana-Champaign: Illinois State Archaeological Survey, Prairie Research Institute, University of Illinois.

Pauketat, T. R. (1998). Refiguring the archaeology of Greater Cahokia. *Journal of Archaeological Research, 6*, 45–89.

Pauketat, T. R. (2002). A fourth-generation synthesis of Cahokia and Mississippianization. *Midcontinental Journal of Archaeology, 27*, 149–170.

Pauketat, T. R. (2003). Resettled farmers and the making of a Mississippian polity. *American Antiquity, 68*, 39–66.

Pauketat, T. R. (Ed.). (2005). *The archaeology of the East St. Louis Mound Center, Part I: the southside excavations*. Urbana: Illinois Transportation Archaeological Research Program, University of Illinois.

Pauketat, T. R. (2007). *Chiefdoms and other archaeological delusions*. Walnut Creek, CA: AltaMira.

Pauketat, T. R. (2013). *An archaeology of the cosmos: rethinking agency and religion in ancient America*. London: Routledge.

Pauketat, T. R. (2018a). Thinking through the ashes, architecture, and artifacts of ancient East St. Louis. In T. E. Emerson, B. H. Koldehoff, & T. K. Brennan (Eds.), *Revealing Cahokia's urbanism: rediscovery and large-scale excavations of the East St. Louis Precinct* (pp. 463–486). Urbana–Champaign: Illinois State Archaeological Survey, Prairie Research Institute, University of Illinois.

Pauketat, T. R. (2018b). In and around Cemetery Mound: The Northside and Southside Excavations at the East St. Louis Precinct.. In T. E. Emerson, B. H. Koldehoff, & T. K. Brennan (Eds.), *Revealing Cahokia's urbanism: rediscovery and large-scale excavations of the East St. Louis Precinct* (pp. 127-146). Urbana–Champaign: Illinois State Archaeological Survey, Prairie Research Institute, University of Illinois.

Pauketat, T. R., & Emerson, T. E. (1991). Ideology of authority and the power of the pot. *American Anthropologist, 93*, 919–941.

Pauketat, T. R., & Lopinot, N. H. (1997). Cahokian population dynamics. In T. R. Pauketat & T. E. Emerson (Eds.), *Cahokia: domination and ideology in the Mississippian world* (pp. 103–123). Lincoln: University of Nebraska Press.

Pauketat, T. R., Fortier, A. C., Emerson, T. E., & Alt, S. M. (2013). A Mississippian conflagration at East St. Louis and its historical implications. *Journal of Field Archaeology, 38*, 208–224.

Pauketat, T. R., Alt, S. M., & Kruchten, J. D. (2015a). City of earth and wood: Cahokia and its material-historical implications. In N. Yoffee (Ed.), *Early cities in comparative perspective, 4000 BCE–1200 CE* (pp. 437–454). Cambridge: Cambridge University Press.

Pauketat, T. R., Boszhardt, R. F., & Benden, D. M. (2015b). Trempealeau entanglements: an ancient colony's causes and effects. *American Antiquity, 80*, 260–289.

Pauketat, T. R., Alt, S. M., & Kruchten, J. D. (2017a). The Emerald Acropolis: elevating the moon and water in the rise of Cahokia. *Antiquity, 91*, 207–222.

Pauketat, T. R., Boszhardt, R. F., & Kolb, M. J. (2017b). Trempealeau's Little Bluff: an early Cahokian terraformed landmark in the upper Mississippi Valley. *Midcontinental Journal of Archaeology, 42*(2), 168–199.

Safran, W. (1991). Diasporas in modern societies: myths of homeland and return. *Disapora: A Journal of Transnational Studies, 1*(1), 83–99.

Simon, M. L. (2014). Reevaluating the introduction of maize into the American Bottom and western Illinois. In Raviele, M. E., and Lovis, W. A. (Eds.), Reassessing the timing, rate, and adoption trajectories of

domesticate use in the Midwest and Great Lakes, (pp. 97-134). Champaign: Midwest Archaeoloical Conference, Occasional Papers 1.

Skousen, B. J. (2016). *Pilgrimage and the construction of Cahokia: a view from the Emerald site*. Urbana: Unpublished Ph.D. dissertation, Department of Anthropology, University of Illinois.

Slater, P. A., Hedman, K. M., & Emerson, T. E. (2014). Immigrants at the Mississippian polity of Cahokia: strontium isotope evidence for population movement. *Journal of Archaeological Science, 44*, 117–127.

Stoltman, J. B. (Ed.). (1991). *New perspectives on Cahokia: views from the periphery*. Madison, WI: Prehistory Press.

Stoltman, J. B. (2000). A reconsideration of the cultural processes linking Cahokia to its northern hinterlands during the period A.D. 1000–1200. In S. R. Ahler (Ed.), *Mounds, Modoc, and Mesoamerica: papers in honor of Melvin L. Fowler* (pp. 439–467). Illinois State Museum: Springfield.

Vanderwarker, A. M., Wilson, G. D., & Bardolph, D. N. (2013). Maize adoption and intensification in the central Illinois River valley: an analysis of archaeobotanical data from the Late Woodland through Early Mississippian periods (A.D. 600–1200). *Southeastern Archaeology, 32*, 147–168.

Walthall, J., Farnsworth, K., & Emerson, T. E. (1997). Constructing (on) the past. *Common Ground, 2*, 26–33.

Weinstein, R. A. (Ed.). (2005). *Lake Providence: a terminal Coles Creek culture mound center, East Carroll Parish, Louisiana*. Baton Rouge, LA: Coastal Environments, Inc..

**Publisher's Note** Springer Nature remains neutral with regard to jurisdictional claims in published maps and institutional affiliations.

Journal of Archaeological Method and Theory (2020) 27:72–89
https://doi.org/10.1007/s10816-019-09431-z

# Diasporic Longings? Cahokia, Common Field, and Nostalgic Orientations

Meghan E. Buchanan[1]

Published online: 9 November 2019
© Springer Science+Business Media, LLC, part of Springer Nature 2019

## Abstract
As Cahokia experienced its prolonged abandonment and violence spread throughout the Midwest and Southeast, thousands of people left the American Bottom region and either established new communities or integrated into others. Tracing where Cahokians went has been difficult to discern archaeologically, begging the questions: How do we distinguish between diasporic and other kinds of population movements? And what might a diasporic community born of thirteenth and fourteenth century violence look like? This article discusses the Common Field site in southeast Missouri and explores the possibility and utility of considering Common Field a diasporic community by highlighting the role of nostalgia in diasporic movements.

**Keywords** Diaspora · Nostalgia · Cahokia · Orientation · Materiality

As Cahokia experienced its prolonged abandonment during the thirteenth and fourteenth centuries and violence spread throughout the Midwest and Southeast, thousands of people left Cahokia and its associated towns, villages, and farmsteads across the broad expanse of Mississippi River floodplain known as the American Bottom. The causes of Cahokia's abandonment have been debated for decades, with some arguing that this was the natural life cycle of chiefly political formation (Milner 1998) and others implicating environmental degradation (Iseminger 1997; Lopinot and Woods 1993; Woods 2004) and climate change (Cobb and Butler 2002; Milner 1998). Considerable evidence, in the form of massive fortifications and burned villages, points to violent upheaval throughout the Mississippian Period Midwest (*e.g.*, Chapman *et al.* 1977; Conrad 1991; Krus 2016; Milner 1999; Morse and Morse 1983), culminating in the mid-fifteenth century with the near complete abandonment of what Stephen Williams (1990) called the "Vacant Quarter" (Fig. 1).

Chapter 5 was originally published as Buchanan, M. E. Journal of Archaeological Method and Theory (2020) 27:72–89. https://doi.org/10.1007/s10816-019-09431-z.

✉ Meghan E. Buchanan
   meb0105@auburn.edu

[1] Department of Sociology, Anthropology, and Social Work, Auburn University, 7030 Haley Center, Auburn, AL 36849, USA

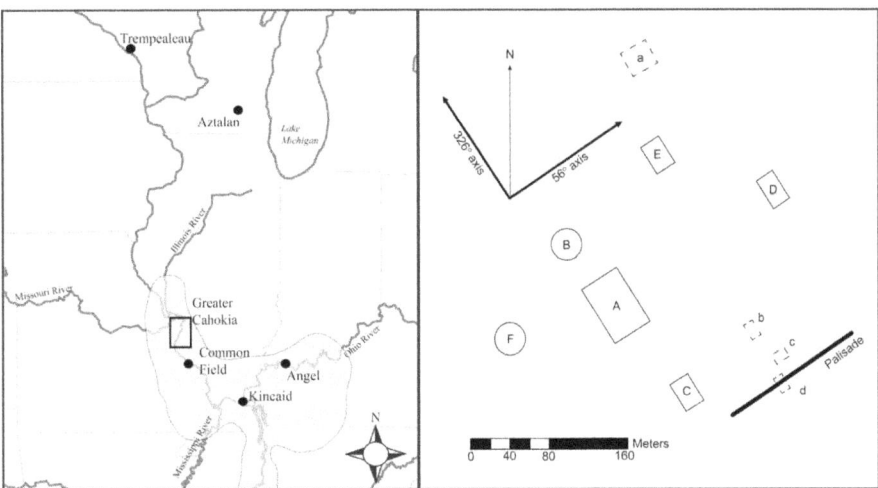

**Fig. 1** Regional map (left) showing sites mentioned in the text as well as the Vacant Quarter shaded in gray (adapted from Cobb and Butler 2002 and Williams 1990). Plan map of the Common Field (right) with site orientation axis and excavation areas a–d illustrated (dashed outline) in Fig. 3 (maps created by the author)

The abandonment of Cahokia and other Mississippian Period sites in the American Bottom was a prolonged affair, beginning at the end of the Stirling Phase (ca. A.D. 1150) with complete Mississippian abandonment of the American Bottom by the end of the Sand Prairie Phase (ca. A.D. 1350). Cahokians leaving the American Bottom would have either established new communities or integrated into others. However, tracing where Cahokians went during those 200 years has been difficult to discern archaeologically. Prior to the abandonment of the Vacant Quarter, some Cahokians likely immigrated to the Central Illinois River Valley (see Wilson *et al.*, this volume) where there is evidence of population increases coincident with American Bottom population decreases. The population increase in the Central Illinois River Valley does not account for all of the people who would have left the American Bottom, nor does it explain relative archaeological invisibility of ex-Cahokians leaving the region just prior to the abandonment of the Vacant Quarter. The relative archaeological invisibility of Cahokians leaving the American Bottom coupled with archaeologically documented regional violence indicates that something beyond mere out-migration (similar to what Wilson and colleagues refer to as "arrows out of Cahokia," this volume) occurred during the thirteenth and fourteenth century exodus.

The Common Field site, a palisaded Mississippian town (Fig. 1), was founded, attacked, and destroyed during this period of Cahokian abandonment and movement (Buchanan 2015a, b). Common Field is one of the few sites where there is relatively unambiguous evidence that it was settled by people who left the American Bottom in the thirteenth century (Buchanan 2015a, b). When the thirteenth and fourteenth century movements of other former Cahokians are difficult to trace archaeologically, what does it mean that Common Field is so identifiably Cahokian? Was Common Field a diasporic community comprised of former Cahokians who left the American Bottom during this tumultuous period of warfare and political collapse? How do we distinguish between diasporas and other kinds of population movements? In order to address these questions, this article explores how anthropological theories of diasporic movements and communities may help to understand the transformation and movement of peoples, things, and other-than-human beings from Cahokia and the establishment of new communities at places like the Common Field site in southeast Missouri. In particular, this article will focus on the nostalgic longings present in most definitions of diasporic communities. I argue that nostalgic orientations provide a material dimension to diasporic movements that help to distinguish (archaeologically) diaspora from other kinds of migration in the past. Common Field's spatial orientations and ceramic practices drew on a nostalgic version of Cahokia's past and transformed those practices in the present in order to affect future outcomes during a period of violence, warfare, and political upheaval. Despite this relocated community's attempts to engage the past to positively affect the future, Common Field was ultimately attacked and burned in a catastrophic event, leading to another migration away from the Mississippi River Valley just prior to the regional abandonment of the Vacant Quarter.

## Diaspora and Nostalgia

Diaspora is a highly contested term within anthropology and there may be as many definitions of diaspora as there are writings about the concept (*e.g.*, Brubaker 2005; Cohen 2008; Dufoix 2008; Safran 1991). Some definitions emphasize the movement or dispersal of populations due to violent expulsion, hostility, or abduction (*e.g.*, Fennell 2007; Safran 1991), what Cohen (2008) refers to as "victim diaspora." The classic example is the Jewish diaspora(s), beginning with the destruction of Jerusalem (and the Temple) in 586 B.C. and the dispersal/exile/captivity of Jews to Babylon and other parts of the Near East. Finding that definition too restrictive, Cohen (2008) argues that there are additional kinds of diaspora, including imperial/colonial diaspora, labor diaspora, trade/business diaspora, and cultural diaspora. However, in this expansion of categories, the utility of the diaspora concept has stretched to the point where all migrations, movements, and dispersals might be considered "diasporic" (*e.g.*, Brubaker 2005; Dufoix 2008; Story and Walker 2016).

Regardless if one is applying the classic definition of diaspora or something more diffuse, there are three characteristics that appear relatively consistent throughout all the definitions. First, diasporic communities are dispersed (perhaps violently) to peripheral or foreign regions; second, diasporic communities have a desire to return to or a nostalgia for a homeland; and third, maintenance of a group identity distinct from their host community (Brubaker 2005; Safran 1991). Engaging in arguments over which kinds of movements "count" as diasporas or which populations fit the criteria of diaspora, we run the risk of overlooking what is meaningful about the concept—its emphasis on the dynamism of culture change and the entanglements between past (nostalgia for an imagined "homeland"), present (life in a new community), and future (nostalgia for a return).

Outside of the trans-Atlantic slave trade (*e.g.*, Fennell 2007), there has been little discussion of diaspora in the archaeology of the Americas. Owen's (2005:Table 1) analysis of Tiwanaku-related diasporic communities offers a series of potential archaeological material correlates. According to Owen, possible correlates of diasporic communities include intrusive material culture developed in the homeland, material culture that changes little over several generations and is distinct from a host population, persistence of rituals from the homeland, trade goods from the homeland, and biological distinctiveness of the diasporic population. Owen's correlates for diaspora are similar to the old "arrows out of Cahokia" narrative (Wilson *et al.*, this volume) or something like a site-unit intrusion whereby small groups of elite Cahokians moved into the Illinois River Valley and maintained material culture traditions distinct from their host communities (*e.g.*, Harn 1991; Stoltman 2000). Problematically, there is little that distinguishes Owen's archaeological correlates of diasporic movements from the material correlates of other kinds of migration. Like the definitional difficulty in parsing diaspora from other kinds of migration, perhaps one reason why archaeologists have been reluctant to explore the processes of diasporas is *because* they look archaeologically similar to other kinds of migrations or to intensive trade and exchange.

Baires and Baltus (this volume) warn against the use of trait lists to identify diasporas and caution in assuming that materials had static or homogenous meanings and instead argue that diasporas are "processes of being." Thus, rather than spinning our teleological wheels in trying to determine whether or not a community was/is diasporic, we might be better served in considering what theorizing about diaspora reveals about dispersed communities, peoples' lives (practices, experiences, affects) in new lands, and dispersed communities' relationships to their historical/imagined/mythologized homeland. If researchers studying modern and historically documented communities struggle with the diaspora concept, how can (and should) archaeologists disentangle diaspora from other kinds of movements? If we jettison the trait lists (as Baltus and Baires advocate in this volume), how do we engage the diaspora concept with the archaeological past?

For Clifford (1994) and Lilley (2006), diaspora is part of a social process structured by movement, whereby one's identity is constructed in relation to difference—difference tied to being alienated from a homeland and living in a new land. Diaspora involve more than diasporic communities recreating their homes and practices in new settings. Thus, while maintenance of group boundaries and identities is often one of the characteristics of diasporic communities, these identities are the result of processes of hybridity and creolization, *not* an adherence to an idealized purity of what once was (cf. Bhabha 1994; Brubaker 2005; Hall 1990), particularly in contexts of violence or forced expulsion. Engagement with new communities (as well as alienation within new communities) results in the flux, creation, and innovation of practices (technological, religious, economic, political, *etc.*) and identities.

Diaspora results in altered identities and practices, but ones that engage in a nostalgia. Nostalgia or desire for a return to a homeland is a characteristic of diasporic movements that can aid archaeologists in distinguishing them from other kinds of immigration. But, nostalgia is more than a desire or remembrance for what came before. Nostalgia involves the mediation of a future-past through material engagements (Berdahl 1999; Stewart 1988, 1993). Future-past refers to the (re)invention or (re)remembrance of past people/places/things through the lens of the present, but intended to orient toward the future: that which once was, in relation to a now, is also a framing for a future to be (Fig. 2a) (*e.g.*, Koselleck 2004). Materials and symbols from a mythologized past or homeland can be given new meanings and transformations in the present in order to affect a desired future. Dillehay (2007) argues that South American Araucanian polities linked together ancestors (including symbolic connections to the Inka) and past knowledge to the present through spatial organization and monumental construction in order to guide behavior and manage the future. Similarly, Randall (2015) contends that the creators of Mount Taylor shell mound sites in Florida engaged in the commemoration of the past through depositional acts of renewal by depositing new layers of shell and other materials and/or through the creation of mortuary mounds atop residential spaces. The bundling of shell, soils, objects, and ancestors not only allowed Mount Taylor people to orient themselves to the past, those commemorative actions were also future oriented since they animated sacred spaces and continued to generate histories.

Rather than replicating lives and materials from before the diaspora, nostalgic materialities allow migrant communities to engage with diversity and difference in their present, to re-envision past realities, and still plan for a future return to the homeland. Fennell (2007) notes different ways in which diasporic enslaved Africans and their descendants engaged in and modified practices from their homelands, hidden from the view of plantation owners. Cached symbolic objects (similar, but not identical to objects used in Africa) buried in the floors of slave dwellings allowed for secret religious practices, some of which connected enslaved people to their ancestors while at the same time invoking the aid of spirits for protection (Fennell 2007). Nostalgia is an orientation—of self, of community, of space, of material engagement. Nostalgia is not a longing held in peoples' heads; it is phenomenological, orienting people to the past, present, and future. This is similar to what people experience during periods of heightened violence and warfare, processes that frequently result in the mass movement of people, displacing them from their homelands. Nordstrom (1997:184) asks, "What happens to people when what they believe makes them human—home, hearth, family, and tradition—has been wrenched from their grasp?" Displaced, diasporic peoples and

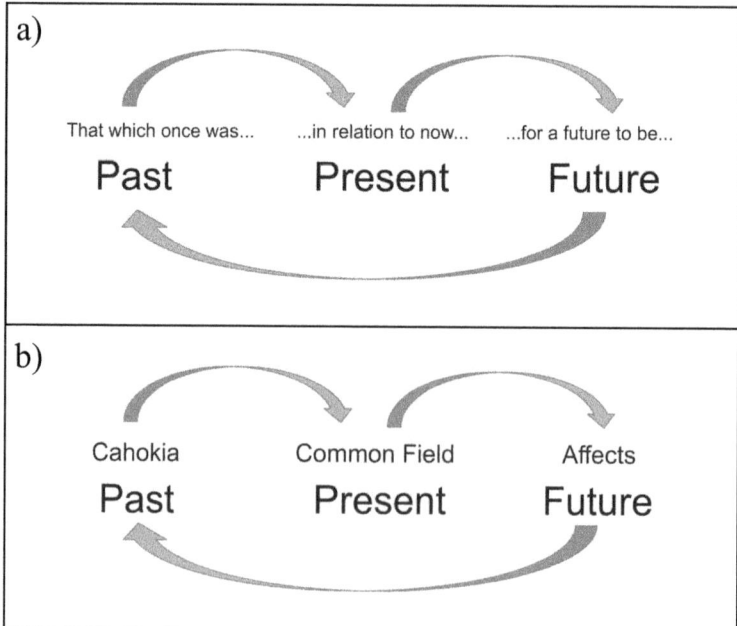

**Fig. 2** (a) Nostalgic orientations. (b) Nostalgic orientations at Common Field

communities long for that which came before, re-form themselves in the present, and imagine that which is possible in the future (Nordstrom 1997:178-193).

Archaeologists studying the Mississippian Period have increasingly acknowledged the role of migration and population movement in the processes of Mississippianization throughout the Midwest and Southeast (*e.g.*, Alt 2006, 2018; Cobb and Butler 2006; Pauketat 2003). The emphasis on theories of chiefdom evolution led to a focus on internal mechanisms for culture change or saw migration as a side effect of chiefly evolution rather than a process of change in and of itself (Alt 2006; Pauketat 2007). More recently, Alt (2006, 2018) has argued that people from the Varney and Yankeetown regions moved to the American Bottom and surrounding uplands and argues that processes of hybridity were in effect as diverse groups of people came together with the early founding of the Cahokian polity and its rural outposts. Similarly, Pauketat *et al.* (2015) have argued that movement of Cahokian missionaries to places like Trempealeau was part of the processes of Mississippianization. Contributors to this volume similarly note the importance of the movement of people and goods during Cahokia's early history as well as the migration of people into Cahokia up until the thirteenth century. Many of these early Cahokian movements could be argued to be diasporic movements; however, how are archaeologists to characterize the later movements of Cahokians as they left the region during a period of violence and upheaval? Were these later movements also diasporic in nature? The Common Field site was established by people leaving the American Bottom during Cahokia's collapse and provides insights into how a displaced community leaving a homeland negotiated and created a new home, drawing on nostalgic orientations from their past.

## Common Field

Common Field's history begins nearly two centuries before the site was inhabited ca. A.D. 1250 (Buchanan 2015a). Before Common Field became a large village on the Mississippi River, the religious and sociopolitical centrifugal forces of Cahokia, the large Mississippian city in the American Bottom, drew in people from throughout the Midwest. The early Lohmann Phase (A.D. 1050–1100) history of Cahokia was characterized by an influx of migrants into the American Bottom floodplain and its surrounding uplands (*e.g.*, Alt 2018; Emerson and Hargrave 2000; Pauketat 2003; Slater *et al.* 2014), as well as a concerted effort at establishing religious missions (Pauketat *et al.* 2015). Pauketat (2004) has argued that the creation of Cahokia and the spread of new religious practices also resulted in a regional *Pax Cahokiana*, widespread peace throughout the Midwest. In contrast, the later Moorehead Phase (A.D. 1200–1300) history of Cahokia was characterized by significant out-migration and eventual abandonment (*e.g.*, Emerson and Hedman 2016; Milner 1998; Pauketat and Lopinot 1997). Population estimates for Cahokia show a precipitous population decline from high of 10–15,000 people during the Lohmann Phase to 3–4500 inhabitants during the Moorehead Phase (A.D. 1200–1300) (Pauketat and Lopinot 1997). Emerson and colleagues (this volume) note a similar dramatic drop in population at the nearby East St. Louis site, declining from estimated 11,000 people during the Stirling Phase (A.D. 1100–1200) to a few hundred individuals during the Moorehead Phase and even fewer during the subsequent Sand Prairie Phase (A.D. 1300–1350). Farming communities in the uplands surrounding the American Bottom were also largely abandoned by A.D. 1150 (Pauketat 2003). Pauketat (2004:153-160) has contended that this massive outmigration involved a wide-scale Cahokian diaspora concurrent with a regional rise in violent encounters and attacks. As contributors in this volume note (Baires and Baltus; Emerson and colleagues), Cahokia was created by multiple immigrant groups and likely never formed a homogenous ethnic "homeland." Thus, the Moorehead and Sand Prairie Phase exodus/diaspora from Cahokia would have been comprised of diverse groups of ex-Cahokians who may have never completely lost their ancestral ethnic identities or cultural associations from prior to moving to the American Bottom (Emerson et al., this volume).

The majority of the occupation at the Common Field site has its genesis in the thirteenth century Cahokian exodus. The Common Field site is a multi-mound, palisaded Mississippian community located outside of modern-day Ste. Genevieve in southeastern Missouri, approximately 80 kilometers south of Cahokia (Fig. 1). Based on my excavations from 2010 to 2012 and a number of radiocarbon dates, the site appears to have been settled in the mid-thirteenth century and burned in a catastrophic event 50 years later (Buchanan 2015a, b). Prior to the Moorehead Phase creation of Common Field, there was a group of small villages making Late Woodland (ca. A.D. 400–1000) pottery located 2 kilometers south of the site (Keslin 1964). A smattering of Terminal Late Woodland and Lohmann Phase Mississippian pottery (Buchanan 2015a; Ferguson 1990) at Common Field indicates that there may have been a small hamlet present for a short period, but no architecture or features dating to that period have been found; there is nothing to indicate a Stirling Phase presence at Common Field. The major settling of Common Field coincides with Cahokia's Moorehead Phase and the mass outmigration from Cahokia and related sites in the American Bottom floodplain. Based on similarities in material culture and architectural practices, Common Field appears to have been largely settled by people who left Cahokia (Buchanan 2015a).

If one were to apply the diaspora checklist advocated by Owen (2005), Common Field may not fulfill one of the primary criteria—namely, maintenance of group identity, distinct from that of the host community. Prior to Common Field, few people were living in the Ste. Genevieve flood plain. There was a small farmstead (the Bauman site) near Common Field where people were making Stirling Phase (A.D. 1100–1200) and Moorehead Phase Cahokian-style artifacts (Voigt 1985). Overall though, the culture history of the Ste. Genevieve floodplain demonstrates that the region was mostly depopulated during Cahokia's Lohmann and Stirling Phases (with the exception of Bauman) and then repopulated during the Moorehead Phase (Buchanan 2015a). The influx of people who created Common Field in the mid-thirteenth century would have outnumbered the people living at the Bauman farmstead. Rather than maintaining an identity distinct from a host community, the people who created Common Field were the primary community. If Cahokia was populated by migrants moving into the American Bottom during the Lohmann Phase, Common Field may be a group of Cahokians returning to their ancestral homeland in the Ste. Genevieve floodplain (see Emerson et al., this volume).

While the Common Field shared many material culture and architectural practices with American Bottom communities, it was not a static continuation of what came before. While we should not necessarily assume that migrant communities replicated the material practices from their places of origin, the practices used at Common Field show a nostalgic longing for a past Cahokia. This nostalgia for Cahokian pasts in Common Field's present is visible in the spatial orientation of the site monuments and architecture and in the construction, decoration, and consumption of ceramic serving wares, all of which had the potentiality for future affects.

## Spatial Orientations

During the Lohmann Phase (ca. A.D. 1050), Cahokia experienced major population growth and the city was organized with a new orientation such that buildings, mounds, plazas, and other monumental constructions were oriented to 5-degrees of azimuth (Baires 2014; Fowler 1997). Other towns and villages in the American Bottom and surrounding uplands incorporated Cahokia's 5-degrees of azimuth or had orientations that referenced lunar and solar phenomena (Pauketat 2013a). Pauketat *et al.* (2017; Pauketat 2013a) argue that the mounds and many of the structures at the Emerald site (located east of Cahokia and constructed ca. AD 1000–1100) were aligned with the moon's 18.6-year cycle, oriented 53-degrees of azimuth. While many of the referents behind the organization of other sites in the region are yet unknown, it is clear that Cahokian sites during the Lohmann and Stirling Phases had cosmological orientating orthodoxies.

Communities were less rigidly organized during the later Moorehead and Sand Prairie Phases. While mounds created during the earlier Lohmann and Stirling Phases kept their original orientations, newly created structures frequently deviated from earlier organizational principles. For example, some of the Moorehead structures at Cahokia's Tract 15B were oriented with their long axis 14-degrees of azimuth (Pauketat 2013b). Moorehead and Sand Prairie Phase neighborhoods in Cahokia's Tract 15A were oriented around newly created monuments (Pauketat 1998) and Cahokia's Tract ICT-II and rural settlements in the American Bottom were organized along topographic features rather than Cahokia's Lohmann Phase community-wide orientation (Collins 1990; Mehrer 1995).

Plan maps from features excavated at Common Field in 2010–2012 (Buchanan 2015a) and a map of features visible on the site surface in 1980 (O'Brien *et al.* 1982:Figure 3) reveal strong, site-wide orientations (Figs. 1 and 3). The mounds and the palisade would have been primary orienting features due to their size and visibility. Mound A, the central feature of the site, was once an imposing 30-foot tall, pyramidal platform mound. Now reduced to approximately 15 feet in height, the mound still retains its basic orientation with the long axis at approximately 326-degrees of azimuth. The southern palisade wall is perpendicular (56-degrees of azimuth) to the long axis of mound A. Structures 22 and 11 (Fig. 3c, d) excavated at Common Field follow this organizational trend, either paralleling the north/south axis of mound A or paralleling the east/west orientation of the palisade. Some of the surface stains from likely structures mapped in 1980 after a flood/scouring event that occurred in 1979 (O'Brien *et al.* 1982:Figure 3) also follow this organizational plan (Fig. 3a). Feature 26 (Fig. 3b) deviates from the dominant orienting trend present in the other structures and mound A and has its long axis at 127-degrees of azimuth.

The site-wide organizational principle at Common Field is reminiscent of early Lohmann Phase orienting orthodoxies like the 5-degrees of azimuth at Cahokia or

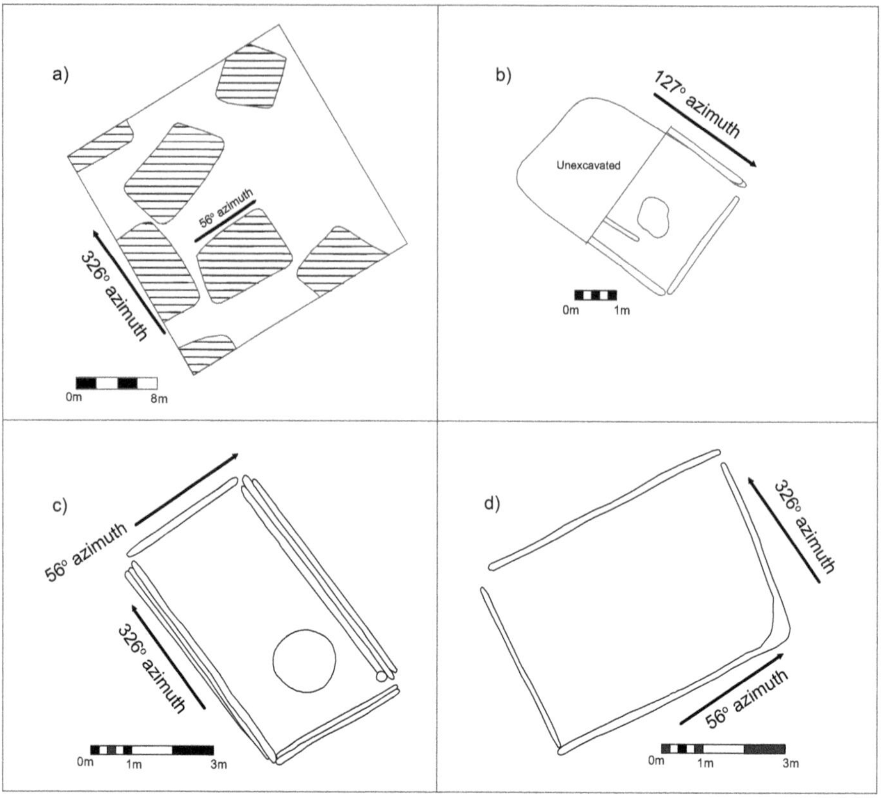

**Fig. 3** Common Field feature orientations. (a) Surface stains mapped in 1980 (modified from O'Brien *et al.* 1982:Figure 3, redrawn and created by the author). (b) Feature 26 (structure) plan map. (c) Feature 22 (structure) plan map. (d) Feature 11 (structure) plan map (maps b–d created by the author)

the 53-degrees of azimuth at Emerald, *not* the contemporaneous Moorehead and Sand Prairie Phase orientations in the American Bottom. Common Field's orientations could have been an attempt on the part of the people of Common Field to create the same kinds of religious affects that Lohmann Phase Cahokia and Emerald's orientations did (cf. Watts Malouchos, this volume). The 3-degree difference between the Common Field 56-degrees of azimuth and the Emerald 53-degrees of azimuth is possibly due to the presence of the bluffs located directly east and west of Common Field. At Emerald, the view to watch the northern maximum moon rise (53-degrees of azimuth) and the southern maximum moon set (231-degrees of azimuth) would have been unobstructed (Pauketat 2013a); at Common Field, the moon would have rose and set from the bluffs, slightly changing the angle and position at which the moon was visible to people in the floodplain. Despite the slight difference in azimuths, it is highly likely the earthen monuments, palisade, and structures at Common Field are oriented to the same lunar northern maximum moonrise and southern maximum moonset as Emerald. Feature 26 with its different orientation, is also within 3-degrees of the minimum southern moonrise, an orientation seen at the Lohmann Phase Lange site located northwest of Emerald (Pauketat 2013a). Common Field was oriented to the cosmological powers of the moon during multiple parts of the 18.6-year lunar cycle.

The spatial orientation at Common Field does more than contain potential cosmo-logical orientations—it emplaces Common Field within the mytho-historical time of an earlier imagined Cahokia, recreating a similar kind of spatial orthodoxy and drawing on the same cosmological powers (the power of the moon). The last building episode of the palisade included the deposition of magico-ritual materials, bundling the affective powers of those objects into a physical/cosmological defensive structure (Buchanan 2015b) while simultaneously orienting the community toward their collective past and the cosmos through the overall site plan. The creation of this nostalgic spatiality allowed for the folding of space and time such that the past, present, and future were entangled (Fig. 2b). A past Cahokian orientation was reimagined in the Common Field community's present (through its spatial organization) for its affective future potential protection from outside harm during a period of violent upheaval and political insta-bility in the Midwest.

## Material Orientations

In many respects, the ceramic assemblage (excavated and surface collected from both domestic and ceremonial contexts) recovered from Common Field looks like contem-poraneous Moorehead and Sand Prairie Phase assemblages from the American Bottom. The vessel shapes and decorative motifs all fit within the kind of variation seen at Cahokia and related sites (Buchanan 2015a). However, the Common Field pottery deviates in a couple of ways. First, Common Field has a high percentage of plates (over 30% of vessels recovered), more than twice as many at contemporaneous assemblages in the American Bottom (Buchanan 2015a:Figure 8.13), whereas jars are the primary vessel types at other Mississippian Period sites in the region. Jars were used primarily for cooking and storage while plates would have been utilized for serving and presentation; plates typically account for less than 15% of the assem-blages (both ceremonial and domestic) at Cahokia and related sites. Second, approx-imately 30% of the plates were tempered with grog, primarily comprised of crushed pieces of old shell-tempered vessels (Buchanan 2015a). Throughout the American Bottom, grog (made from shell sherds) was not a common tempering agent. At Cahokia's Tract 15B, less than 10% of the plates recovered from Moorehead contexts were tempered with grog (Pauketat 2013b:Appendix J) and that pattern generally holds at other Moorehead and Sand Prairie Phase American Bottom sites. The potters at Common Field incorporated the past (crushed shell-tempered sherds) into the very clay fabric of their serving vessels.

Third, almost 63% of the plate rims recovered from Common Field were decorated with line-filled triangles and chevrons, a ceramic type known as Wells or O'Byam Incised/Engraved. While decoration is not uncommon in American Bottom assem-blages, it consistently represents a smaller percentage of vessels than seen at Common Field. For example, at Cahokia's Tract 15B (interpreted as a ceremonial precinct), only 12% of the plates were decorated (Pauketat 2013b:215). The ceramics from Common Field were recovered from a combination of excavations in domestic contexts and surface collections from domestic neighborhoods and ceremonial (mound and plaza)-related contexts. Thus, decorated serving vessels were not restricted to ceremonial precincts; they were used in large numbers in domestic contexts as well.

                                                           Springer

The decorations present on the plates highlight significant reorientations in the symbolic and religious repertoire during the Moorehead Phase at Common Field and Cahokia. Prior to the early A.D. 1200s, Ramey Incised jars were iconographically potent vessels created in the American Bottom and distributed throughout the Midwestern and Southeastern United States (Emerson 1997a, b; Pauketat 2004; Pauketat and Emerson 1991). These relatively rare vessels brought together symbolism, vessel form, and bodily movement to convey certain ideas about the cosmos. These jars were semi-globular with sharply inslanting, decorated shoulders. Pauketat and Emerson (1991; Pauketat 2013a) argue that the designs on these vessels were arranged in a quadripartite division and frequently blended together Upper (birds, Thunderer beings, sky vaults) and Under World (serpents, marine shells, water) themes. The orifice of the vessel served as an axis mundi located in the center of the quadripartite division, connecting the physical and sensuous aspects of reaching into a vessel, through the design motif on the shoulders, and tapping into the powers of the cosmos and the materials held within the pot. Ramey vessels may have reflected particular Cahokian narratives about the cosmos and their attempts to spread that narrative (Pauketat and Emerson 1991).

After the early 1200s, the production of Ramey Incised vessels in the American Bottom ceased. Instead, long rimmed plates with triangular, line-filled decorations became much more common in the American Bottom and portions of the central Mississippi, Illinois, and Ohio River valleys (Hilgeman 2000; Vogel 1975). The incised (Wells and O'Byam Incised/Engraved) and painted versions of these plates have been interpreted as sun or sacred fire motifs (Emerson 1997b:227; Hilgeman 2000; Kelly 1984:10, cited in Hilgeman 2000). While sun symbolism was not unknown at Cahokia, Emerson (1997b) points out that the dominance of sun symbols after 100 years of Ramey symbolism (balancing Upper and Under World motifs) would have marked a major shift. But the triangle motifs (Fig. 4) on Wells and O'Byam Incised plates were not without contemporaneous analogues in other parts of the Midwest (*e.g.*, Benn 1995; Hall 1991), nor were they that dissimilar from Upper World motifs on Ramey Incised jars where they have been interpreted as avian symbols, with the triangles representing feather, tail, and wing elements of raptors (Pauketat and Emerson 1991). One Wells Incised plate rim recovered from Cahokia's Tract 15B (Pauketat 2013b:Figure 6.50) even depicts a bird man (human-bird hybrid or a human in the guise of a bird) with outstretched wings represented by line-filled triangles. Avian symbolism throughout the

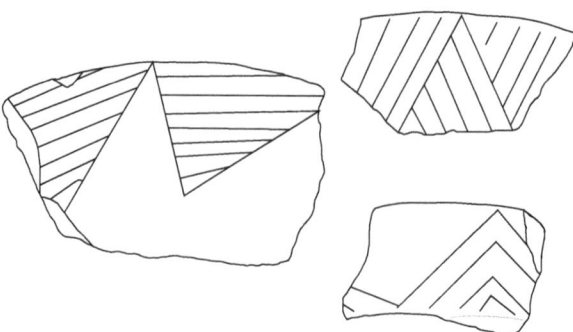

**Fig. 4** Examples of three plate rim decorations from Common Field

Mississippian Midwest and Southeast was associated with warfare, warriors, and leadership status (Cobb and Giles 2009; Emerson 1997b; Knight 1986; Strong 1989).

Rather than a major shift to sun symbolism, decorated plates like those found at Common Field reinterpret or reposition earlier Ramey Incised iconography (and its concomitant cosmic entanglements) through designs alluding to Upper World beings like hawks, falcons, and Thunderer beings (all associated with warfare), while excluding the Under World elements that were critical to the cosmic balance and hierarchy embodied in Ramey vessels. The form of the plates does not allow for the physical, experiential aspects of Ramey; one cannot transcend the Upper World, through This World, and reach into the Under World with an incised plate (Baltus 2018; Buchanan 2015a). Rather than a single or few users reaching into a Ramey jar, the large serving plates would have been viewed and used to feed large numbers of people who were present at and participating in ceremonies. Dye (2007:153-154) has argued that warfare rituals in the Mississippian southeast were aimed at reducing anxiety, bolstering group solidarity, purifying warriors, and appealing to supernatural powers through practices of feasting, fasting, and purification (see also LaFlesche 1939). Serving vessels would have been an ideal medium for depicting the prominent role of the Upper World during this turbulent period of political fragmentation and warfare.

The comparatively high percentage of grog tempered and decorated serving wares at Common Field shows that there were new material orientations emplaced in the community. The construction of the vessels would have invoked the past in the present through the literal incorporation of old vessels as temper and through the elevated prominence of Upper World, war-related iconography. The placement of that warfare-related iconography on a highly visible media would have been used to reinforce certain narratives and relationships between people at Common Field, their relationships with people in other polities, and their place in an out of balance world fraught with warfare and political fragmentation. The association between war-related and Upper World imagery and the foods served within vessels may have imparted those foods with certain powers, preparing people to go to war, to protect against attacks, or to solidify and/or create group communal identities in a rapidly changing social landscape. Like the spatial orientation of the Common Field community, the use of grog-tempered serving plates with warfare-related imagery engaged nostalgic orientations through the physical incorporation of past practices (grog temper from old shell-tempered vessels) and the reinterpretation of earlier Cahokian symbolisms on a new vessel medium, likely involving newly created ceremonies aimed at affecting future events (*e.g.*, battles, raids) (Fig. 2b).

## Nostalgic Longings?

Was the Common Field village simply the result of people migrating away from Cahokia (due to political collapse or climate change) or was it the home of a Cahokian diasporic community? If Common Field was something like a site unit intrusion or the migration of a large group of people from Cahokia setting up a new community, we might expect that these Cahokians would replicate their lives with the full suite of Moorehead Phase attributes. We would expect the spatial layout to resemble the layout of Moorehead Phase Cahokia and its neighboring sites; loosely organized along topographic features or around monuments (*e.g.*, mounds, wooden post monuments). Common Field does not have a Moorehead Phase American Bottom spatial layout. If Common Field was simply the migration of Moorehead Phase Cahokians, ceramic traditions would also conform to Moorehead Phase assemblages; primarily comprised of jars, vessels almost exclusively constructed with shell temper, and a small percentage of decorated plates. In contrast, the Common Field assemblage was dominated by decorated plates, many of which were tempered with mixtures of shell and grog (often grog made from shell-tempered vessels).

The difficulties in interpreting Common Field arise because the site, while recognizably related to Cahokia and almost certainly settled by people who left the American Bottom region, does not replicate Moorehead Phase Cahokian practices. Why does Common Field look so Cahokian and yet differ in the ways that it does? If the people who moved to Common Field in the thirteenth century were returning to a homeland their ancestors left in the eleventh century, diaspora and its nostalgic orientations were being enacted in multiple ways. The move to the Ste. Genevieve floodplain itself would have been a realization of the desired return to (and nostalgia for) their ancestral homeland (see Emerson *et al.*, this volume). At the same time, the people moving to the region also had Cahokian histories and identities, having had a history in the American Bottom region for 150 years. Thus, the movement to Common Field was also a diaspora away from Cahokia, replete with a different kind of nostalgia; a longing for an earlier Cahokia during a period of time when palisades and defensive structures were not a part of daily life.

When the people of Common Field created their community in the mid-thirteenth century, they did so in a way that modified an older version of Cahokia rather than exactly replicating contemporaneous Moorehead Phase American Bottom ways of life and engaged in processes and practices that had diasporic, nostalgic qualities. Something drove or inspired people to leave the American Bottom and construct the large, fortified town at Common Field. The *Pax Cahokiana* that was achieved through new religious, political, and social orderings at A.D. 1050 was no more and relations between Cahokians, other polities, and the cosmos were in the process of being disentangled and transformed (*e.g.*, Baltus 2015). After A.D. 1200, people left the American Bottom in droves, palisades were constructed throughout the Midwest, and violent encounters occurred. Were the people of Common Field simply re-returning to a homeland their ancestors left in the eleventh century? Were they attempting to create a new homeland through mythopraxis or new cosmological and material entanglements? Or was it both—returning to a homeland while also emplacing it within mythic dimensions that engaged the powers of past Cahokia and the moon (through spatial orientation) in order to affect the future through those powers? American Bottom Moorehead Phase structure orientations did not tap into the same kinds of cosmological powers that Lohmann Phase orientations did. The orientation of the mounds and domestic structures at Common Field drew on the power of the moon and evoked a Cahokian worldview and ethos that undergirded the Lohmann Phase creation of places like Emerald Mound. The organization of Common Field was retro, nostalgic for the way things were in the eleventh century when there was a *Pax Cahokiana* and ceremonial and daily lives were tied to the cosmos. This nostalgia was not entirely backward looking; the past and present anticipated and projected toward the future. By engaging the mytho-historical past of Cahokia, Common Field was attempting to create

new futures by drawing on the same lunar powers concentrated and bundled into Emerald and Cahokia. Even the act of creating ceramic vessels entangled the past into present and projected toward the future as potters reused old vessels for temper in the production of plates decorated with warfare and Upper World cosmological imagery. The serving and consumption of foods from those plates during ceremonies may have been intended to provide spiritual and cosmological protection in the present and the future.

Might this be what nostalgia for a mythologized homeland look like; the co-opting of past Cahokian practices/ideologies/powers and the reimagining in the Common Field present to affect future happenings? While the people of Common Field were not foreigners transplanted to a new community or region, their actions in creating their community and objects embodied diasporic, nostalgic qualities. The new spatial and material orientations at Common Field drew on the past, present, and future through the deployment of symbols with historical roots, the reorganization of cosmological relations in the present, and the intended consequences of assemblages of people, actions, and materials aimed at affecting and effecting something in their near or distant future. Nostalgia was in action as the identities of people, objects, and places were negotiated through community organization, the construction of ceramic vessels, reimagined use of symbols, and new ceremonial orderings.

Ultimately, the attempts of the Common Field community to affect their future were met with hostility. Despite the cosmological orientation of the town, the burial of magico-sacred materials in the fortification trench, and the ceremonies of war, the result for Common Field was the catastrophic conflagration and destruction of the town, likely with significant loss of life (Buchanan 2015a, b). This event would have had an even more profound effect on peoples' daily practices and their nostalgic remembrances of a homeland. As Pauketat (2007:128) notes, "when a town such as…Common Field was destroyed, people didn't relocate en masse to another place, transferring their social relations to other people and places intact. No. Things must have been mixed up, with cultural standards and referents abandoned and reformulated and daily practices adjusted to new realities in other places." When the people of Common Field created their community, they did so in a way that hearkened back to Lohmann Phase American Bottom practices, connecting past, present, and future. After Common Field's destruction, the historical and material links were severed as the site was destroyed. The bundling together of the mythical past of Cahokia, the power of the moon, and war-related ceremonies involving plates did not create a safe and renewable future—it did not save the future of those who died in the fire and those who survived altered their lives dramatically. Those who escaped the destruction did not leave behind a trail of archaeological breadcrumbs pointing to where they went next—there are no overtly obvious arrows out of Common Field. Wherever the survivors moved to, they abandoned those nostalgic orientations emplaced at Common Field.

Dhegihan Siouan peoples lived west of the Cahokian region historically, but their histories place them somewhere east of the Mississippi River in their past (LaFlesche 1917), leading many to suggest that the Osage, Omaha, Ponca, and other Siouan peoples are some of the probable descendants of Cahokians (*e.g.*, Bailey 1995; Kehoe 2007; Pauketat 2004). However, between Cahokia and Common Field's abandonment, the Vacant Quarter, and the documentation of Dhegihan origin histories, we have an archaeological and historical gap. Missing from the migration stories of

Dhegihan Siouan peoples are any mentions of a place that sounds like Cahokia (see Emerson *et al.*, this volume). If the settling of Common Field was the return of a group of people to their homeland as well as a diasporic movement from Cahokia, the movements that took place after the destruction of Common Field involved the collective forgetting or obscuring of their catastrophic past.

LaFlesche's (1921:59-61) account of origin of the Osage's tribal organization may contain hints at a kind of Vacant Quarter diaspora. In this account, the Water, Land, and Sky peoples were wandering the earth when they encountered a strange people (who would become known as the Isolated Earth clan) living in a village surrounded by the bleaching bones of animals and humans. The leader of these strange people recounted how his people destroyed everything they encountered. The Water leader, not liking the strangers' habits of destroying life, suggested that the strangers move with them to a land free of death and violence. The strangers, the Isolated Earth clan, joined the others and moved to this new land. The Isolated Earth clan looked back at their land of violence and death, turned, and moved forward toward a new land and a united tribal life. Is this origin story telling part of the Cahokian diaspora? Is the land of death and violence a remembrance (albeit, not nostalgic) of a departed homeland? Regardless of whether this story speaks of places like Common Field or Cahokia, the broader themes of diaspora are there—violence, remembrance of a homeland, and the creation of new traditions in a new land.

Archaeological studies of diasporic communities frequently focus on historical and post-colonial case studies where they have the benefit of knowing from the outset if populations were part of diasporic movements.

However, the features and processes of diaspora (*e.g.*, expulsion, movement, alienation, nostalgia) were not unique to colonial and modern contexts. When studying pre-Contact or prehistoric societies, different forms of evidence are necessary to differentiate between diasporic and other kinds of migrations in order to interpret the nature and consequences of population movements. In the case of Cahokia's collapse, the materiality of nostalgia provides a way to distinguish diasporic movements from other kinds of migration. Cahokia was the largest Native American city north of Mexico. It was comprised of local and immigrant populations who came together and created a city that harnessed the power of the cosmos and time through city planning, monumental construction, architecture, and a host of religious and quotidian practices (Pauketat 2013a, b). When people left Cahokia and violence gripped the region, their movements had consequences. As Emerson and colleagues argue (this volume), immigrants may have returned to their ancestral lands, completing diasporas begun in the eleventh century. Common Field may have been a return to an ancestral homeland, but it was also a migration away from a more recent homeland in the American Bottom. At Common Field, the diaspora was continued as the site was constructed in a way that harnessed the materiality of nostalgia—the myth, history, and power of an earlier Cahokia, aimed at creating new futures.

**Acknowledgments**  Excavations at the Common Field site were funded by a Wenner-Gren Foundation Dissertation Field Work Grant (Gr. 8366), an Indiana University Department of Anthropology David Skomp Research Feasibility Grant, and a Foundation for the Restoration of Ste. Genevieve Research Grant. The Roth Family has been gracious in allowing me access to the Common Field site and the time to analyze artifacts from the site. Susan Alt and Timothy Pauketat provided feedback on early stages of this article—their critical

and helpful comments are much appreciated. Thank you to the three anonymous reviewers who provided valuable comments and helpful feedback. All mistakes and errors within are mine alone.

# References

Alt, S. M. (2006). The power of diversity: the roles of migration and hybridity in culture change. In B. M. Butler & P. D. Welch (Eds.), *Leadership and polity in Mississippian society* (Occasional Paper 33 (pp. 289–308). Carbondale: Center for Archaeological Investigations.

Alt, S. M. (2018). *Cahokia's complexities: ceremonies and politics of the first Mississippian Farmers*. Tuscaloosa: University of Alabama Press.

Bailey, G. A. (1995). *The Osage and the invisible world from the works of Francis La Flesche*. Norman: University of Oklahoma Press.

Baires, S. E. (2014). Cahokia's Rattlesnake causeway. *Midcontinental Journal of Archaeology, 39(1)*, 1–19.

Baltus, M. R. (2015). Unraveling entanglements: reverberations of Cahokia's big bang. In M. E. Buchanan & B. J. Skousen (Eds.), *Tracing the relational: the archaeology of worlds, spirits, and temporalities* (pp. 146–160). Salt Lake City: University of Utah Press.

Baltus, M. R. (2018). Vessels of change: everyday relationality in the rise and fall of Cahokia. In M. R. Baltus & S. E. Baires (Eds.), *Relational engagements of the indigenous Americas: alterity, ontology, and shifting paradigms* (pp. 63–85). Lanham: Lexington Books.

Benn, D. W. (1995). Woodland people and the roots of the Oneota. In W. Green (Ed.), *Oneota archaeology: past, present, and future* (Office of the State Archaeologist Report 20 (pp. 91–139). Iowa City: Office of the State Archaeologist.

Berdahl, D. (1999). '(N)Ostalgie' for the present: memory, longing, and East German things. *Ethnos, 64(2)*, 192–211.

Bhabha, H. K. (1994). *The location of culture*. New York: Routledge.

Brubaker, R. (2005). The 'diaspora' diaspora. *Ethnic and Racial Studies, 28(1)*, 1–19.

Buchanan, M. E. (2015a) Warfare and the materialization of daily life at the Mississippian Common Field site. Unpublished Ph.D. dissertation, Department of Anthropology, Indiana University.

Buchanan, M. E. (2015b). War-scapes, lingering spirits, and the Mississippian vacant quarter. In M. E. Buchanan & B. J. Skousen (Eds.), *Tracing the relational: the archaeology of worlds, spirits, and temporalities* (pp. 85–99). Salt Lake City: University of Utah Press.

Chapman, C. H., Cottier, J., Denman, D., Evans, D. R., Harvey, D. E., Regan, M. B., Rope, B. L., Southard, M. D., & Waselkov, G. A. (1977). Investigation and comparison of two fortified Mississippian tradition archaeological sites in southeast Missouri: a preliminary compilation. *Missouri Archaeologist, 38*, 1–346.

Clifford, J. (1994). Diasporas. *Cultural Anthropology, 9(3)*, 302–338.

Cobb, C. R., & Butler, B. M. (2002). The vacant quarter revisited: late Mississippian abandonment of the lower Ohio valley. *American Antiquity, 67*, 625–641.

Cobb, C. R., & Butler, B. M. (2006). Mississippian migration and emplacement in the lower Ohio valley. In B. M. Butler & P. D. Welch (Eds.), *Leadership and polity in Mississippian society* (Occasional Paper 33 (pp. 328–347). Carbondale: Center for Archaeological Investigations.

Cobb, C. R., & Giles, B. (2009). War is shell: the ideology and embodiment of Mississippian conflict. In A. E. Nielsen & W. H. Walker (Eds.), *Warfare in cultural conflict: practice, agency, and the archaeology of violence* (pp. 84–108). Tucson: University of Arizona Press.

Cohen, R. (2008). *Global diasporas: an introduction*. New York: Routledge.

Collins, J. M. (1990). *The archaeology of Cahokian Mounds ICT-II: site structure* (Illinois Cultural Resources Study 10). Springfield: Illinois Historic Preservation Agency.

Conrad, L. A. (1991). The middle Mississippian cultures of the central Illinois river valley. In T. E. Emerson & R. B. Lewis (Eds.), *Cahokia and the hinterlands: middle Mississippian cultures of the Midwest* (pp. 119–156). Urbana: University of Illinois Press.

Dillehay, T. D. (2007). *Monuments, empires, and resistance: the Araucanian polity and ritual narratives*. Cambridge University Press.

Dufoix, S. (2008). *Diasporas*. Berkeley: University of California Press.

Dye, D. H. (2007). Ritual, medicine, and the war trophy iconographic theme in the Mississippian southeast. In F. K. Reilly III & J. F. Graber (Eds.), *Ancient objects and sacred realms: interpretations of Mississippian iconography* (pp. 152–173). Austin: University of Texas Press.

Emerson, T. E. (1997a). *Cahokia and the archaeology of power.* Tuscaloosa: University of Alabama Press.

Emerson, T. E. (1997b). Cahokian elite ideology and the Mississippian cosmos. In T. R. Pauketat & T. E. Emerson (Eds.), *Cahokia: domination and ideology in the Mississippian world* (pp. 190–228). Lincoln: University of Nebraska Press.

Emerson, T. E., & Hargrave, E. (2000). Strangers in paradise? recognizing ethnic mortuary diversity on the fringes of Cahokia. *Southeastern Archaeology, 19,* 1–23.

Emerson, T. E., & Hedman, K. (2016). The dangers of diversity: the consolidation and dissolution of Cahokia, native North America's first urban polity. In R. K. Fuslseit (Ed.), *Beyond collapse: archaeological perspectives on resilience, revitalization, and transformation in complex societies* (Occasional Paper 42) (pp. 147–175). Carbondale: Center for Archaeological Investigations.

Fennell, C. C. (2007). *Crossroads and cosmologies: diasporas and ethnogenesis in the New World.* Gainesville: University Press of Florida.

Ferguson, J. A. (1990) Pottery classification, site patterns, and Mississippian interaction at the Common Field site (23SG100), eastern Missouri. Unpublished Master's thesis, Department of Anthropology, University of Missouri Columbia.

Fowler, M. L. (1997). *The Cahokia atlas: a historical atlas of Cahokia archaeology* (Illinois Transportation and Archaeological Research Program Studies in Archaeology Series 2). Urbana: University of Illinois Press.

Hall, S. (1990). Cultural identity and diaspora. In J. Rutherford (Ed.), *Identity: community, culture, difference* (pp. 222–237). London: Lawrence & Wishart.

Hall, R. L. (1991). Cahokia identity and interaction models of Cahokia Mississippian. In T. E. Emerson & R. B. Lewis (Eds.), *Cahokia and the hinterlands: middle Mississippian cultures of the Midwest* (pp. 3–34). Urbana: University of Illinois Press.

Harn, A. D. (1991). The Eveland site: inroad to Spoon River Mississippian society. In J. B. Stoltman (Ed.), *New perspectives on Cahokia: views from the periphery* (pp. 129–153). Madison: Prehistory Press.

Hilgeman, S. L. (2000). *Pottery and chronology at Angel.* Tuscaloosa: University of Alabama Press.

Iseminger, W. R. (1997). Culture and environment in the American Bottom: the rise and fall of Cahokia Mounds. In A. Hurley (Ed.), *Common fields: an environmental history of St. Louis* (pp. 38–57). St. Louis: Missouri Historical Society Press.

Kehoe, A. B. (2007). Osage texts and Cahokia data. In F. K. Reilly III & J. F. Graber (Eds.), *Ancient objects and sacred realms: interpretations of Mississippian iconography* (pp. 246–261). Austin: University of Texas Press.

Kelly, J. E. (1984) Wells Incised or O'Byam Incised, variety Wells, and its context in the American Bottom. Paper presented at the Paducah Ceramic Conference.

Keslin, R. O. (1964). Archaeological implications on the role of salt as an element of cultural diffusion. *Missouri Archaeologist, 26,* 1–181.

Knight Jr., V. J. (1986). The institutional organization of Mississippian religion. *American Antiquity, 51(4),* 675–687.

Koselleck, R. (2004). *Futures past: on the semantics of historical time.* New York: Columbia University Press.

Krus, A. M. (2016). The timing of pre-Columbian militarization in the U.S. Midwest and southeast. *American Antiquity, 8,* 375–388.

LaFlesche, F. (1917). Omaha and Osage traditions of separation. In F. W. Hodge (Ed.), *Proceedings of the nineteenth international congress of Americanists* (pp. 459–462). Washington DC: Government Printing Office.

LaFlesche, F. (1921). *The Osage tribe: rite of the chiefs; sayings of the ancient men* (Thirty-sixth annual report) (pp. 35–604). Washington DC: Bureau of American Ethnology, Government Printing Office.

LaFlesche, F. (1939). *War ceremony and peace ceremony of the Osage Indians* (Bulletin 101). Washington DC: Bureau of American Ethnology, Government Printing Office.

Lilley, I. (2006). Archaeology, diaspora and decolonization. *Journal of Social Archaeology, 6(1),* 28–47.

Lopinot, N. H., & Woods, W. I. (1993). Wood overexploitation and the collapse of Cahokia. In C. M. Scarry (Ed.), *Foraging and farming in the eastern woodlands* (pp. 206–231). Gainesville: University of Florida Press.

Mehrer, M. W. (1995). *Cahokia's countryside: household archaeology, settlement patterns, and social power.* DeKalb: Northern Illinois University Press.

Milner, G. R. (1998). *The Cahokia chiefdom: the archaeology of a Mississippian society.* Washington D. C.: Smithsonian Press.

Milner, G. R. (1999). Warfare in prehistoric and early historic eastern North America. *Journal of Archaeological Research, 7,* 105–151.

Morse, D. F., & Morse, P. A. (1983). *Archaeology of the central Mississippi valley.* New York: Academic Press.

Nordstrom, C. (1997). *A different kind of war story.* Philadelphia: University of Pennsylvania Press.

O'Brien, M. J., Beets, J. L., Warren, R. E., Hotrabhavananda, T., Barney, T. W., & Voigt, E. E. (1982). Digital enhancement and grey-level slicing of aerial photographs: techniques for archaeological analysis of intrasite variability. *World Archaeology, 14*(2), 173–190.

Owen, B. D. (2005). Distant colonies and explosive collapse: two stages of the Tiwanaku diaspora in the Osmore drainage. *Latin American Antiquity, 16*(1), 45–80.

Pauketat, T. R. (1998). *The archaeology of downtown Cahokia: the Tract 15A and Dunham Tract excavations.* (Illinois Transportation Archaeological Research Program Studies in Archaeology 1. Urbana: University of Illinois.

Pauketat, T. R. (2003). Resettled farmers and the making of a Mississippian polity. *American Antiquity, 68*, 39–66.

Pauketat, T. R. (2004). *Ancient Cahokia and the Mississippians.* London: Cambridge University Press.

Pauketat, T. R. (2007). *Chiefdoms and other archaeological delusions.* Lanham: Altamira Press.

Pauketat, T. R. (2013a). *An archaeology of the cosmos: rethinking agency and religion in ancient North America.* New York: Routledge.

Pauketat, T. R. (2013b). *The archaeology of downtown Cahokia II: the 1960 excavation of Tract 15B* (Studies in Archaeology No. 8). Urbana: Illinois State Archaeological Survey.

Pauketat, T. R., & Emerson, T. E. (1991). The ideology of authority and the power of the pot. *American Antiquity, 93*(4), 919–941.

Pauketat, T. R., & Lopinot, N. H. (1997). Cahokian population dynamics. In T. R. Pauketat & T. E. Emerson (Eds.), *Cahokia: domination and ideology in the Mississippian world* (pp. 103–123). Lincoln: University of Nebraska Press.

Pauketat, T. R., Bozhardt, R. F., & Benden, D. M. (2015). Trempealeau entanglements: an ancient colony's causes and effects. *American Antiquity, 80*(2), 260–289.

Pauketat, T. R., Alt, S. M., & Kruchten, J. D. (2017). The Emerald Acropolis: elevating the moon and water in the rise of Cahokia. *Antiquity, 91*(355), 207–222.

Randall, A. R. (2015). *Constructing histories: Archaic freshwater shell mounds and social landscapes of the St. Johns River, Florida.* Gainesville: University of Florida Press.

Safran, W. (1991). Diasporas in modern societies: myths of homeland and return. *Diaspora, 1*(1), 83–99.

Slater, P. A., Hedman, K. M., & Emerson, T. E. (2014). Immigrants at the Mississippian polity of Cahokia: strontium isotope evidence for population movement. *Journal of Archaeological Science, 44*, 117–127.

Stewart, K. (1988). Nostalgia: a polemic. *Cultural Anthropology, 3*(3), 227–241.

Stewart, S. (1993). *One longing: narratives of the miniature, the gigantic, the souvenir, the collection.* Durham: Duke University Press.

Stoltman, J. B. (2000). A reconsideration of the cultural processes linking Cahokia to its northern hinterlands during the period A. D. 1000-1200. In S. R. Ahler (Ed.), *Mounds, Modoc, and Mesoamerica: papers in honor of Melvin L. Fowler* (Scientific Papers) (Vol. 28, pp. 439–467). Springfield: Illinois State Museum.

Story, J., & Walker, I. (2016). The impact of diasporas: markers of identity. *Ethnic and Racial Studies, 39*(2), 135–141.

Strong, J. A. (1989). The Mississippian bird-man theme in cross-cultural perspective. In P. Galloway (Ed.), *The southeastern ceremonial complex: artifacts and analysis* (pp. 211–238). Lincoln: University of Nebraska Press.

Vogel, J. O. (1975). Trends in Cahokia ceramics: preliminary study of the collections from Tracts 15A and 15B. *Perspectives in Cahokia Archaeology, Bulletin, 10*, 31–125.

Voigt, E. E. (1985). *Archaeological testing of the Bauman site (23STG158), Ste. Genevieve County, Missouri.* Cultural Resource Management Reports No. 23. St. Louis District: United States Army Corps of Engineers.

Williams, S. (1990). The vacant quarter and other late events in the lower valley. In D. H. Dye & C. A. Cox (Eds.), *Towns and temples along the Mississippi* (pp. 170–180). Tuscaloosa: University of Alabama Press.

Woods, W. I. (2004). Population nucleation, intensive agriculture, and environmental degradation: the Cahokia example. *Agriculture and Human Values, 21*, 255–261.

**Publisher's Note**     Springer Nature remains neutral with regard to jurisdictional claims in published maps and institutional affiliations.

Journal of Archaeological Method and Theory (2020) 27:90–110
https://doi.org/10.1007/s10816-019-09440-y

# Transregional Social Fields of the Early Mississippian Midcontinent

Gregory D. Wilson[1] · Dana N. Bardolph[2] · Duane Esarey[3] · Jeremy J. Wilson[4]

Published online: 7 January 2020

## Abstract

This paper employs concepts from Bourdieu's theory of social fields and contemporary research on transnationalism to explore the complicated history of population movement, culture contact, and interaction that fueled the origins of Mississippian society in the greater Cahokia area and closely related socio-political developments in the Central Illinois River Valley (CIRV) of west-central Illinois. We offer a new take on Mississippian origins and the history of culture contact in the CIRV, arguing that interregional simultaneity and inter-group collaboration played an important part of the early processes of Mississippianization in the North American Midwest. By decentering Cahokia in our explanation of Mississippian origins in the greater Midwest, we argue for a long-term persistence of traditional pre-Mississippian practices in the CIRV region, beginning with the first documented engagement among Cahokians and Illinois Valley groups in the early eleventh century until the beginning of the thirteenth century AD.

**Keywords** Cahokia · Mississippian · Migration · Culture contact · Identity · Social fields

This study employs concepts from Bourdieu's theory of social fields (*e.g.*, Bourdieu 1977; Bourdieu 1982; Bourdieu and Wacquant 1992) and contemporary research on transnationalism (*e.g.*, Bauböck and Faist 2010; Faist 2013; Levitt and Schiller 2004; Lubbers et al. 2018; Schiller 2005; Schiller et al. 1992) to explore the complicated history of population movement, culture contact, and interaction that fueled the origins of Mississippian societies in the greater Cahokia area and closely related socio-political developments in the Central Illinois River Valley (henceforth referred to as CIRV) of west-central Illinois. The early

Chapter 6 was originally published as Wilson, G. D., Bardolph, D. N., Esarey, D. & Wilson, J. J. Journal of Archaeological Method and Theory (2020) 27:90–110. https://doi.org/10.1007/s10816-019-09440-y.

✉ Gregory D. Wilson
  gdwilson@anth.ucsb.edu

[1] Department of Anthropology, University of California, Santa Barbara, CA 93106-3210, USA

[2] Department of Anthropology, Northern Illinois University, DeKalb, IL 60115, USA

[3] Dickson Mounds Museum, Lewistown, IL 61542, USA

[4] Indiana University–Purdue University Indianapolis, Indianapolis, IN 46202, USA

Mississippian period in the eleventh and twelfth centuries AD comprised an era during which many Native American groups throughout the Midwest and Southeast altered their quotidian lifeways, religious beliefs, and socioeconomic relationships in response to engagement with each other, new ideas, and practices. Cahokia, the earliest and most complex Mississippian polity (see Emerson 1997; Fowler 1997; Kelly 1990a; Milner 1990; Pauketat 2004; Pauketat and Emerson 1997), played an important role in these far-flung negotiations, although recent scholarship continues to reframe our understanding of this historical process. Indeed, culture contact (*sensu* Lightfoot 1995; Gosden 2004; Loren 2008)[1] and population movements both to and from Cahokia are now being viewed as critical to the development of Mississippian culture, with local hinterland groups actively contributing to this process (Alt 2002, 2006; Emerson 1999). By the eleventh century, Cahokia was as much a religion coming-into-being as it was the complex society that came to re-fashion Indigenous identity and history across a large portion of North America, and a number of poorly connected Native American groups became better integrated through the establishment of new forms of religious ceremonialism in newly established or transformed monumental spaces during this time. The American Bottom and neighboring regions such as the CIRV thus present an excellent context for evaluating the complex dynamics of pre-Columbian Native American culture contact, with implications for how we might conceptualize and investigate Cahokia's relationship with other hinterland groups specifically (Fig. 1), and the archaeology of indigenous and immigrant populations in non-colonial contexts more broadly.

To this end, we draw on a productive set of literature from contemporary migration studies, the most prominent of which addresses transnational social fields. Anthropologists have long recognized the existence of important social, political, religious, and economic relationships crosscutting territorial boundaries of societies. Indeed, scholars of transnationalism (*e.g.*, Levitt and Schiller 2004; Lubbers et al. 2018; Schiller 2005) have laid bare the shortcomings of an older, 'container-view' of culture that equates the spatial limits of social-evolutionary processes with the regional political boundaries of modern nation states (see for example Beck 2000; Faist 2000). They convincingly argue that such *methodological nationalism* reifies and naturalizes regionally bounded societies as the appropriate macro-unit of investigation, thus analytically disassociating far-flung people, places, and things with historically meaningful entanglements (Guarnizo 1997; Schiller 2005; Vertovec 1999; Wimmer and Glick Schiller 2003. Not limited to the perimeter of a nation-state, the field is a more abstract concept that allows for the methodological autonomization of a space of activity (Sapiro 2018), defined in relational terms and historically grounded.

Glick Schiller et al. (1992:1-2) define transnationalism as the process by which immigrants build social fields that link together their country of origin and their country of settlement. Such migrants develop and maintain multiple relations (kin-based, economic, religious, political, *etc.*) that span borders, and these migrants take actions, make decisions, and develop identities within social networks that connect them to two or more societies simultaneously. Scholars in a range of disciplines, including anthropology and archaeology, have adopted transnational field perspectives in order to frame various

---

[1] In this paper, we subscribe to a broad definition of the term culture contact that encompasses the many small- and large-scale encounters and cultural entanglements of different groups of people with each other in the past, while recognizing the baggage associated with the term "contact" (Silliman 2005) and not restricting its usage to capitalist or colonial contexts.

  Springer

**Fig. 1** Important sites and cultural areas in late Prehistoric eastern North America

population movements in ways that attempt to counter essentialist thinking about identity (*i.e.*, that it is fixed and unchanging) and instead consider multiple, overlapping, and decentered identities that resist traditional models of either/or classification.

Aspects of this critique are not new to Mississippian archaeologists, particularly those scholars working in the Midwestern area of Mississippian culture where Cahokia has been variably cast as a center of religious pilgrimage (Skousen 2016) and missionization (Pauketat et al. 2015), an economic core (Dincauze and Hasenstab 1989), and a gateway city by different scholars (Kelly 1991). However, we argue that while Cahokia has been reconceptualized from various multi-regional theoretical perspectives, there often remain unquestioned assumptions about hierarchy and developmental timing that lead scholars to envision Cahokians as the primary authors of Mississippian culture while deeply connected hinterland groups are regarded as simply being acculturated to various extents. Both Alt (2002, 2006) and Pauketat (2000) deserve credit for explicitly interrogating the intentionality and directionality of the early Mississippian processes of culture making in the American Bottom region. However, we argue that such conceptualization must now be applied outside the boundaries of the American Bottom to reconsider the transregional processes of culture making that have traditionally led scholars to divide eleventh century Native American groups into categories of *Mississippians versus Mississippianized.*

In an attempt to sidestep these theoretical limitations, we employ the social field concept while also drawing on contemporary research on transnationalism in our discussion of Mississippian origins in the North American Midwest. Informed by the work of Bourdieu's (1977) theory of practice, we define a social field as the social and spatial contexts in which agents operate and in which they are hierarchically positioned. Relevant to the transregional focus of our current research, fields are multidimensional, encompassing structured interactions of differing forms and breadth. Indeed, the spatial configuration of a social field need not correspond with the regional political boundaries of a society but may include many other direct or indirect interactions and influences that crosscut otherwise well-demarcated territorial boundaries. Examples of a social field include but are not limited to political and religious institutions, shared areas of work and play, and social groups (see de Nooy 2003; Hilgers and Manez 2014). These cultural practices and social experiences occupy space, and bodies, objects, and other physical features distributed in space comprise fields where identities are reconfigured and history is made (see Pauketat 2008).

An interesting recent avenue of archaeological and ethnohistoric research takes up transnational considerations of regional cultural systems or social fields. Various case studies describe cultural complexes characterized by material similarities and differences at various spatial extents, characterizing a number of communities that are both distinct and intimately connected. For example, in his consideration of Asian immigrants in mid-nineteenth century North America, Ross (2013) uses a transnational framework to explore how immigrant workers at the Ewen Cannery in Richmond, British Columbia, formed new cultural identities in the face of displacement, demonstrating how some traditional practices persisted while others changed in response to new contextual factors, reflecting the complexity of migrant experiences. At both Chinese and Japanese camps in the region, Ross found evidence of a heavy reliance on traditional meals, along with a large volume of imported Asian ceramics; however, each community also made use of English ceramics as servingwares and consumed Western-style condiments. Furthermore, both Chiense and Japanese communities combined Asian and Western medicines and adopted Western-style domestic and work clothes, albeit in distinct ways.

In her discussion of interaction and social fields in San Pedro de Atacama in Northern Chile (*ca.* AD 100–1000), Stovel (2008) takes inspiration from the Sepik Coast social field concept outlined by Terrell and colleagues (Terrell 2001; Terell and Welsch 1990; Welsch and Terrell 1998). In the Papua New Guinea case, scholars describe a social network characterized by varying levels of material and cultural similarity after many generations of close-knit trade and social relations, although multiple communities also hold a wide range of mutually unintelligible languages. Stovel draws on this example in her consideration of persistent, low-level, and long-term inclusion of non-local vessels from the same regional communities into the graves of the precolumbian inhabitants of San Pedro de Atacama. According to Stovel (Stovel 2008:996), the Algarrobo cultural complex of San Pedro resembles the Sepik Coast social field "in its abundant long-term interaction, consumption of non-local staples rather than or in addition to exotic goods, [and] its focus on kinship, rather than exclusively trade relations, and its consideration of an entire region rather than a grouping of individual communities."

An important element of the Papuan and Northern Chilean examples described above is that multiethnic regional configurations were maintained without social, economic, or political inequality. As outlined by Bourdieu (1977), individuals within a social field develop an understanding of the rules of interaction (*doxa*) through their experiences moving through it and by engaging with others. In a single field, individuals tend to share a common *doxa* but can take positions to transform power relations to attempt to change these rules for their own benefit. It is important to recognize that an individual's position in a field is determined not only by these rules of interaction but also by the amount and kinds of capital they possess. Moreover, certain kinds of capital are variably valued within different fields. For example, within Mississippian societies, knowledge of distant lands and the customs of foreign dignitaries may have been valued in certain chiefly political fields while experience making and using weaponry may have been valued within militaristic fields of combat. On the other hand, knowledge of celestial movements and alignments as well as certain arcane ritual practices and spiritually charged locations and objects may have been valued within certain priestly religious fields.

There are a series of relationships and social dynamics that have been documented within both the scholarly literature on social fields and transnationalism that are useful to consider when investigating the *kinds* of population movements and interactions related to Cahokia's trajectory of development. Among these noted relationships is the observation that there are many different types of social fields that could potentially characterize a group's relationships: with a distant land; with its inhabitants; to a region of origin; and to fellow migrants, pilgrims, and other travelers. Moreover, the modal qualities of these fields can change over time. For example, nonlocal groups may be large or small, dispersed, or aggregated (Anthony 1990; Clark 2001; Neuzil 2008). They may include political or religious representatives and/or refugees, and their political intent may be diplomatic or enacted under asymmetrical power relations. With respect to Cahokia, there were probably many centrifugal and centripetal population movements and interactions associated with its rise and fall (Alt 2006; Emerson 1991; Pauketat et al. 2015); indeed, recent dental chemistry evidence indicates that roughly one third of Cahokia's population was nonlocal in origin throughout its entire history of occupation (Slater et al. 2014). Thus, if we are to evaluate the transregional interactions associated with Midwestern Mississippian origins from a social field perspective, we should attempt to identify and map out the different kinds of social fields that connected

distant lands and peoples, each of which was characterized by its own historical and modal properties with specific forms of social capital (see Bourdieu and Wacquant 1992).

Another important observation that has come out of the transnational literature is that depending on their place in transregional social fields, individuals can be expected to make situational and strategic pivots between localized and more far-flung connections and interests (Levitt and Schiller 2004:1011). Thus, the identities of, and relationships among, locals and nonlocals should not be essentialized (see Voss et al. 2018). This observation has important implications for conceiving of Cahokian and broader Mississippian identity politics. What did it mean in terms of social membership to be a Cahokian living hundreds of miles north of the American Bottom? How did Cahokian migrants, pilgrims, or other travelers conceptualize or represent their connections to their homeland *and* to local groups? What did it mean in terms of social identity and group membership to be a member of a local indigenous community from the northern Midwest (*e.g.*, the CIRV), but directly engaged with Cahokian visitors or to be traveling to or living in the American Bottom region? Under what conditions did nonlocal connections overshadow local ones and *vice versa*?

Another tactic we incorporate from recent scholarship on culture contact and colonialism is to avoid conceptualizing the generation and maintenance of transregional social phenomenon in unidirectional or teleological terms. All social relationships are products of negotiation and co-construction, even those under politically asymmetrical conditions (Voss 2005:461; see also Panich 2013; Silliman 2005; Wilcox 2009). Moreover, the historical outcomes of long-distance engagements may not always proceed directly from the social intents of all or any of the participants. Such a critique is particularly relevant to conceptualizing the origins and spread of what archaeologists recognize as Mississippian culture. Scholars (*e.g.*, Emerson 1997; Mehrer 1995; Milner 1998; Pauketat 1994, 1997) have referred to an explosive flashpoint in the mid-eleventh century as the "Big Bang," a period in which Cahokia coalesced rapidly, evidenced archaeologically by the construction of multiple large monuments, the structural reorganization of social relations and religious ideology, and significant changes in population densities. Pauketat (2000) posits that this flurry of centralized monumental constructions and other ritual gatherings at early Cahokia were exaggerated but broadly inclusive forms of traditional ceremonial practices that culminated in the empowerment of certain individuals or groups. In other words, such events were not the outcomes of elite co-option but instead themselves generated the material and social circumstances from which hierarchical social relations later emerged (see also Baltus and Wilson 2019). Indeed, archaeologists have documented the clearest indications of social and economic inequalities and institutionalized leadership positions in the later Mississippian period occupation of the region (Emerson 1997; Trubitt 2000).

We see important implications of this reasoning for understanding the far-flung interactions among the earliest Cahokians and contemporaneous local indigenous groups living in the CIRV and elsewhere in the northern Midwest. Rather than evidence of polity expansion, we argue that initially these distant interactions helped constitute the social means through which Mississippian political culture emerged in the greater Cahokia area and beyond. Accordingly, our discussion attempts to transcend an older *Arrows out of Cahokia* narrative that conjured up notions of high-status Cahokians

                                              Springer

heading off to distant lands with fully formed Mississippian ideas and practices that were then simply emulated to various degrees by hinterland groups.

We pursue these research principles through a discussion of the early Mississippian period (1000–1200 AD) of population movement and culture contact connecting the greater Cahokia area to the CIRV, and beyond (Fig. 2). We begin with a discussion of the tenth century Terminal Late Woodland period that immediately preceded the Mississippian period and is manifested archaeologically as a variety of minimally hierarchical, *tribal* groups in both regions, groups that had little evidence of direct interaction (see Benn and Thompson 2014; Fortier and Fortier and McElrath 2002). We then evaluate the eleventh century, which corresponds with the initial establishment of

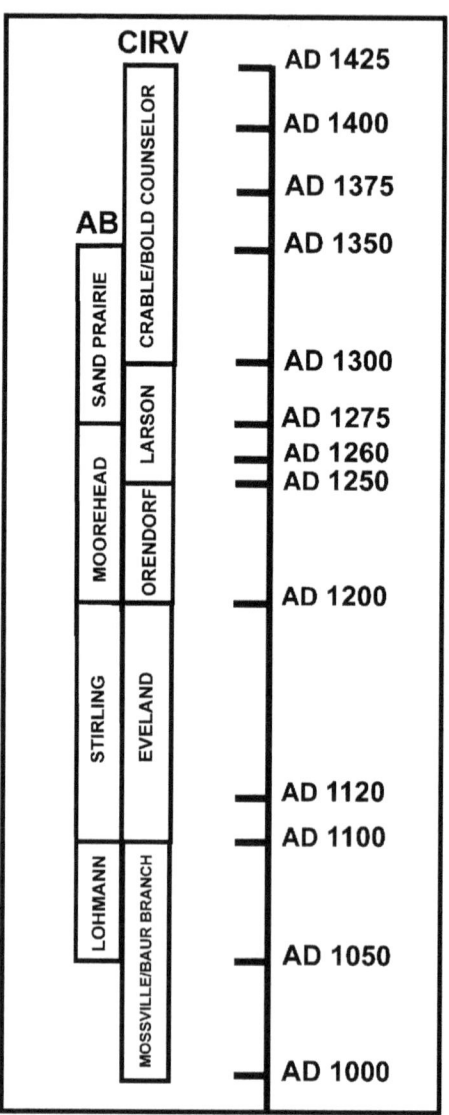

**Fig. 2** Phase based chronologies for the American Bottom and the Central Illinois River Valley

Cahokia as an early Mississippian urban center and the first evidence of a developing social field connecting groups from the American Bottom and the CIRV (see Conrad 1991; McConaughy 1991; McConaughy et al. 1993; Pauketat 1994). We also discuss the twelfth century, which is typically conceived of as Cahokia's *Classic* period and its peak of sociopolitical complexity and corresponds with the widespread appearance of Mississippian material culture throughout the CIRV (Conrad 1991; Emerson 1997).

In doing so, we offer a new take on Mississippian origins and the history of culture contact in the CIRV. Previous scholarship has overemphasized the role of Cahokian migrants as agents of Mississippianization in the CIRV (Conrad 1991), while not sufficiently acknowledging the agency of local CIRV groups acting as initial and persistent contributors to this process. We argue that this framing is a teleological problem that stems from projecting Cahokia's *Classic* era core/hinterland dynamics upon its early Mississippian *Formative* era. Considering that centrifugal and centripetal population movements and other far-flung interactions were key generative elements of Cahokia's emergence (Alt 2002, 2006; Pauketat et al. 2015), we contend that interregional simultaneity and inter-group collaboration played an important part of the early processes of Mississippianization in the North American Midwest.

In decentering Cahokia in our explanation of Mississippian origins in the greater Midwest, we also argue for a long-term persistence of traditional pre-Mississippian practices in the CIRV region, beginning with the first documented engagement among Cahokians and Illinois Valley groups in the early eleventh century until the beginning of the thirteenth century. This diversity is represented by a deep history (a full century) of stylistically mixed Mississippian-Woodland assemblages and household organizational traditions at CIRV sites that we discuss below.

## Late Woodland Antecedents to Mississippian Culture

To set the stage for examining local indigenous interactions with Cahokians in the early Mississippian period CIRV, we draw on settlement patterns and ceramic stylistic traditions that designate the presence of distinct indigenous groups in the region. During the Terminal Late Woodland period (approximately the tenth century AD), two contemporaneous local indigenous groups occupied the CIRV. Manifested archaeologically as Bauer Branch and Maples Mills groups based on distinct ceramic production techniques, these neighboring groups resided in the southern and northern part of the CIRV and adjacent uplands, respectively (Green and Nolan 2000; Esarey 2000; Bardolph and Wilson 2015; Wilson et al. 2017). Settlement patterns for both groups consisted of river-edge villages in addition to small settlements dispersed throughout the adjacent uplands (Esarey 2000:398; Green and Nolan 2000:362). Excavations at Southern CIRV Bauer Branch sites revealed that local residents constructed single-post flexed pole domiciles, and neighboring households used shared clusters of deep pit features as earth ovens and for storage (Green 1987:133, 251; Green and Nolan 2000).

This communal organization of domestic foodways also was characteristic of contemporaneous Late Woodland period settlements in the American Bottom, where indigenous groups cooked in earth ovens and stored food in spaces spatially segregated from dwellings (Kelly 1990b; Mehrer 1995). There is a clear lack of overlap or mixing of material culture between the Maples Mills and Bauer Branch groups at excavated archaeological sites in the CIRV. Distinct pottery styles and production techniques (*e.g.*, vessel form, temper, rim form, surface decoration, *etc.*) do not overlap among these two groups, indicating distinct communities of practice (*sensu* Roddick and Stahl 2016) with limited interaction between these groups. In fact, Bauer Branch and Maples Mills groups may have actively avoided interactions, at times engaging in hostilities; mortuary evidence for sporadic violence (*e.g.*, Cole and Deuel 1937:191–198; Esarey 2000; Wilson 2012, 2015) indicates that a strategy of social avoidance resulting in periodic bellicosity was employed for much of this era, although such violence was small in scale.

Our ability to evaluate the Terminal Late Woodland era from a social fields perspective is limited by the paucity of archaeological research that has focused on this regional time period to date. Maples Mills and Bauer Branch groups represent social groups that occupied distinct portions of the regional landscape, but we know little about how they were organized or how their constituents interacted with their fellow kin and community members, aside from intrasite organizational conventions related to communal cooking in earth ovens and shared storage in deep pit features. On the basis of the current evidence, however, it would appear that there were few transregional social fields in place at this time that served to crosscut ethnic boundaries. In contrast to the broad regional networks witnessed during the earlier Middle Woodland (200 BC to 400 AD) Hopewell interaction sphere (Braun 1986; Caldwell 1964; Dancey 2005; Hall 1980), interactions between Late Woodland groups were scaled back to the point of social avoidance in the tenth century AD. Thus, the inter-regional connections that were forged beginning in the early eleventh century (discussed below) were truly revolutionary by historical standards, with the political consolidation of Cahokia in the American Bottom sending shock waves throughout much of the Midwest and Midsouth and into the Plains (Pauketat 2004).

## The Eleventh and Twelfth Centuries in the Midwest

The mid eleventh century American Bottom region was fundamentally reorganized through the establishment of a series of mounded ceremonial centers, which included the sprawling urban multi-mound centers at the Cahokia and East St. Louis sites as well as numerous smaller mound sites and nodal farmsteads in the rural countryside. Two multi-mound sites dubbed "shrine complexes" devoted to religious ceremonialism also were founded at this time in the uplands immediately east of the American Bottom (Alt and Pauketat 2017; Pauketat 2013; Pauketat et al. 2017a, b). Recent scholarship has revealed that this monumentalization of the landscape was part of the establishment of a new social and religious movement that emerged out of the interactions among groups from various portions of the North American Midwest and Midsouth (Betzenhauser 2017; Skousen 2016).

Indeed, early eleventh century sites in the American Bottom region yield a variety of nonlocal ceramic types from surrounding regions, a pattern that is increasingly interpreted as evidence for the arrival of migrant groups into the region (Alt 2002, 2006; Emerson 1991; Kelly 1991). Population movements to and from the American Bottom appear to have been continuous during the decades following Cahokia's mid

eleventh century regional consolidation. Alt's (2006, 2018) research has primarily emphasized the movement of Varney groups from southeastern Missouri and northeastern Arkansas into the American Bottom. Recent scholarship, however, also has documented the presence of Terminal Late Woodland ceramics from the CIRV in the Northern American Bottom region, a pattern Wilson et al. (2017:117) have tentatively interpreted as evidence of northern visitors to the region (migrants or pilgrims) who likely played a role in the transregional process of Mississippianization in both the American Bottom region and in their Illinois Valley homeland.

Not coincidentally, this is the same time we see the first clear evidence of a strong transregional connection between the greater Cahokia area and the northern CIRV, best known from a small number of early eleventh century sites in Peoria County referred to archaeologically as Mossville phase (Esarey 2000; see also Conrad 1991). The best documented Mossville-phase site is Rench, where excavations by McConaughy (McConaughy 1991; McConaughy et al. 1993) uncovered a small farmstead of local inhabitants actively mixing and matching Woodland and Mississippian traditions (Fig. 3). The two structures excavated at the site were small, rectangular buildings that

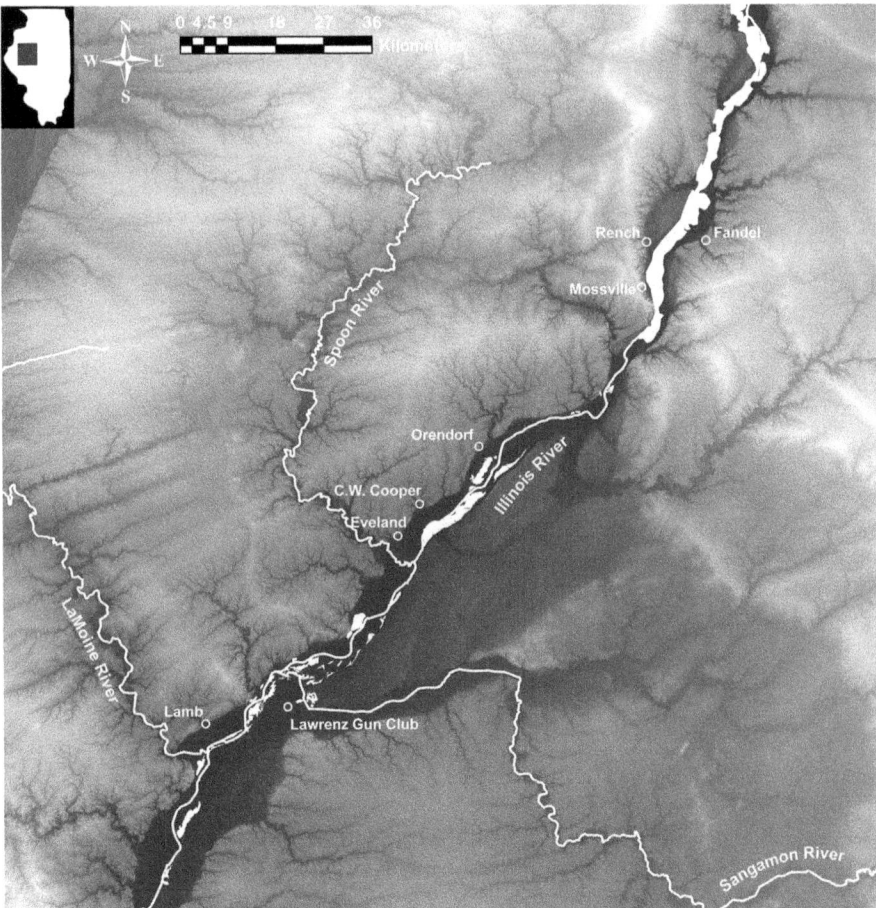

**Fig. 3** The Central Illinois River Valley

Springer

exhibited a combination of wall-trench and single-post architectural techniques. Pottery assemblages from the two buildings and associated pit features were primarily composed of grit-tempered plain and cordmarked jars, exhibiting signs that local potters were continuing traditional modes of production but also emulating early Mississippian vessel forms, as well as receiving Mississippian vessels from the American Bottom (Fig. 4). Thin section analysis by James Stoltman determined that a minimum of 21 Cahokia style vessels in the Rench assemblage most likely originated in the American Bottom (McConaughy 1991:110–111).

Our recent research in the Peoria Lake area has identified a previously undocumented Mossville-phase mound site directly east across Upper Lake Peoria from Rench (see Fig. 3). The Fandel Mounds (11WD4) site consists of three low rectangular platforms (Fig. 5) and an associated Mossville-phase village area. Remote sensing of the site revealed the clear rectangular footprints of two of the mounds; these mounds share a similar alignment with an unplowed platform mound located 230 m to the northwest

**Rench Site Jar Rims**

**Fandel Site Rims**

**Fig. 4** Selected Rim sherds from the Fandel and Rench sites (Rench site: row 1: Mossville Cordmarked, Rench site: row 2: Mossville Plain, Rench site row 3: Mossville Cord Impressed, Fandel site: row 1: Lohmann phase Mississippian jar and bowl rim sherds, Fandel site: row 2: Mossville Plain and Mossville Cordmarked rim sherds, Fandel site: row 3: Mossville Cord Impressed rim sherds (note row 2, item 6 is a shell tempered hybrid Mossville Cordmarked jar rim)

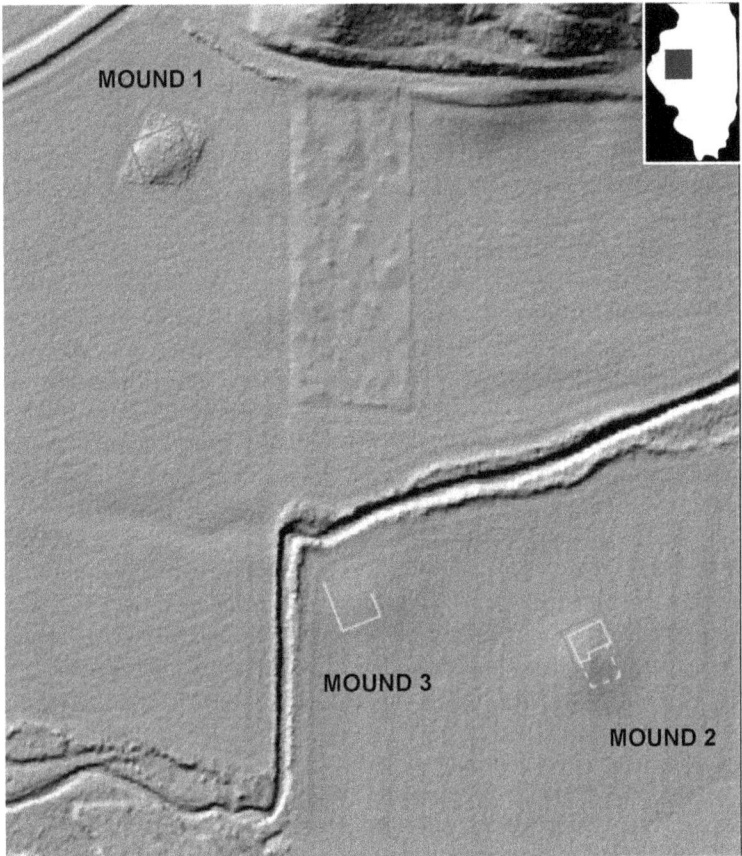

**Fig. 5** Fandel Mounds (11Wd4) platform mound alignments as evidenced by contours (Md 1) and magnetometry (Mds 2 and 3). Magnetometry and LiDar contour work courtesy Illinois State Archaeological Survey

(intact due to the small nineteenth century cemetery on its summit). Insights from preliminary analysis of materials excavated in 2018 and 2019 by G. Wilson, Bardolph, and Esarey indicate that artifact assemblages consist primarily of local Burlington chert and locally made grit-tempered and cordmarked jars with a small minority of early Mississippian Cahokia-made vessels and ceremonial items (including a chunkey gaming stone from the American Bottom region that is stylistically identical to those recovered from Mound 72 at Cahokia) (see Fig. 4). Overall, there is little evidence to suggest the presence of large numbers of Cahokians at Fandel. However, the recent discovery of ceremonial buildings with wall-trench foundations that were ritually sanctified with crushed yellow limonite and red hematite indicates that Fandel's eleventh century inhabitants were knowledgeable practitioners of very specific forms of religious ceremonialism that were simultaneously occurring in the greater Cahokia area (see Pauketat et al. 2017a, b; Skousen 2016).

A wealth of research at several late eleventh century and early twelfth century sites has led to a better understanding of the events that followed the enigmatic contact dynamic at Fandel Mounds and related Mossville-phase sites in the northern CIRV (Bardolph 2014; Bardolph and Wilson 2015; Caldwell 1967a, b; Conrad 1989, 1991;

Conrad and Harn 1972; Esarey 1996, Esarey 2000; Harn 1975, 1978, 1991; Wilson et al. 2017; Wray and MacNeish 1958). By the end of the eleventh century, mound construction and Terminal Late Woodland associations with Mississippian artifacts and organizational conventions became more widespread throughout the Illinois valley (Conrad 1989, 1991; Friberg 2018). However, the emulation and incorporation of Cahokia-centered lifeways were highly selective and uneven in its adoption. Our most detailed glimpse of the new social landscape comes from the Lawrenz Gun Club (11Cs4) site (henceforth Lawrenz), in the southern CIRV (see Fig. 3). J. Wilson's recent extensive remote sensing survey and small-scale excavations documented an early Mississippian structure complex consisting of ~15 to 20 buildings on three floodplain ridges adjacent to the Sangamon River. The complete excavation of one of these buildings revealed a small wall-trench structure that matches the size and rectangular dimensions (*i.e.*, 2.5 × 4.5 m) of contemporaneous early Mississippian domiciles in the American Bottom. Pottery from this structure was dominated by Mississippian jars that are stylistically identical to late Lohmann/early Stirling horizon vessels from the northern American Bottom (Fig. 6). Scarce but still present in this assemblage are traditional Woodland-style grit-tempered, cordmarked jar forms that, earlier in the century, had been majority types in the CIRV.

It is notable that among these sherds are examples from both southern CIRV Bauer Branch and northern Mossville tradition vessels, indicating a level of engagement among these two groups that was unprecedented prior to the eleventh century. Evidence of intensified interactions among these local groups is important, as it mirrors observations of late eleventh and early twelfth century contacts among numerous other sites emplaced across the upper Midwest (Claflin 1991; Delaney-Rivera 2000; Douglas 1976; Esarey 2000; Friberg 2018; Millhouse 2012). Notably missing from the Lawrenz assemblage are the bowls, bottles, pans, stumpware, and funnels that routinely comprise early Mississippian assemblages from the greater Cahokian area. The ceramic pattern identified at Lawrenz also defines subsequent early and middle twelfth century sites in the region such as Eveland and Lamb (11SC24) (Bardolph 2014; Esarey 2000; Wilson 2015; Wilson et al. 2017) (see Fig. 6). While *stylistically* these assemblages appear Cahokian, they continue to display *functional* continuity with local Late Woodland traditions, when ceramic assemblages were composed primarily of jars and had not been fundamentally reorganized to emphasize the ceremonial dimensions of commensal politics. Unlike the ceramics at Rench, thin section analysis of sherds from Eveland indicates that Mississippian-style vessels were manufactured using local clays by local potters, which was presumably the case at other early twelfth century sites in the region (Harn 1991:143). In all, three sites dating to this extended time period, Lawrenz, Eveland, and Lamb, among others, display variable forms of contextual and ceramic hybridity, suggesting that complex sets of social relations and identity politics likely crosscut kin groups and communities.

These transregional interactions, involving social groups and ceremonial locations from the American Bottom, Illinois Valley, and neighboring regions are well suited for evaluation from a social fields' perspective. During the eleventh century, a number of poorly connected Native American groups began to become better integrated through the establishment of new forms of religious ceremonialism in newly established or transformed monumental spaces. These spaces like Fandel, Eveland, Cahokia, and Emerald (and the ceremonial practices that occurred there) can be conceived of as

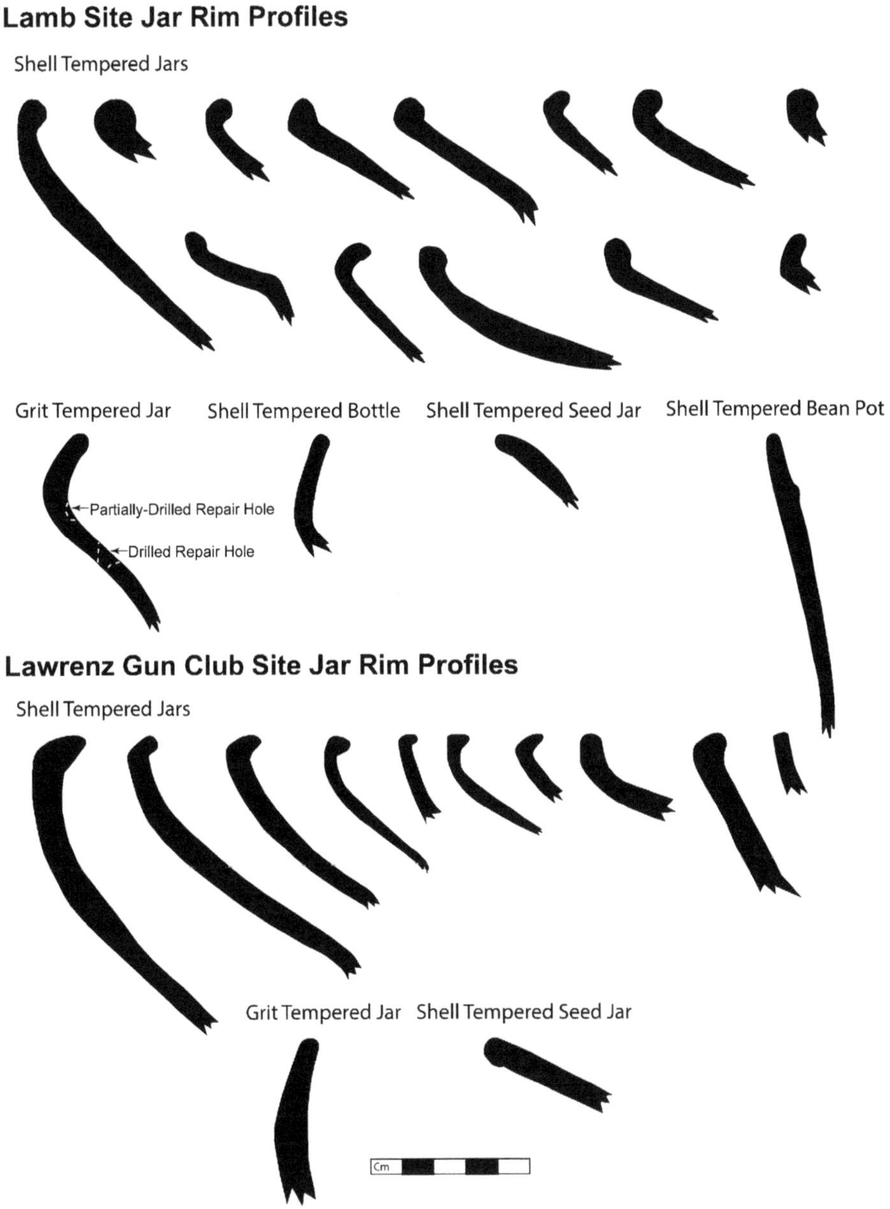

## Lamb Site Jar Rim Profiles

Shell Tempered Jars

Grit Tempered Jar    Shell Tempered Bottle    Shell Tempered Seed Jar    Shell Tempered Bean Pot

←Partially-Drilled Repair Hole

←Drilled Repair Hole

## Lawrenz Gun Club Site Jar Rim Profiles

Shell Tempered Jars

Grit Tempered Jar   Shell Tempered Seed Jar

Cm

**Fig. 6** Selected rim sherd profiles from the Lamb and Lawrenz Gun Club sites

social fields as they represent the social and spatial contexts in which various groups interacted and generated the transregional connections, beliefs, and practices that came to define what archaeologists now recognize as Mississippian culture. Indeed, the act of entering into and moving through these fields was likely the very process that dismantled older, more territorially delimited ethnic boundaries and forged more inclusive ones. The common denominators at these sites include the construction and use of celestially aligned substructural platform mounds, religious buildings of various shapes, sizes, and purposes, politico-religious ceremonialism involving the game of chunkey, and the use of different kinds of color symbolism (*via* mineral pigments and clays) to line the floors and foundations of special buildings, pits, earthen mounds, and causeways (Pauketat et al. 2017a, b; Skousen 2016). Knowledge of the cosmological dimensions of this monumentalism, and the religious rites associated with shrines, temples, council houses, games, cosmically charged artifacts, and raw materials represent the obvious forms of social capital that people would have valued within these fields.

However, membership in these newly established transregional fields did not exclude simultaneous participation in other preexisting localized fields. Indeed, alongside the rapidly shifting identities and relationships in the region is evidence for a rural persistence of traditional household and community organization related to foodways. As discussed above, the ceramic data from Lawrenz and Lamb reveal that foodways in the CIRV during the eleventh and twelfth century were embedded in local Late Woodland *organizational* conventions that involved cooking, storing, and serving in multi-purpose jars. This consideration also extends to other household conventions; in contrast to corresponding Stirling-phase settlement data from the American Bottom that indicate shifts toward restricted and privatized cooking and storage practices within dwellings by the early Mississippian period (*e.g.*, at the Cahokia ICT-II residential tract, see Mehrer and Collins 1995). Contemporaneous inhabitants of the CIRV retained traditional communal modes of outdoor cooking and storage in large earth ovens and storage pits (Bardolph 2014; see Green 1987; Green and Nolan 2000:362), a pattern also noted in the excavation of the wall-trench structure at Lawrenz.

The social and spatial changes to the CIRV landscape witnessed during the latter part of the early Mississippian period likely resulted from the expansion of transregional ceremonial social fields enacted through the establishment of temple complexes and associated mortuaries such as the Eveland and Dickson Mounds sites in Fulton County. Such religiously charged locations perhaps enabled ongoing centrifugal and centripetal movements between the CIRV, American Bottom, and other regional locales in the broader Southeast and Midwest. Throughout much of the eleventh and twelfth centuries, Illinois Valley groups may have made pilgrimages to Cahokia, where they would have not only witnessed but helped generate increasing hierarchical complexity, and upon returning home, selectively syncretized what they had seen and participated in, overlaying and combining new meanings and cultural practices onto their local traditions. Indeed, the presence of Terminal Late Woodland ceramics from the CIRV in the northern American Bottom suggests the presence of northern migrants or pilgrims who likely played a role in the processes of Mississippianization in the greater Cahokia area (Wilson et al. 2017:117). Moreover, small numbers of Cahokians also likely were present throughout the 12th CIRV, perhaps in a capacity similar to that seen in the Peoria Lake area in the early Lohmann horizon.

## Discussion and Conclusion

Cahokia's Big Bang (*ca.* 1050 AD) emerged from and was enabled by a complex series of still poorly understood interactions among minimally ranked Terminal Late Woodland groups from a broad swath of the Midwest and Midsouth. Cahokia ultimately

loomed as the most complex by regional polity in this network, but this situation is not how the process began and it is probably a teleological error to assign too much design or intentionality to this outcome. Moreover, Cahokia's emerging complexity would have been shaped by the diversity of its migrants and pilgrims (Alt 2002, 2006). Such connections no doubt also facilitated the movement of small groups of "new" Cahokians northward beginning in the early to mid-eleventh century. These journeys to and from the American Bottom had a profound impact on the regional inhabitants of the Illinois Valley, who quickly began to selectively incorporate early Mississippian lifeways. In addition, differential hinterland syncretic processes may well have related to the variable effect of having extended kin in the American Bottom actively contributing to the rise and maintenance of Cahokia. In this sense, nearby hinterlands such as the CIRV would have continued to play an important role in mediating the successful tenure of Cahokia, as well as potentially conditioning the format of its ultimate dissolution. This consideration allows us to sidestep the dichotomy of *Mississippians versus Mississippianized*, an important goal of our continued work that seeks to identify the roles that hinterland groups played in the formation of what it meant to be a member of various Mississippian social fields (religious, political, economic, *etc.*) as early as the mid-tenth century AD, with membership that neither excluded simultaneous participation in other pre-existing local fields nor required immediate hierarchical reorganization of participating groups. Indeed, the presence of Late Woodland groups in the American Bottom during the formation of Cahokia merits further investigation and is a goal of this project moving forward.

The patterns summarized above highlight the transregional and relational nature of identity construction during the early Mississippian-period CIRV and reveal the degree to which individuals were capable of strategically pivoting between localized and more far-flung social fields, each of which had different modal properties and forms of capital. Over at least a century (mid-tenth through mid-eleventh centuries), indigenous inhabitants in the CIRV appear to have negotiated identities that responded to important changes and influences from Cahokia and elsewhere, while retaining elements of traditional social and economic organization and biological continuity (Steadman 1998, 2001). This phenomenon articulates with a critical element of the politics of postcolonial and indigenous archaeologies, the recognition that even in overtly asymmetrical colonial encounters, influence and change from dominant groups is not all-encompassing. Groups selectively adopt and filter objects and ideas through their local perspectives, cultural referents are altered, and historical traditions become reconfigured (Lightfoot 1995; Oland 2017).

The last 20 years of archaeological research has revealed that migrations, pilgrimages, and other far-flung interactions were important parts of the developmental history of the ancient world (Bauer and Stanish 2001; Cabana and Clark 2011; Skousen 2016; Van Dyke 2018). Accordingly, we contend that investigating the articulation between transregional social fields and more locally defined ones will contribute to a more nuanced, historical understanding of the ancient past. As for the formative history of the Mississippian Midwest, many questions remain. It is becoming increasingly clear that the developmental dynamics of the early Mississippian period were far more rapid and expansive than we are currently able to track archaeologically. Future research should concentrate not only on the eleventh century locations and interactions that generated Mississippian culture, but also on the localized regional histories that immediately precede Mississippian beginnings. It is only through tacking back and forth between these two centuries as well as the relevant regional locations that we will transcend our current, more regionally and historically circumscribed understanding of this phenomenon.

**Acknowledgements** Thank you to Sarah Baires, Melissa Baltus, and Jayur Mehta for the invitation to participate in this special issue. We acknowledge Dorothy Lamb, the Heinz and Fandel families, and the Hardwick and Robertson families for providing support and permission to conduct research at the Lamb, Fandel, and Lawrenz Gun Club sites, respectively. We also aknowledge support from the Illinois State Archaeological Survey. We appreciate the thoughtful comments of the peer reviewers and editor Margaret Beck as well as feedback on earlier drafts by Amber VanDerwarker and Kaitlyn Brown. Lawrence Conrad, Alan Harn, and Bill Green provided advice at various stages of this research as well. Archaeological projects discussed in the text were supported by the National Science Foundation under Grant Nos. 1062290 and 1262530; the University of California, Santa Barbara Academic Senate and Institute for Social, Economic, and Behavioral Research; and the Cornell Institute of Archaeology and Material Science Hirsch Fund.

# References

Alt, S. M. (2002). Identities, traditions, and diversity in Cahokia's uplands. *Midcontinental Journal of Archaeology, 27*, 217–235.

Alt, S. M. (2006). The power of diversity: The roles of migration and hybridity in culture change. In B. M. Butler & P. D. Welch (Eds.), *Leadership and Polity in Mississippian Society. Occasional paper no. 33* (pp. 289–308). Carbondale: Southern Illinois University.

Alt, S. M. (2018). *Cahokia's complexities: Ceremonies and politics of the first Mississippian farmers.* Tuscaloosa: The University of Alabama Press.

Alt, S. M., & Pauketat, T. R. (2017). The elements of Cahokian shrine complexes and the basis of Mississippian religion. In S. B. Barberand & A. A. Joyce (Eds.), *Religion and politics in the ancient Americas* (pp. 51–74). London: Routledge.

Anthony, D. W. (1990). Migration in archeology: The baby and the bathwater. *American Anthropologist, 92*(4), 895–914.

Baltus, M. R., & Wilson, G. D. (2019). The Cahokian crucible: Burning ritual and the emergence of Cahokian power in the Mississippian Midwest. *American Antiquity, 84*(3), 438–470.

Bardolph, D. N. (2014). Evaluating Cahokian contact and Mississippian identity politics in the late prehistoric Central Illinois River Valley. *American Antiquity, 79*(1), 69–89.

Bardolph, D. N., & Wilson, G. D. (2015). The Lamb site (11SC24): Evidence of Cahokian contact and Mississippianization in the Central Illinois River valley. *Illinois Archaeology, 27*, 138–149.

Bauböck, R., & Faist, T. (Eds.). (2010). *Diaspora and transnationalism: Concepts, theories and methods.* Amsterdam: Amsterdam University Press.

Bauer, B. S., & Stanish, C. (2001). *Ritual and pilgrimage in the ancient Andes: The islands of the sun and the moon.* Austin: University of Texas Press.

Beck, U. (2000). The cosmopolitan perspective: Sociology in the second age of modernity. *British Journal of Sociology, 51*(1), 79–107.

Benn, D. W., & Thompson, J. B. (2014). What four late late woodland sites reveal about tribal formation processes in Iowa. *Illinois Archaeology, 26*, 1–55.

Betzenhauser, A. (2017). Cahokia's beginnings: mobility, urbanization, and the Cahokian political landscape. In G. D. Wilson (Ed.), *Mississippian Beginnings* (pp. 71-96). Gainesville: University Press of Florida.

Bourdieu, P. (1977). *Outline of a theory of practice.* Cambridge: Cambridge University Press.

Bourdieu, P. (1982). Les Règles de l'art : Genèse et structure du champ littéraire. Paris: Seuil. In English: 1996. The Rules of Art. Translated by S. Emanuel. Stanford: Stanford University Press.

Bourdieu, P., & Wacquant, L. (1992). *An invitation to reflexive sociology.* Chicago: University of Chicago Press.

Braun, D. (1986). Midwestern Hopewellian exchange and supralocal interaction. In C. Renfrew & J. Cherry (Eds.), *Peer polity interaction and socio-political change* (pp. 117–126). Cambridge: Cambridge University Press.

Cabana, G. S., & Clark, J. J. (Eds.). (2011). *Rethinking anthropological perspectives on migration.* Gainesville: University Press of Florida.

Caldwell, J. R. (1964). Interaction spheres in prehistory. In J. R. Caldwell & R. Hall (Eds.), *Hopewellian Studies, Scientific Papers, vol. 12, no. 2* (pp. 133–143). Springfield: Illinois State Museum.

Caldwell, J. R. (1967a). The house that "X" built. *The Living Museum, 28,* 139–142.

Caldwell, J. R. (1967b). New discoveries at Dickson mounds. *The Living Museum, 29,* 139–142.

Claflin, J. (1991). The Shire site: Mississippian outpost in the Central Illinois prairie. In J. B. Stoltman (Ed.), *New perspectives on Cahokia: Views from the periphery* (pp. 155–176). Madison: Prehistory Press.

Clark, J. (2001). *Tracking prehistoric migrations: Pueblo settlers among the Tonto Basin Hohokam. Anthropological papers of the University of Arizona Number 65.* Tucson: The University of Arizona Press.

Cole, F. C., & Deuel, T. (1937). *Rediscovering Illinois: Archaeological explorations in and around Fulton County.* Chicago: University of Chicago Press.

Conrad, L. A. (1989). The southeastern ceremonial complex on the northern middle Mississippian frontier: Late prehistoric politico-religious systems in the Central Illinois River Valley. In P. Galloway (Ed.), *The southeastern ceremonial complex: Artifacts and analysis* (pp. 93–11). Lincoln: University of Nebraska Press.

Conrad, L. A. (1991). The middle Mississippian cultures of the Central Illinois Valley. In T. E. Emerson & R. B. Lewis (Eds.), *Cahokia and the hinterlands: Middle Mississippian cultures of the Midwest* (pp. 119–156). Urbana: University of Illinois Press.

Conrad, L. A., & Harn, A. D. (1972). *The Spoon River culture in the Central Illinois River valley. Unpublished manuscript on file.* Lewiston: Dickson Mounds Branch of the Illinois State Museum.

Dancey, W. S. (2005). The enigmatic Hopewell of the eastern woodlands. In T. R. Pauketat & D. Loren (Eds.), *North American archaeology* (pp. 108–137). Malden: Blackwell.

De Nooy, W. (2003). Fields and networks: Correspondence analysis and social network analysis in the framework of field theory. *Poetics, 31,* 305–327.

Delaney-Rivera, C. (2000). Mississippian and late woodland cultural interaction and regional dynamics: A view from the lower Illinois River valley. Unpublished Ph.D. Dissertation, Department of Anthropology, University of California, Los Angeles.

Dincauze, D. F., & Hasenstab, R. J. (1989). Explaining the Iroquois: Tribalization on a prehistoric periphery. In T. C. Champion (Ed.), *Centre and periphery: Comparative studies in archaeology* (pp. 67–87). London: Unwin Hyman.

Douglas, J. G. (1976). Collins: A Late Woodland ceremonial complex in the Woodfordian northeast. Unpublished Ph.D. Dissertation, Department of Anthropology, University of Illinois, Urbana.

Emerson, T. E. (1991). Some perspectives on Cahokia and the northern Mississippian expansion. In T. E. Emerson & R. B. Lewis (Eds.), *Cahokia and the hinterlands: Middle Mississippian cultures of the Midwest* (pp. 221–236). Urbana: University of Illinois Press.

Emerson, T. E. (1997). *Cahokia and the archaeology of power.* Tuscaloosa: University of Alabama Press.

Emerson, T. E. (1999). The Langford tradition and the process of Tribalization on the middle Mississippian Borders. *Midcontinental Journal of Archaeology, 24*(1), 3–56.

Esarey, D. E. (1996). *Summary of the 1957–1995 investigations at the Eveland site (11F353): A site management tool. Quaternary studies program technical report no. 96–000-6.* Springfield: Illinois State Museum.

Esarey, D. E. (2000). The Late Woodland Maples Mills and Mossville Phase sequence in the Central Illinois River Valley. In T. E. Emerson, D. L. McElrath, & A. C. Fortier (Eds.), *Late Woodland Societies: Tradition and Transformation across the Midcontinent* (pp. 387–412). Lincoln: University of Nebraska Press.

Faist, T. (2000). *The volume and dynamics of international migration.* New York: Oxford University Press.

Faist, T. (2013). Transnationalism. In S. J. Gold & S. J. Nawyn (Eds.), *Routledge international handbook of migration studies* (pp. 463–473). New York: Routledge.

Fortier, A. C., & McElrath, D. L. (2002). Deconstructing the emergent Mississippian concept: The case for the terminal late woodland in the American bottom. *Midcontinental Journal of Archaeology, 27,* 172–215.

Fowler, M. L. (1997). *The Cahokia atlas, revised: A historical atlas of Cahokia archaeology. Illinois transportation archaeological research program, studies in archaeology 2.* Urbana: University of Illinois Press.

Friberg, C.M. (2018). Igniting interaction through Mississippian tradition-making: An interregional analysis at the Audrey site (11GE20). Unpublished Ph.D. Dissertation, Department of Anthropology, University of California, Santa Barbara.

Gosden, C. (2004). *Archaeology and colonialism: Cultural contact from 5000 BC to the present*. Cambridge: Cambridge University Press.

Green, W. (1987). Between Hopewell and Mississippian: Late Woodland in the prairie peninsula as viewed from the Western Illinois uplands. Unpublished Ph.D. dissertation, University of Wisconsin, Madison.

Green, W., & Nolan, D. J. (2000). Late Woodland peoples in west-Central Illinois. In T. E. Emerson, D. L. McElrath, & A. C. Fortier (Eds.), *Late Woodland Societies: Tradition and Transformation across the Midcontinent* (pp. 345–386). Lincoln: University of Nebraska Press.

Guarnizo, L. (1997). The emergence of a transnational social formation and the mirage of return migration among Dominican transmigrants. *Identities, 4*(2), 281–322.

Hall, R. L. (1980). An interpretation of the two-climax model of Illinois prehistory. In D. L. Browan (Ed.), *Early native Americans* (pp. 401–462). The Hague: Mouton.

Harn, A. D. (1975). Cahokia and the Mississippian emergence in the Spoon River area of Illinois. *Transactions, Illinois State Academy of Science, 68*(4), 414–434.

Harn, A. D. (1978). Mississippian settlement patterns in the Central Illinois River Valley. In B. D. Smith (Ed.), *Mississippian Settlement Patterns* (pp. 233–268). New York: Academic Press.

Harn, A. D. (1991). The Eveland site: Inroad to Spoon River Mississippian society. In J. B. Stoltman (Ed.), *New Perspectives on Cahokia: Views from the Periphery. Monographs in world archaeology no. 2* (pp. 129–153). Madison: Prehistory Press.

Hilgers, M., & Manez, E. (2014). Introduction to Pierre Bourdieu's theory of social fields. In *Bourdieu's theory of social fields: Concepts and applications* (pp. 1–35). London: Routledge.

Kelly, J. E. (1990a). The emergence of Mississippian culture in the American bottom. In B. D. Smith (Ed.), *The Mississippian emergence* (pp. 113–152). Washington, D.C.: Smithsonian Institution Press.

Kelly, J. E. (1990b). Range phase features. In J. E. Kelly, S. J. Ozuk, & J. A. Williams (Eds.), *The Range Site 2: The Emergent Mississippian and Range Phase Occupations (11-S- 47). American bottom archaeology FAI- 270 site reports 20* (pp. 313–386). Urbana: University of Illinois Press.

Kelly, J. E. (1991). Cahokia and its role as a gateway center in interregional exchange. In T. E. Emerson & R. B. Lewis (Eds.), *Cahokia and the hinterlands: Middle Mississippian cultures of the Midwest* (pp. 61–80). Urbana: University of Illinois Press.

Levitt, P., & Schiller, N. G. (2004). Conceptualizing simultaneity: A transnational social field perspective on society. *The International Migration Review, 38*(3), 1002–1039.

Lightfoot, K. G. (1995). Culture contact studies: Redefining the relationship between prehistoric and historical archaeology. *American Antiquity, 60*, 199–192.

Loren, D. D. (2008). *In contact: Bodies and spaces in the sixteenth-and seventeenth-century eastern woodlands*. Lanham: Rowman Altamira.

Lubbers, M. J., Verdery, A. M., & Molina, J. L. (2018). Social networks and transnational social fields: A review of quantitative and mixed-methods approaches. *International Migration Review.* https://doi.org/10.1177/0197918318812343

McConaughy, M. A. (1991). The Rench site: Late late woodland/Mississippian farming hamlet from the Central Illinois River Valley: Food for thought. In J. B. Stoltman (Ed.), *New Perspectives on Cahokia: Views from the Periphery (pp. 101-128). Monographs in world archaeology, no. 2*. Madison: Prehistory Press.

McConaughy, M. A., Martin, T. J., & King, F. B. (1993). Late Late Woodland/Mississippian Component. In M. A. McConaughy (Ed.), *Rench: A Stratified Site in the Central Illinois River Valley* (pp. 76–130). Springfield: Illinois State Museum Reports of Investigations No. 49.

Mehrer, M. W. (1995). *Cahokia's countryside: Household archaeology, settlement patterns, and social power*. Dekalb: Northern Illinois University Press.

Mehrer, M. W., & Collins, J. M. (1995). Household archaeology at Cahokia and its hinterlands. In J. D. Rogers & B. D. Smith (Eds.), *Mississippian communities and households* (pp. 23–57). Tuscaloosa: University of Alabama Press.

Millhouse, P. G. (2012). The John chapman site and creolization on the northern frontier of the Mississippian world. Unpublished Ph.D. Dissertation, Department of Anthropology, Urbana: University of Illinois.

Milner, G. R. (1990). The late prehistoric Cahokia polity of the Mississippi River valley: Foundations, florescence, and fragmentation. *Journal of World Prehistory, 4*, 1–43.

Milner, G. R. (1998). *Cahokia chiefdom*. Washington D.C.: Smithsonian Press.

Neuzil, A. (2008). *In the aftermath of migration: Renegotiating ancient identity in Southeastern Arizona. Anthropological papers of the University of Arizona Number 73*. Tucson: University of Arizona Press.

Oland, M. (2017). The olive jar in the shrine: Situating Spanish objects within a 15th-17th century Maya worldview. In C. N. Cipolla (Ed.), *Foreign objects: Rethinking indigenous consumption in American archaeology* (pp. 127–142). Tucson: University of Arizona Press.

Panich, L. M. (2013). Archaeologies of persistence: Reconsidering the legacies of colonialism in native North America. *American Antiquity, 78*(1), 105–122.

Pauketat, T. R. (1994). *The ascent of chiefs*. Tuscaloosa: University of Alabama Press.

Pauketat, T. R. (1997). Specialization, political symbols, and the crafty elite of Cahokia. *Southeastern Archaeology, 16*, 1–15.

Pauketat, T. R. (2000). The tragedy of the commoners. In M. A. Dobres & J. Robb (Eds.), *Agency in Archaeology* (pp. 113–129). London: Routledge.

Pauketat, T. R. (2004). *Ancient Cahokia and the Mississippians*. Cambridge: Cambridge University Press.

Pauketat, T. R. (2008). The grounds for agency in Southwestern archaeology. In M. D. Varien & J. R. Potter (Eds.), *The social construction of communities: Agency, structure, and identity in the Prehispanic southwest* (pp. 233–249). Lanham, MD: Altamira.

Pauketat, T. R. (2013). *An archaeology of the cosmos: Rethinking agency and religion in ancient America*. London: Routledge.

Pauketat, T. R., & Emerson, T. E. (1997). *Cahokia: Domination and ideology in the Mississippian world*. Lincoln: University of Nebraska Press.

Pauketat, T. R., Boszhardt, R. F., & Benden, D. M. (2015). Trempealeau entanglements: An ancient colony's causes and effects. *American Antiquity, 80*(2), 260–289.

Pauketat, T. R., Alt, S. A., & Kruchten, J. D. (2017a). The Emerald acropolis: Elevating moon and water in the rise of Cahokia. *Antiquity, 91*, 207–222.

Pauketat, T. R., Boszhardt, R. F., & Kolb, M. (2017b). Trempealeau's little bluff: An early Cahokian terraformed landmark in the upper Mississippi Valley. *Midcontinental Journal of Archaeology, 42*(2), 168–199.

Roddick, A. P., & Stahl, A. B. (Eds.). (2016). *Knowledge in motion: constellations of learning across time and place*. Tucson: University of Arizona Press.

Ross, D. E. (2013). *An archaeology of Asian transnationalism*. Gainsville: University Press of Florida.

Sapiro, G. (2018). Field theory from a transnational perspective. In T. Medvetz & J. J. Sallaz (Eds.), *The Oxford Handbook of Pierre Bourdieu* (pp. 161-185). Oxford: Oxford University Press.

Schiller, N. G. (2005). Transnational social fields and imperialism: Bringing a theory of power to transnational studies. *Anthropological Theory, 5*(4), 439–461.

Schiller, N. G., Basch, L., & Blanc-Szanton, C. (1992). Transnationalism: A new analytic framework for understanding migration. *Annals of the New York Academy of Sciences, 645*(1), 1–24.

Silliman, S. W. (2005). Culture contact or colonialism? Challenges in the archaeology of native North America. *American Antiquity, 70*(1), 55–74.

Skousen, B. J. (2016). Pilgrimage and the construction of Cahokia: A view from the emerald site. Unpublished Ph.D. Dissertation, Department of Anthropology, Urbana: University of Illinois.

Slater, P. A., Hedman, K. M., & Emerson, T. E. (2014). Immigrants at the Mississippian polity of Cahokia: Strontium isotope evidence for population movement. *Journal of Archaeological Science, 44*, 117–127.

Steadman, D. W. (1998). The population shuffle in the Central Illinois Valley: A diachronic model of Mississippian biocultural interactions. *World Archaeology, 30*(2), 306–326.

Steadman, D. W. (2001). Mississippians in motion? A population genetic analysis of interregional gene flow in west-Central Illinois. *American Journal of Physical Anthropology, 114*(1), 61–73.

Stovel, E. (2008). Interaction and social fields in San Pedro de Atacama, northern Chile. In H. Silverman & W. Isbell (Eds.), *The Handbook of South American Archaeology* (pp. 979–1002). New York: Springer.

Terell, J., & Welsch, R. L. (1990). Trade, networks, areal integration, and diversity along the north coast of New Guinea. *Asian Perspectives, 29*(2), 155–165.

Terrell, J. (2001). Ethnolinguistic groups, language, boundaries and culture history: A sociolinguistic model. In J. Terell (Ed.), *Archaeology, language and history: Essays on culture and ethnicity* (pp. 199–221). Westport: Bergin & Garvey.

Trubitt, M. B. D. (2000). Mound building and prestige goods exchange: Changing strategies in the Cahokia chiefdom. *American Antiquity, 65*(4), 669–690.

Van Dyke, R. (2018). From enchantment to agencement: Archaeological engagements with pilgrimage. *Journal of Social Archaeology, 18*(3), 1–12.

Vertovec, S. (1999). Conceiving and researching transnationalism. *Ethnic and Racial Studies, 22*(2), 447–462.

Voss, B. L. (2005). From *Casta* to *Californio*: Social identity and the archaeology of culture contact. *American Anthropologist, 107*, 461–474.

Voss, B. L., Kenedy, J. R., Tan, J., & Ng, L. W. (2018). The archaeology of home: *Qiaoxiang* and nonstate actors in the archaeology of the Chinese diaspora. *American Antiquity, 83*(3), 407–426.

Welsch, R. L., & Terrell, J. (1998). Material culture, social fields, and social boundaries on the Sepik coast of New Guinea. In M. T. Stark (Ed.), *The archaeology of social boundaries* (pp. 50–77). Washington, D.C.: Smithsonian Institution Press.

Wilcox, M. (2009). Marketing conquest and the vanishing Indian: An indigenous response to Jared Diamond's *Guns, Germs, and Steel* and *Collapse*. *Journal of Social Archaeology, 10*, 92–117.

Wilson, G. D. (2012). Living with war: The impact of chronic violence in the Mississippian period Central Illinois River Valley. In T. R. Pauketat (Ed.), *The Oxford handbook of north American archaeology* (pp. 523–533). Oxford: Oxford University Press.

Wilson, G. D. (2015). Lamb site ceramics: Mississippianization in the Central Illinois River Valley. *Illinois Archaeology, 27*, 174–200.

Wilson, G. D., Delaney, C. M., & Millhouse, P. G. (2017). The Mississippianization of the Illinois and Apple River valleys. In G. D. Wilson (Ed.), *Mississippian Beginnings* (pp. 97–129). Gainesville: University Press of Florida.

Wimmer, A., & Glick Schiller, N. (2003). Methodological nationalism, the social sciences and the study of migration: An essay in historical epistemology. *International Migration Review, 37*(3), 576–610.

Wray, D. E., & MacNeish, R. S. (1958). *The Weaver site: Twenty centuries of Illinois prehistory. Unpublished manuscript on file*. Lewiston: Dickson Mounds Museum.

**Publisher's Note**     Springer Nature remains neutral with regard to jurisdictional claims in published maps and institutional affiliations.

Journal of Archaeological Method and Theory (2020) 27:111–127
https://doi.org/10.1007/s10816-019-09433-x

# Creating and Abandoning "Homeland": Cahokia as Place of Origin

Melissa R. Baltus[1]  · Sarah E. Baires[2]

Published online: 10 December 2019
© Springer Science+Business Media, LLC, part of Springer Nature 2019

## Abstract

"Diaspora" is typically used in reference to large-scale population dispersals across borders of modern nation-states. This concept has particular connotations with regard to political dynamics and the creation of social identities of difference; however, similar movements of people who retain an identity of a collective "homeland" may be useful for understanding some aspects of cultural influence and complexity in the Mississippian Southeast. Here, we consider the debate over concepts of "diaspora" and "homeland," identifying aspects of diaspora theory that provide a useful lens through which to understand Cahokia's impact in the greater Southeast, specifically in the construction of a physical, ancestral, and/or metaphorical Place of Origin as referential "homeland." We then consider the implications of this Central Place in the context of abandonment and small-scale out-migrations within the Greater Cahokia region. While certain non-human bodies and material practices are "carried away," others are abandoned altogether. We consider what these choices can tell us about the process of dissolution of this once-created Place of Origin, Cahokia.

**Keywords** Cahokia · Diaspora

The symposium that led to this special issue encouraged participants to engage with theories of diaspora to frame our understanding of Cahokia, one of North America's largest cities in terms of both occupied land and population density (Fig. 1), and its greater impact across the Southeast, Plains, and Midwest. The outcome of that symposium was a varied application of diaspora theory to critically engage with the ways people materially construct or deconstruct their social identities in relation to others within the context of physical movement, as well as the ways in which regional

Chapter 7 was originally published as Baltus, M. R. & Baires, S. E. Journal of Archaeological Method and Theory (2020) 27:111–127. https://doi.org/10.1007/s10816-019-09433-x.

✉ Melissa R. Baltus
   melissa.baltus@utoledo.edu

1   University of Toledo, Toledo, OH, USA

2   Eastern Connecticut State University, Willimantic, CT, USA

movement foments social change in local places. Most contributions focused on the use of diaspora to understand Cahokian connections outside of the American Bottom; along with Emerson *et al.* (2020), we focus on the concept of "homeland" in the context of population movements. This focus is less about seeking material connections back to Cahokia that may be considered diasporic and more of a consideration of local place-identity as a continually emerging process of weaving together local and non-local people, ideas, and materials. Utilizing the lens of diaspora, we consider the concept of homeland as a created Place of Origin and how Cahokia-as-homeland was transformed by people entering and leaving the city. We trace how the movements of Cahokian or American Bottom materials, substances, persons, and non-human bodies converged in the relational creation of Cahokian identities within and immediately outside of the Cahokian homeland. Finally, we consider the processes by which humans and other-than-humans left the city, including processes of termination and transformation.

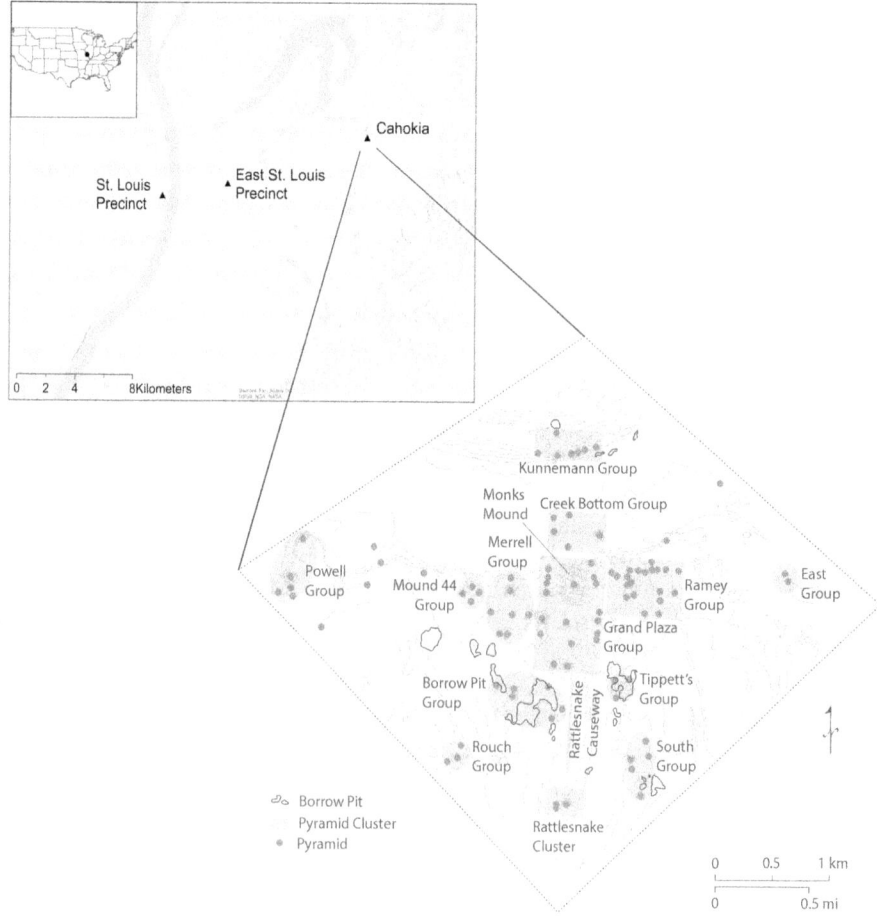

**Fig. 1** Map of the City of Cahokia

## Considering Diaspora

"Diaspora" as a concept emerged from a specific historical-academic context, rapidly becoming a term expanded well beyond its original usage and utilized in topics ranging from regional studies, to migration, to tourism (see Butler 2001). Such breadth, Lilley (2004: 287) argues, makes diaspora a particularly useful term for studying the past "because it offers archaeologists a greater number of intellectual avenues to consider in their approaches to past population dispersals." Diaspora studies include diverse approaches that range from a focus on diaspora "as a type of society characterized by particular attributes [to] a social condition produced by experiencing such attributes" (Lilley 2004: 289). At its most general, diaspora refers to communities living outside of a recognized and imagined homeland that maintain some cohesive identity in relation to that homeland. Safran (1991) offers up a set of defining characteristics that include dispersal, memories and/or myths of a homeland, distinction from the host society, and possible return to, maintenance of, and a continuing relationship with the homeland (see also Lilley 2004). To that end, diaspora is both "'social condition and social process'…structured by movement and 'the experience of being from one place and of another…where one is constructed in and through difference'" (Lilley 2004: 291 citing Anthias 1998:565, emphasis original).

Diaspora refers to the movement(s) of groups of people related through ties of origin and has its historical, anthropological, and sociological roots in the lived experiences of people within the modern era. Specifically, the term originates in the study of the dispersal and long-term separation of the Jews from Israel, their historically recognized homeland (Dufoix 2008). This concept has been expanded to include the forcible removal and geographical spread of Africans through the slave trade, the sometimes, but not always, voluntary movement of people for economic opportunity or political freedom (for example people of Chinese or Indian descent), actions of conquest and genocide leading to the spread of refugee populations beyond their modern borders (*e.g.*, Armenians, Bosnians, Syrians), and the *en masse* migrations of colonizing peoples like the French, Dutch, Portuguese, and British (Dufoix 2008; Gilroy 1993; González-Tennant 2011; Kumar 2005; Lilley 2004).

Given the multiple, diverse populations and historical experiences explored through the lens of diaspora, it may be—and has been—argued that the term is too broadly used, losing potential for effectual meaning (see Dufoix 2008; see also Butler 2001). Born from a modern concept, diaspora describes entanglements with nation-states, colonialist practices and paradigms, imagined but reified boundaries, and ongoing ethnogenesis in the wake of globalization as defined in relation to observable populations with documented histories (*e.g.*, the Black Atlantic [see Gilroy 1993]).

Limited exploration of diaspora in "more ancient times," as Lilley (2004) describes it, considers movements of peoples largely in terms of migrations, colonization, and/or dispersal. Perhaps Bender (2001) comes the closest to examining something like a diaspora in a pre-modern context when she explores "landscapes on the move." Through this concept, she considers the dynamics of these movements in relation to the creation of place as a sensorial relationship between persons and the places they move through, leave behind, and settle in. Perhaps the most important take-away from these scholars' early works on applications of diaspora to the pre-modern past is that diasporas are "characterized by fluid identities and hybridity," qualities detectable through patterns of artifact dispersal and landscape use (Lilley 2004: 304). To bring the discussion of diaspora into the precontact archaeological realm, we must necessarily focus on the materiality of diaspora. But, we must do so cautiously, with the caveat that identities, boundaries, and even movements of populations in pre-modernity differ in how they were defined, understood, and experienced, recognizing additionally that identities and boundaries are fluid constructs.

Insight into applying and examining the term diaspora in the pre-contact past can be gleaned from historic archaeology studies on the material culture of African, Irish, and Chinese diasporas to tease apart different types of movements of past peoples. Archaeologists engaged in exploring the African Diaspora highlight the dangers of uncritically assigning material culture to one particular ethnicity, race, or social group; rather a critical consideration of hybridity (or creolization), active identity construction/maintenance, and cultural persistence is required (see Franklin and McKee 2004; Orser 1998). Therefore, much of our focus here concerns the movement of non-human bodies as pieces of a Place of Origin, which constitute those material connections to shared, albeit differentially expressed, identity(ies). Additionally, we recognize the entanglement of those non-human bodies within the ongoing construction of identities in the context of population coalescence at, and dispersal from, Cahokia.

While the motivations, mechanisms, and experiences of population movements and migrations may be variable (even for people within the same diasporic population, see González-Tennant 2011), some key shared elements among migrating populations unite them under the rubric of "diaspora." Those key to our discussion here include:

1. Dispersal from an original homeland
2. A collective memory about the homeland, including its location and history (what Buchanan (2020) refers to as *nostalgia for* a homeland)
3. A strong ethnic group consciousness sustained over a long time and based on a sense of distinctiveness (Owen 2005: 47; see also Brubaker 2005; Cipolla 2017; Clifford 1994; Cohen 1997; Lilley 2006; Safran 1991)

The two elements of greatest consideration here are homeland—a Place of Origin that is as much imagined and constructed as it is a physical reality—and shared identity tied to that Place of Origin. Typically, this shared identity is presumed to be discursively expressed.

While diaspora necessarily requires processes of migration, migration does not necessarily equate to diaspora. Here, we take inspiration from Clifford (1994) in considering what aspects of population movements in relation to Cahokia may be considered diasporic. Clifford (1994) notes that while a series of requisite attributes have been used to identify diaspora among extant populations, they do not always and at all times hold true, even for those populations used to define diaspora (*e.g.*, a desire to return to the homeland among Jewish populations). Seemingly, though, at least one aspect of shared identity in reference to history and place is necessary to identify a population in diaspora. Simultaneously, we may try to recognize the "diasporic dimensions" of longing, memory, and (dis)identification in "practices…of displacement" (such as migration) even if the community itself might not be identified as diasporic (Clifford 1994:303).

For our purposes here, we see diaspora as a form of entanglement (sensu Hodder 2012), a network of social relationships linked together by their connection to a remembered homeland "reimagined [for] contemporary purposes and new generations" (Story and Walker 2016: 136). Diaspora thus includes not just ties between human populations referencing a shared historical identity, but continuing relations with and

between place (including pieces of place as well as other-than-human occupants of that place). How long these connections and identities are maintained in relation to memory and place in order to be considered diasporic remains in question, especially given the lack of fine-grained temporal detail in pre-contact North American archaeology. As experiences of diaspora are not monolithic, our discourse of diaspora must remain polythetic and consider the "particular maps and histories" involved in population movements around Cahokia (Clifford 1994).

Archaeologically, we could begin our discussion of "Cahokian diaspora" by identifying shared material traits or markers that provide concrete evidence of people spreading out into the greater Southeast, Plains, and northern Midwest from the Cahokian homeland, or by looking for examples of immigrant communities and enclaves with shared characteristics present at Cahokia that might mark them as "other" (see Alt 2006). Those markers might include building styles and practices of construction, community plan, Cahokian-style pottery, or other iconographic paraphernalia. Such markers might be boldly obvious or may manifest subtly on a single sherd of pottery. These material objects, community plans, and building styles may be evidence of "a strong ethnic group consciousness sustained over a long time and based on a sense of distinctiveness, a common history" (Owen 2005: 47). We must be cognizant, however, that these material practices are not simply the result of rote socialized behavior, but rather involve conscious choice and negotiation of history and circumstance. It is in these choices that people create and recreate a particular kind of group identity. If we accept the premise that diaspora should materialize as a movement of people with shared identities outward from, and with continued reference back to a common origin while maintaining that shared identity, then such places should be easy enough to identify archaeologically. Yet, these sorts of criteria assume that this sense of community identity is maintained over time in a linear fashion, that "their origins, in other words, lie in a completed past, rather than in the present lives of participants" (Ingold 2000: 135). As such, we must not only question the historical contexts within which populations migrated but consider the contingencies by which identities were created, negotiated, or maintained. González-Tennent (2011:512) describes a diasporic framework that considers the way imagined communities can move beyond simple center-periphery relations by understanding how "each geographic context results in unique experiences, drawing on a mixture of emigrant-area traditions reconfigured through contact with various host societies." As such, discursive maintenance of an "ethnic identity" by the migrating population, different than that of a local or "host" community, will vary depending on historically contingent circumstances. Additionally, the material "signatures" of identity may be fleeting in temporal usage or otherwise be lacking; intentional disconnect from such material signatures may have been a necessary part of the population movement.

We argue, following Dufoix (2008), that diaspora should be a concept of plurality—meaning there are innumerable historical contingencies, motivations, processes, and identities entangled with population movements in the past as well as the present. Even concepts like homeland were likely not monolithic. We also argue that diasporas (in the plural) are not solely defined by their 'straight-line' material connections to a homeland; instead, we must look to the relationships, as embodied by and through the material world, among community members and their homeland to consider not only how people seemingly "stayed the same," but more than likely changed due to a reimagining of a shared historical experience. Similarly, we must also consider how diasporic populations were complicit in enacting change outside of the homeland. The "relational turn" can be helpful here; diasporas are movements and processes "continually coming into being" (à la Ingold 2000: 142; see also Deleuze and Guattari 1987; Pauketat 2013a, b). The creation of a diasporic identity occurs in relation to a homeland (itself a fluid construct), movement, and other populations. Importantly, Dufoix (2008: 29, 33) and Lilley (2006) remind us that diasporas are also composed of difference—sex, gender, and class—in both perception and construction of identity. Further, "markers of identity are fluid and contingent" rather than stable or fixed representations of a group or individual (Story and Walker 2016: 140). Rather than specific material markers of "Cahokian-ness," we should consider the materiality of diasporic dimensions—*i.e.*, discursive and nondiscursive references to Cahokia as Place of Origin and participation in the dispersed Cahokian community (whether "real" or "imagined"). Despite potential shortcomings, however, diaspora theory provides a useful framework for thinking about the intersections of movements, temporalities, and social identity in relation to place. Diasporic communities, in their indeterminacy, occupy interstitial temporal and physical spaces, simultaneously mitigating pasts, presents, and futures in spaces between home and foreign worlds (see Clifford 1994). Diasporic movements are the embodied convergences of lives lived, and imagined or alternative futures (Sassaman 2012, see also Buchanan 2020). That being said, let us turn to the Cahokian homeland for a consideration of the creative spaces that population movements may afford as well as the historical contingencies by which we may gain a better understanding of the centrifugal and centripetal forces of Places of Origin and specifically that of Cahokia.

## Cahokia as Diaspora

Rather than considering diaspora as a specific blanket theory to understand the appearance of Cahokian objects and practices outside of the American Bottom, we suggest the diasporic lens is more broadly useful as a means of engaging the process of homeland creation, imagining, and dissolution as entangled with the creation of different kinds of persons (human and otherwise). By focusing on this aspect of diaspora—the idea of an ancestral homeland—we can problematize and reconsider the diversity notable in the dispersal of bodies (human and otherwise) outside of the American Bottom.

Beginning as a large agricultural village along Cahokia Creek in the Mississippi River floodplain of modern Illinois, the growth of Cahokia to become the largest Native American city north of Mexico was not a simple organic process. Large-scale construction projects, wholesale reorientation of space to cosmic alignments, and regional population movements characterized the creation of this place as a Place of Origin. The universe—conceptualized as Upper World, Terrestrial or 'Here' World, and Below World—was made physical at Cahokia through mounds, plazas, and borrow pits (see Baires 2017 for a review; Hall 1997: Pauketat 2013a, b). Human bodies were fully engaged in the process of calling forth the universe, creating a physical dwelling place for spirits, forces, ancestral beings, and other-world heroes. The narratives surrounding this central place, likely embedded in material objects and practices (Pauketat 2004), spread throughout the midcontinent during early growth and later dispersal from Cahokia. Here, we explore the movement of bodies—human and other-than-

human—that create and recreate places like Cahokia, both as physical space as well as imagined homelands.

Shortly before 1050 CE, people began coalescing in the wide floodplain of the Mississippi River, known locally as the American Bottom, to build earthen pyramids and carve out plaza spaces. Monks Mound, the largest earthen construction north of the Rio Grande, was initiated and built within a generation (Schilling 2013). Simultaneously, a 19-hectare Grand Plaza was sculpted from the ridge-and-swale topography of the floodplain (Dalan *et al.* 2003). Previous residential neighborhoods were appropriated for public buildings (Pauketat 2008, 2013a) and new neighborhoods were created (Collins 1990); these new architectural features—from mounds to domiciles—were aligned to a central grid which cited the movement of celestial bodies (Baires 2017; Pauketat 2013b; Romain 2015). New construction methods for building houses—using continuous trenches to hold walls rather than individually dug postholes—were introduced to the region; significantly, both earthen platform mounds and wall-trench construction are found in the southern Mississippi Valley trench (Coles Creek culture, Plum Bayou site of Toltec) prior to their appearance at Cahokia (Pauketat 2004). Along with new construction methods, novel buildings are formalized as politico-religious spaces, including circular sweatlodges and rotundas, L- and T-shaped medicine lodges or homes of political-religious specialists, charnel houses, temples, and shrines (Emerson 1997; Pauketat and Alt Forthcoming).

Additional material practices that emerged during the early coalescence at Cahokia included the increasing popularity of using crushed mussel shell as a tempering agent in pottery and novel vessel forms indicative of changing cuisines. Emerson *et al.* (2020) highlight these similarities in pottery and architecture as a process of homogenization of disparate peoples in the creation of a "new mythic Cahokian homeland". Local and regional lithic sources were a clear preference for stone tools—especially Burlington chert which ranges from bright white to multicolored; other regional sources include Mill Creek for agricultural hoes and igneous materials from the St. Francois Mountains for groundstone tools. Notably, these resources are quarried from topographically (and seemingly cosmologically) powerful places. Non-local pottery types produced with local clays, local and non-local projectile point types made on combinations of local and non-local cherts, and exotic materials like copper and marine shell indicate wide ranging entanglements throughout the midcontinent, substantiated by isotopic evidence for immigrant populations at Cahokia (Alt 2006; Emerson *et al.* 2020; Slater *et al.* 2014).

As Susan Alt (2006) aptly identified, migrations of foreign populations into the American Bottom during the early 11th century CE created a "Third Space" (à la Bhabha) from which new identities and new histories were forged. Emerging from these population movements and practices of community (*e.g.*, feasting and building mounds) was a newly shared "Cahokian" identity; however, we must also recognize the likelihood for gender, kinship, personhood, and social status difference to be redefined as new relationships were forged. While material evidence exists in practices of pottery production, foodways, and community organization that clearly indicate non-local populations in the Cahokia area, are these necessarily discursive references to a homeland such that we can consider them to be diasporic as well? Were all of these new arrivals permanent residents or was there an expectation to return home after participating in the Cahokian universe (see Emerson *et al.* 2020)? For it is in these initial population movements that we might frame our later understanding of what it meant to resettle and relate to new groups of people. Likewise, it is in these early movements and novel ways of relating to other humans (and Other-than-Humans) that Cahokia as Place and potential homeland began. Arguably, the large-scale reorganization of space-as-social-relationship that initiated with earthen pyramid construction, plaza leveling, causeway building, and neighborhood realignment was as much an intentional creation of a shared homeland as it was the creation and recreation of a cosmological ordering (see Emerson *et al.* 2020). This cosmological creation of Cahokia produced a homeland both imagined and physical. Cahokia also became homeland to other-than-human bodies created through the gathering of the deceased in ridge-top mounds, the carving of flint-clay figurines, the shaping of shell and copper into Long Nose Gods, and the pressing of copper plates. Transformations in practices of relating during the creation of the Cahokian homeland included the innovation of new pottery types and uses (born of the transformative space afforded by gatherings of foreign populations). Significant among these was the iconic Ramey Incised jar during the twelfth century Stirling phase, which Pauketat and Emerson (1991) argued embodied Upper World and Below World. Many have identified this material piece of Cahokia as a means of relating back to the physical (and cosmological) Place of Origin. Ramey Incised vessels found outside of the American Bottom have been discussed as trade items, emulations, and messengers in missionizing (Pauketat and Emerson 1991). Alongside these vessels are other materials, objects, and practices identified as key pieces of Cahokia—including Burlington and Mill Creek cherts, bi- and tri-notched projectile points, platform mound construction, and wall-trench buildings.

Movement in and out of the city was continuous throughout the history of Cahokia. Public facilities built in the core of downtown to accommodate gatherings of residents, pilgrims, and immigrants—including the Grand Plaza, monumental rotundas, and a wooden Post-circle Monument—displaced residential spaces during the eleventh and twelfth century (Pauketat 2008, 2013a). During these same periods, evidence suggests people also moved out of the city. These movements took place on local as well as regional scales, with Cahokian objects and practices, and local emulations of such, recovered from sites from Minnesota to Mississippi, Missouri to Tennessee.

The long-distance movement of objects identified as Cahokian ("Cahokian calling cards" according to Pauketat 2004) has long called into question the social and historical processes behind those movements. Early theories included centering Cahokia as a gateway to trade between the Plains and Eastern Woodlands as well as along the Mississippi River (Kelly 1990), highlighting the out-migration of Cahokian residents themselves (Conrad 1990) as political refugees (Emerson 1991) or political emissaries (Pauketat 2004), or more recently, considering the circulation of material pieces and persons through missionizing and pilgrimages (Baires *et al.* 2013; Butler 2017; Pauketat 2013b; Pauketat *et al.* 2015). Notably, these theories of population movement typically reference processes occurring in the eleventh and twelfth century Lohmann and Stirling phases. These movements continued to create Cahokia as a Place of Origin through the dispersal of meaningful materials and the persons carrying those materials. People outside of the city of Cahokia received these messages and, in some cases, adopted the object and associated practices (*e.g.*, Aztalan, Wisconsin [Goldstein and Richards 1991; Richards 1992]) creating lines of citation back to the city center. Yet, questions remain regarding the processes of abandonment that occurred in the late thirteenth and early fourteenth centuries. How did the process of abandonment effect

the things (and ideas) people carried away? And further, what transformations took place as new generations moved on and away from Cahokia?

## Leaving the Homeland

A sudden shift in religious-politics on the cusp of the thirteenth century corresponded with fortifications and conflagrations to the north in the Central Illinois River Valley (Wilson 2012), the construction of a palisade around a select portion of the Downtown Cahokia precinct, and a major burning event in the East St. Louis precinct (Emerson *et al.* 2020; Fowler 1997; Pauketat *et al.* 2013). Using spatial data and estimated population numbers Dalan *et al.* (2003), along with Pauketat and Lopinot (1997), suggested large-scale population dispersals from Cahokia took place during the course of the twelfth century Stirling phase. Recent work in the East St. Louis precinct demonstrated a rapid depopulation of that area with only a minor occupation and continued use of Mound 11 after major burning and ensuing destruction (Emerson et al. 2018). All told, Cahokia underwent major changes during the late twelfth and early thirteenth centuries that began the processes of out-migrations and the re-occupation (although in much smaller numbers) of smaller sections of Cahokia [like the East Plaza and the Spring Lake Tract (Kelly and Brown 2010; Baires *et al.* 2017)], which ultimately led to the depopulation of the city center.

In the following section, we examine the dynamics of abandonment within the city by focusing on the material practices and pieces of Cahokia carried away. What people take with them and/or jettison from their lives at times of abandonment varies according to necessity, scale of migration, and likely attachment to homeland; analysis of these materials aids in explicating the processes of depopulation and abandonment of an intentionally constructed homeland while allowing us to take stock of the materials (and ideas) that may constitute that homeland. Cahokia provides a unique case study because of its rapid abandonment. Archaeologists (Dalan *et al.* 2003; Emerson 1997, 2019; Pauketat 2013a, b; Pauketat and Lopinot 1997) generally accept that people began leaving the city during the late thirteenth century at an expeditious pace, leaving behind the accumulated stuff of urban life and the physical mounds and households of the cityscape. But what of the cultural ideas of Cahokia and the portable materials that created this Place of Origin? We explore this question below by examining the termination of certain types of architecture, pottery and symbolic objects, and the re-bundling of cultural ideals into new materials.

## Disconnecting from Homeland

While populations decline throughout the Stirling phase, the major depopulation event in Greater Cahokia coincides with a variety of termination practices involving fire and earth. The use of fire for termination is apparent at the East St. Louis precinct as highlighted by Pauketat *et al.* (2013) (see also Emerson *et al.* 2020), where as many as 70 small storage structures enclosed within a walled compound were burned at once. We see other examples of buildings terminated by fire in the American Bottom region, the percentage of which increases during the later years of Cahokia's occupation, especially after 1200 CE (Baltus and Wilson 2019). At Greater Cahokia, examples of fire-terminated buildings (aside from the complex of storage buildings referenced

above) include possible temples (Brennan 2018), and domiciles of community leaders [*e.g.*, Feature 181 in the East St. Louis precinct, Structure 4, near the east palisade and Structural Feature 178 in ICT-II in the Cahokia precinct (Brennan 2018 ; Collins 1990; Pauketat 1987)]. In the Spring Lake Tract of Cahokia, a Stirling phase building of extra-domestic importance given the presence of a clay bench along at least one wall was cleansed of objects (with the exception of a single Ramey Incised sherd) and burned. Similar signatures in the magnetometry data suggest that multiple other buildings in this tract were terminated via fire. In this same neighborhood, selected soils (grey clay) were used to cleanse the floor of a large public building prior to its dismantling in the Late Stirling phase. This use of soils to cleanse and terminate important places is magnified in the addition of large caps on most mounds at Cahokia at the Stirling to Moorhead phase transition, effectively closing down their use (Dalan *et al.* 2003).

A broader outcome of this termination process is the nearly instantaneous discontinuation of the uniquely Cahokian "architecture of power" in the form of circular, L-, and T-shaped buildings embedded within the emergence of this city (Emerson 1997). This suite of building types was an early marker of Cahokian-ness that embodied particular religious-politico ideas and practices (see Emerson 1997; Pauketat 2013a, b). Termination of these structure types via fire—and discontinued construction of those specific forms—indicates the intentional end to a set of Cahokian religious politics embodied by specific people, objects, and architecture (see Baltus 2014; Pauketat *et al.* 2013). Pauketat *et al.* (2013) argue that this may correspond with the out-migration of specific social groups who were empowered by and through those structures and their attendant practices (see also Emerson *et al.* 2020). However, a few examples of circular sweatlodge buildings persist outside of the American Bottom post-1200 CE, specifically in Southeast Missouri at sites like Lilbourn (Cottier 1977) which may comprise sites occupied by a certain subset of Cahokian population leaving Cahokia and intentionally maintaining particular religious practices.

Additional transformations around this 1200 CE period include the just-as-rapid replacement of Ramey Incised pottery with globular cordmarked jars with angled and everted rims and red slipped interiors, as well as a new plate form with decorated flanges. Ramey vessels [deftly explored by Pauketat and Emerson (1991)] were quintessential Cahokian pots that, like the aforementioned "architecture of power," came into being with the rise of this early city. The design motifs of these vessels served as portals to unite the upper world, living world, and underworld, a quality desired by, and indeed emulated by, potters in regions to the north, thus recapitulating Cahokia's new religious ideology (though often with local interpretations) (see Pauketat and Emerson 1991). The abandonment of these vessels at Cahokia's end suggests a severing with the deeply entangled Cahokian universe, and the termination of their production and replacement with seemingly plain globular jars and modestly (though likely no less potently) decorated plates can be understood as part of the dismantling of that universe and reconstruction of it through new material means. As Baltus (2014) suggests, the abandonment of Ramey for the plates and globular jars indicates a shift in group dynamics that involved more communal means of engaging with one another—as well as with cuisine—through serving wares as opposed to special-use jars.

## Small-scale movements

In juxtaposition to the termination of large areas of Cahokia and East St. Louis, certain areas at Cahokia maintained a population or even resurgence in use during the thirteenth century. For example, Kelly and Brown (2010) demonstrate continued occupation and ceremonial use of the East Plaza area of downtown Cahokia—especially around Mound 34; additionally, large residences were constructed over former public structures in Tract 15B (Pauketat 2013a, b), and the Spring Lake Tract southeast of the Woodhenge location appears to have been occupied through the Moorehead phase (Baires *et al.* 2017). A number of sites located in the surrounding floodplain and uplands were founded or reoccupied beginning in the Moorehead phase as well (see Baltus 2014). As early as the twelfth century Stirling phase, we see a shift away from the Cahokia grid and toward more local mound and plaza groups (Collins 1990); this re-orientation may have been a contributing factor to eventual dissolution of the city. There was a short period of building re-alignment to cardinal or near-cardinal orientations at the Moorehead phase cusp; however, this is not maintained, and small neighborhood hamlets internally reorganized away from Cahokia's original grid alignment reappear.

Evidence at Cahokia and surrounding Moorehead phase sites indicates an increase in commensal activities using the new plate forms (Pauketat 2013a) as well as limited mound building in Cahokia's East Plaza (Kelly and Brown 2010) and in the uplands to the east (Baltus 2014; Emerson and Hargrave 2000). Notably, there continues to be evidence for non-local people engaging in mound-related activities in the region. New connections were honed and in-migration continued with populations from Northern Illinois, Ohio River Valley, and potentially the Mid-South (Emerson and Hargrave 2000). Many of these later sites were either mortuary focused or had major mortuary components to them. For example, the East St. Louis Stone Quarry and Florence Street sites consisted of charnel structures and surrounding burials (Emerson *et al.* 1983; Milner 1983), stone box graves and pit burials were part of the Copper site occupation alongside new mound construction (Baltus 2014), and Kane Mounds held the remains of a number of individuals from or culturally influenced by Northern Illinois Langford peoples (Emerson and Hargrave 2000). While some (perhaps many) groups cut ties with the city and seemingly all it stood for, fully abandoning the region, Cahokia and the surrounding area were maintained as an active—though transformed—homeland for others. Despite (or perhaps because of) the population decline, newly created spaces paved over locations of previous Cahokian religious-politics and made the city anew in ways that emphasized community through commensality and continued use of large square council-house-like buildings.

The major depopulation event in the early 1200s coincides with the founding or major growth of sites elsewhere in the Midwest and Southeast (*e.g.*, Moundville, Angel). People leaving the city at this moment in Cahokia's history, or during its eventual (and seemingly intentional) abandonment, carried with them differing memories, traditions, and material practices from those who left in earlier eras. Perhaps most interesting to consider are the choices people made to take certain things and leave behind others. The abandonment of the "architecture of power" and the Ramey Jar style and form are two very Cahokian things that do not survive (at least in their original iterations) beyond the city's termination. But, people did take with them male flint-clay figurines with repurposed or transformed bodies to participate in smoking ceremonies (Pauketat 2004), and heroes of the Braden style whose origins can be traced to the American

Bottom and Cahokia (Brown 2004). These pieces-of-place potentially served as ties to and reminders of Cahokia-as-homeland where central ideas of the way the world works (*e.g.*, upper, middle, lower) were carried as talisman to new communities in the Eastern Woodlands and Southeast. Perhaps the figure of Birdman—interpreted as a supernatural being associated with the culture hero of Morning Star/Red Horn—embodied in copper, marine shell, and stone provides the most tangible example of Cahokia as Place of Origin. The object-body and its attendant knowledge worked to create an "imagined community" by relocating and re-imagining the culture-hero's homeland through the creation and use of this iconography in locations outside of, though with clear references to, Cahokia (Blitz 2010; see also Brown 2004; Kelly *et al.* 2007). The presence of Birdman and the warrior and shaman-style male flint-clay figurines reflect a disjuncture with Cahokia's early Green Corn Ceremonialism embodied by the female flint clay figurines (*e.g.*, Earth mother imagery) and Ramey Jars tied to Cahokia's emergence (see Emerson 1997). Many have speculated about this ideological shift and its meanings (see Blitz 2010 for summary; see also Knight *et al.* 2001) suggesting that war and war-cults became the focus of post-Cahokian communities. While this may have been the case, these materials likely also became part of the negotiation of identity in new places through processes of "unbundling" old ideas and re-bundling them with new materials and practices (see Pauketat 2013b for discussion of bundling in the context of Cahokia). Cahokia as Place of Origin remained in the reimagining of this iconography.

From the material record alone, it is difficult to discern whether the discontinuation of certain objects (*e.g.*, Ramey Pots), building styles, and site alignments indicate an active forgetting or remembering of Cahokia as Place of Origin. Perhaps this should not be the point of our analysis. Instead we might consider these materials and practices as active agents in the choices and processes of community and identity building, which aid in creating connections to new places as well as negotiating connections to the old. The materials, building styles, and practices discussed above were active participants in the dissolution of Cahokia and worked to reimagine ways of life in new contexts. "Meaning and, by extension, memories are defined by the experiences of people…it is the ongoing incorporation of that object into routinized practice that generate meaning" (Kuijt 2008: 173; see also Blake 1998). Therefore, through the process of movement, meanings and uses of specific materials will change; those transformations may emphasize connection to Place of Origin for some people but may serve to sever those connections for others.

## Discussion and Final Thoughts

While processes of in-migration and out-migration superficially appear similar between the twelfth century Stirling phase and the thirteenth century Moorehead phase, there are some qualitative difference with regard to socio-political environment (a point expertly made by Emerson *et al.* 2020). During the Stirling phase, an apparent draw to the city is likely tied to large public gatherings associated with mound ceremonialism, feasting, and religious performance, while visible outmigration may be effects of temporary pilgrimage populations and missionizing. After 1200 CE, the regional atmosphere includes conflict, conflagration, and perhaps outmigration of certain—possibly religiously or politically disenfranchised—groups. We must ask ourselves how processes of trade, missionizing, expatriatism, and emulation may be understood as different from diaspora—or even if they necessarily are (see Emerson *et al.* 2020). How long does one need to be at a place like Cahokia to consider it a homeland? Does someone need to have been to Cahokia to trace their origins there? How can we rethink diaspora in the context of pilgrimage? How are bodies and persons (including other-than-humans) transformed by their movement from homeland to other-land? Perhaps we should consider these other processes as means of relating to an "imagined" homeland that is at once a physical Place and a location of cosmological origin. Diaspora, then, need not be understood only as a materialized perpetuation of shared characteristics brought from a homeland to a new place; we must be aware of differential experience and embodiment of practices. In particular, how these things transform based on geography, time, and generational change. This recognition of difference, contingency, and consideration of diasporas as processes of being deconstructs overly simplified models of diaspora as solely products of population dispersal. From this premise, we might consider how a person's "emplacement in the world" along with their actions contribute to shared interpretations of histories and memories that then create diaspora (Ingold 2000: 144).

We recognize that all population movements (including those traditionally described as diasporic) are multivalent and historically contingent. More nuanced understandings of these processes of movements of bodies explore technological styles of seemingly non-local objects and architecture—including "exotic" styles at Cahokia and Cahokian styles elsewhere—noting the hybrid nature of many of these objects and suggesting processes of "creolization" or multi-directional integration of technological (and perhaps metaphysical) knowledge (*e.g.*, Alt 2006; Millhouse 2012; Zych 2013). Rather than "unit intrusion" it is clear that social identities and relationships outside of Cahokia are being materially negotiated in a variety of different ways depending on local traditions (see Wilson *et al.* 2020). Arguably, Cahokia itself emerges from these negotiations through a bundling process (sensu Pauketat 2013b; see Emerson *et al.* 2020) drawing together old and new traditions, practices which engage the cosmos, and people from throughout the midcontinent to reinvent themselves and the city as Cahokian. The emergence of Cahokia may in some ways be considered diasporic in this gathering process—bringing together people, practices, and materials which simultaneously reference originating homelands and create anew a Place of Origin. Cahokia was itself constructed as a homeland or origin point (whether physical or imagined) for emerging identities and newly created persons (after Fowler 2004) tying themselves in some way to this place, whether through pilgrimage, resettlement, trade, or political alliance. While Emerson and colleagues (2020) argue that Cahokia was not a diasporic homeland in a traditional sense, given the lack of continued reference to the city in historic memory, we argue that the reference to this Place of Origin was embedded within practices maintained and revitalized in communities across the Midwest and Midsouth (see for example Watts Malouchos 2020). We recognize, however, that these references occur only in *some* populations, each differing from the other with regard to what is maintained, what is transformed, and what is forgotten in the course of movement.

This creation of a homeland to which identities are attached, or towards which those identities are oriented, need not require a physical origination, but rather a construction of an imagined origin point of a people united by a centering Place. Through this Origin Place creation, Cahokia had reverberations across the midcontinent, archaeologically visible as unique objects and practices which reference Cahokia in various ways—architectural alignments that cite Cahokian cosmos (Watts-Malouchos 2020), ear ornaments that mimic those of a narrative hero (see Knight *et al.* 2001), figural carvings (Emerson 1982), iconographic pottery, and embossed copper plates (Brown 2011). Given the origin of Cahokia in movement and convergence of human and material bodies, perhaps the continued circulation of these object-bodies—alongside the human bodies with whom they traveled—was a persistence of the processes by which Cahokia emerged; Central Place and homeland reimagined and rewoven in the places in which those bodies settled.

We question whether we should expect continued "boundary maintenance" between former Cahokians and their new communities in all instances. At parts of Cahokia, rapid transformations to house style and homogenization of pottery assemblages indicate intentional creation and adoption of a local Cahokian identity (Emerson *et al.* 2020). Simultaneously, evidence at sites peripheral to Cahokia suggests that some participants did not "lose" their material identities but rather continued their traditional settlement practices and foodways until they dispersed from the region (Alt 2002, 2006). This does not mean they were unchanged from their time near Cahokia, but perhaps those transformations they take away with them will not be visible to us in the ways we expect (for example pottery or house styles).

Similarity in material goods alone does not make a diaspora; likewise, we cannot assume a static meaning attached to material culture as symbolic of ethnic identity. In examining the potential for diaspora theory to inform the movements of human and nonhuman bodies in relation to Cahokia, we highlight how an archaeology of diaspora can (and should) be self-reflexive in considering the connections among past peoples across long distances. Therefore, we suggest that diaspora is best conceptualized as a plurality (see Dufoix 2008) where notions of a homogeneous homeland fail to capture the dynamism that was (and is) the movement of people, the exchange of ideas, and the trade of artifacts. James Clifford (1994) notes that the origins of diaspora theory are rooted in specific maps and histories, and warns against the construction and maintenance of "ideal" types. Instead of seeking such ideal types of diaspora in the archaeological past, we should recognize "diasporic dimensions to practices and culture of displacement" (Clifford 1994: 303) and explore different histories and experiences of travelling and dwelling. As Lilley (2006: 37) "people literally are their history, the latter being read as patterns of interaction among people and relationships between people and place over time." We thus need to consider the local histories of those who might reference Cahokia as a Place of Origin, inspired by diaspora theory's focus on the transformative effects of movement.

# References

Alt, S. M. (2002). Identities, Traditions and Diversity in Cahokia's Uplands. *Midcontinental Journal of Archaeology, 27*, 217–236.

Alt, S. M. (2006). The Power of Diversity: The Roles of Migration and Hybridity in Culture Change. In B. M. Butler & P. D. Welch (Eds.), *Leadership and Polity in Mississippian Society* (pp. 289–308. Center for Archaeological Investigations, Occasional Paper No. 33). Carbondale: Southern Illinois University.

Anthias, F. (1998). Evaluating "diaspora": Beyond ethnicity? *Sociology, 32*, 557–580.

Baires, S. E. (2017). *Land of Water, City of the Dead: Religion and Cahokia's Emergence*. Tuscaloosa: University of Alabama Press.

Baires, S. E., Butler, A. J., Skousen, J., & Pauketat, T. R. (2013). Fields of Movement in the Ancient Woodlands of North America. In B. Alberti, A. M. Jones, & J. Pollard (Eds.), *Archaeology after Interpretation: Returning Materials to Archaeological Theory* (pp. 197–218). Walnut Creek: Left Coast Press.

Baires, S. E., Baltus, M. R., & Watts-Malouchos, E. (2017). Exploring new Cahokian neighborhoods: Structure density estimates from the spring lake stract, Cahokia. *American Antiquity, 82*(4), 742–760.

Baltus, M. R. (2014). Transforming Material Relationships: 13th Century Revitalization Cahokian Religious-Politics. Ph.D. Dissertation. Department of Anthropology, University of Illinois at Urbana-Champaign. Urbana-Champaign.

Baltus, M. R., & Wilson, G. D. (2019). The Cahokian crucible: Burning ritual and the emergence of Cahokian power in the Mississippian midwest. *American Antiquity, 84*(3), 438–470.

Bender, B. (2001). Landscapes on-the-move. *Journal of Social Archaeology, 1*(1), 75–89.

Blake, E. (1998). The Material expression of Cult, Ritual, and Feasting. In E. Black & A. B. Knapp (Eds.), *The Archaeology of Mediterranean prehistory* (pp. 102–129). Oxford: Blackwell.

Blitz, J. H. (2010). New Perspectives in Mississippian Archaeology. *Journal of Archaeological Research, 18*(1-39).

Brennan, T. (2018). East St. Louis precinct (11S706) Mississippian features. New Mississippi river bridge technical report No. 5. Illinois state archaeological survey, Prairie Research Institute, University of Illinois, Urbana-Champaign.

Brown, J. A. (2004). Exchange and Interaction until 1500. In R. D. Fogelson (Ed.), *Handbook of North American Indians* (Vol. 14, pp. 677–685). Washington D.C.: Southeast, Smithsonian Institution Press.

Brown, J. A. (2011). The Regional Culture Signature of the Braden Art Style. In G. E. Lankford, F. Kent Reilly III, & J. F. Garber (Eds.), *Visualizing the Sacred: Cosmic Visions, Regionalism, and the Art of the Mississippian World* (pp. 37–63). Austin: University of Texas Press.

Brubaker, R. (2005). The 'diaspora' diaspora. *Ethnic and Racial Studies, 28*(1), 1–19.

Buchanan, M. E. (2020). Diasporic Longings? Cahokia, Common Field, and Nostalgic Orientations. *Journal of Archaeological Method and Theory, 27*(1). https://doi.org/10.1007/s10816-019-09431-z.

Butler, K. D. (2001). Defining diaspora, refining a discourse. *Diaspora, 10*(2), 189–219.

Butler, A. (2017). The Mission Should you Accept it: The built space of a Mississippian Mission. Paper presented at the Midwest Archaeological Conference, Indianapolis.

Cipolla, C. N. (2017). Native American Diaspora and Ethnogenesis. Oxford Online.

Clifford, J. (1994). Diasporas. *Cultural Anthropology, 9*(3), 302–338.

Cohen, R. (1997). *Global Diasporas: An Introduction*. London: UCL Press.

Collins, J. M. (1990). The archaeology of the Cahokia mounds ICT-II: Site structure. Illinois cultural resources study, 1. Illinois Historic Preservation Agency. Springfield, IL.

Conrad, L. A. (1990). The Middle Mississippian Cultures of the Central Illinois River Valley. In T. E. Emerson & R. B. Lewis (Eds.), *Cahokia and the Hinterlands: Middle Mississippian Cultures of the Midwest* (pp. 119–156). Urbana: University of Illinois Press.

Cottier, J. (1977). Continued Investigations at the Lilbourn Site, 1973. *The Missouri Archaeologist, 38*, 155–185.

Dalan, R. A., Holley, G. R., Woods, W. I., Watters Jr., H. W., & Koepke, J. A. (2003). *Envisioning Cahokia: A Landscape Perspective*. DeKalb: Northern Illinois University Press.

Deleuze, G., & Guattari, F. (1987). *A Thousand Plateaus: Capitalism and Schizophrenia*. Minneapolis: University of Minnesota Press.

Dufoix, S. (2008). Diasporas. In *Translated by William Rodarmor*. Berkley: University of California Press.

Emerson, T. E. (1982). Mississippian Stone Images in Illinois. Illinois Archaeological Survey Circular 6. University of Illinois, Urbana.

Emerson, T. E. (1997). *Cahokia and the Archaeology of Power*. Tuscaloosa: University of Alabama Press.

Emerson, T. E., & Hargrave, E. (2000). Strangers in Paradise? Recognizing Ethnic Mortuary Diversity on the Fringes of Cahokia. *Southeastern Archaeology, 19*(1), 1–23.

Emerson, T. E., Milner, G. R., & Jackson, D. K. (1983). The Florence Street Site. In *American Bottom Archaeology FAI-270 Site Reports* (Vol. 2). Urbana: University of Illinois Press.

Emerson, T. E., Koldehoff, B. H., & Brennan, T. K. (ed) (2018). Revealing greater Cahokia, North America's first native city: Rediscovery and large-scale excavations of the east St. Louis precinct. Illinois state archaeological survey studies in archaeology No. 12, the archaeology of the New Mississippi river bridge. University of Illinois at Urbana-Champaign.

Emerson, T. E., Hedman, K. M., Brennan, T. K., Betzenhauser, A. M., Alt, S. M., & Pauketat, T. R. (2020). Interrogating Diaspora and Movement in the Greater Cahokian World. *Journal of Archaeological Method and Theory, 27*(1). https://doi.org/10.1007/s10816-019-09436-8.

Fowler, M. L. (1997). The Cahokia atlas: a historical atlas of Cahokia archaeology. Illinois transportation archaeological research program studies in archaeology number 2. Univerity of Illinois at Urbana-Champaign.

Fowler, C. (2004). *The Archaeology of Personhood: An Anthropological Approach*. London: Routledge.

Franklin, M., & McKee, L. (2004). Introduction African Diaspora Archaeologies: Present Insights and Expanding Discourses. *Historical Archaeology, 38*(1), 1–9.

Gilroy, P. (1993). *The Black Atlantic: Modernity and Double Consciousness*. London: Verso.

Goldstein, L., & Richards, J. D. (1991). Ancient Aztalan: The Cultural and Ecological Context of a Late Prehistoric Site in the Midwest. In T. E. Emerson & R. Barry Lewis (Eds.), *Cahokia and the Hinterlands: Middle Mississippian Cultures of the Midwest* (pp. 193–206). Urbana: University of Illinois Press.

González-Tennant, E. (2011). Creating a Diasporic Archaeology of Chinese Migration: Tentative Steps across Four Continents. *International Journal of Historical Archaeology, 15*, 509–532.

Hall, R. L. (1997). *An archaeology of the soul: North American Indian belief and ritual*. Champaign: University of Illinois Press.

Hodder, I. (2012). *Entangled: An Archaeology of the Relationships between Humans and Things*. Malden: Wiley-Blackwell.

Ingold, T. (2000). *The Perception of the Environment: Essays on Livelihood, Dwelling and Skill*. London: Routledge.

Kelly, J. E. (1990). Cahokia and its Role as a Gateway Center in Interregional Exchange. In T. E. Emerson & R. B. Lewis (Eds.), *Cahokia and the Hinterlands: Middle Mississippian Cultures of the Midwest* (pp. 61–80). Urbana: University of Illinois Press.

Kelly, J. E., & Brown, J. A. (2010). Just in Time: Dating Mound 34 at Cahokia. *Illinois Antiquity, 45*, 3–8.

Kelly, J. E., Brown, J. A., Hamlin, J. M., Kelly, L. S., Kozuch, L., Parker, K., & Van Nest, J. (2007). Mound 34: The context for the early evidence of the southeastern ceremonial complex at Cahokia. In A. King (Ed.), *Southeastern ceremonial complex: chronology, content, context* (pp. 57–87). Tuscaloosa: The University of Alabama Press.

Knight, V. J., Brown, J. A., & Lankford, G. E. (2001). On the subject matter of Southeastern Ceremonial Complex art. *Southeastern Archaeology, 20*, 129–141.

Kuijt, I. (2008). The Regeneration of Life: Neolithic Structures of Symbolic Remembering and Forgetting. *Current Anthropology, 49*(2), 171–197.

Kumar, P. P. (2005). Introduction. In P. P. Kumar (Ed.), *Religious Pluralism in the Diaspora* (pp. 1–12). Brill Academic Publishers.

Lilley, I. (2004). Diaspora and Identity in Archaeology. In L. Meskell & R. Purcell (Eds.), *A Companion to Social Archaeology* (pp. 287–312). Massachusetts: Blackwell Publishing.

Lilley, I. (2006). Archaeology, Diaspora and Decolonization. *Journal of Social Archaeology, 6*(1), 28–47.

Millhouse, P. (2012). The John Chapman site and Creolization on the Northern Frontier of the Mississippian World. Ph.D. Dissertation, Department of Anthropology, University of Illinois at Urbana-Champaign.

Milner, G. R. (1983). The East St. Louis Stone Quarry Site Cemetery (11-S-468). In *American Bottom Archaeology FAI-270 Site Reports* (Vol. 1). Urbana: University of Illinois Press.

Orser Jr., C. E. (1998). The Archaeology of the African Diaspora. *Annual Review of Anthropology, 27*, 63–82.

Owen, B. (2005). Distant Colonies and Explosive Collapse: The Two Stages of the Tiwanaku Diaspora in the Osmore Drainage. *Latin American Antiquity, 16*(1), 45–80.

Pauketat, T. R. (1987). A Burned Domestic Dwelling at Cahokia. *Wisconsin Archaeologist, 68*(3), 212–237.

Pauketat, T. R. (2004). *Ancient Cahokia and the Mississippians*. New York: Cambridge University Press.

Pauketat, T. R. 2008 The Archaeology of Downtown Cahokia I: The Tract 15A and Dunham Tract Excavations. In *Studies in Archaeology No. 1, Illinois Transportation Archaeological Research Program*. Urbana: University of Illinois.

Pauketat, T. R. (2013a). The Archaeology of Downtown Cahokia II: The 1960 Excavation of Tract 15B. In *Studies in Archaeology No. 8, Illinois State Archaeological Survey*. Urbana: University of Illinois.

Pauketat, T. R. (2013b). *An Archaeology of the Cosmos: Rethinking Agency and Religion in Ancient America*. London: Routledge.

Pauketat, T. R., & Alt, S. M. (Forthcoming). Religious Innovation at the Emerald Acropolis: Something New under the Moon. In D. Yerxa (Ed.), *Submitted for Something New under the Sun: Perspectives on the Interplay of Religion and Innovation*. London: Bloomsbury Press.

Pauketat, T. R., & Emerson, T. E. (1991). The Ideology of Authority and the Power of the Pot. *American Anthropologist, 93*(4), 919–941.

Pauketat, T. R., & Lopinot, N. (1997). Cahokian Population Dynamics. In T. R. Pauketat & T. E. Emerson (Eds.), *Cahokia: Domination and Ideology in the Mississippian World* (pp. 103–123). Lincoln: University of Nebraska Press.

Pauketat, T. R., Fortier, A. C., Alt, S. M., & Emerson, T. E. (2013). A Mississippian Conflagration at East St. Louis and its Political-Historical Implications. *Journal of Field Archaeology, 38*(3), 210–226.

Pauketat, T. R., Boszhardt, R., & Benden, D. (2015). Trempealeau Entanglements: An Ancient Colony's Causes and Effects. *American Antiquity, 80*, 260–289.

Richards, J. D. (1992). Ceramics and Culture at Aztalan: A Late Prehistoric Village in Southeast Wisconsin. PhD dissertation, University of Wisconsin-Milwaukee.

Romain, W. (2015). Moonwatchers of Cahokia. In T. R. Pauketat & S. M. Alt (Eds.), *Medieval Mississippians: The Cahokian World* (pp. 33–42). Santa Fe: School for Advanced Research Press.

Safran, W. (1991). Diasporas in modern societies: Myths of Homeland and return. *Diaspora, 1*, 83–99.

Sassaman, K. (2012). Futurologists Look Back. *Archaeologies, 8*, 250–268.

Schilling, T. (2013). The chronology of monks mound. *Southeastern Archaeology, 32*, 14–28.

Slater, P. A., Hedman, K. M., & Emerson, T. E. (2014). Immigrants at the Mississippian Polity of Cahokia: Strontium Isotope Evidence for Population Movement. *Journal of Archaeological Science, 44*, 117–127.

Story, J., & Walker, I. (2016). The Impact of Diasporas: Markers of Identity. *Ethnic and Racial Studies, 39*(2), 135–141.

Watts Malouchos, E. (2020, this issue). Angel Ethnogenesis and the Cahokian Diaspora. *Journal of Archaeological Method and Theory, 27*(1).

Wilson, G. D. (2012). Living with War: The Impact of Chronic Violence in the Mississippian-Period Central Illinois River Valley. In T. R. Pauketat (Ed.), *The Oxford Handbook of North American Archaeology* (pp. 523–532). Urbana-Champaign: Oxford University Press.

Wilson, G. D., Bardolph, D. N., Esarey, D., & Wilson, J. J. (2020, this issue). Early Mississippian diasporas of the North American midcontinent. *Journal of Archaeological Method and Theory, 27*(1).

Zych, T. J. (2013). The Construction of a Mound and a New Community: An Analysis of the Ceramic and Feature Assemblages from the Northeast Mound at the Aztalan Site. Unpublished M.S. Thesis, Department of Anthropology, University of Wisconsin Milwaukee.

**Publisher's Note** Springer Nature remains neutral with regard to jurisdictional claims in published maps and institutional affiliations.

Journal of Archaeological Method and Theory (2020) 27:128–156
https://doi.org/10.1007/s10816-020-09443-0

# Angel Ethnogenesis and the Cahokian Diaspora

Elizabeth Watts Malouchos [1]

Published online: 30 January 2020
© Springer Science+Business Media, LLC, part of Springer Nature 2020

## Abstract

The rise of Cahokia, the largest precontact Native American city north of Mexico, was precipitated by centripetal and centrifugal mobilizations of peoples, ideas, objects, and practices. To interrogate outward Cahokian movements as diasporic, I reassess relationships between Cahokia and the Angel polity on the northeastern Mississippian frontier. I approach Mississippian communities through a relational framework as ever-emerging assemblages constituted by both human and non-human actors. This framework emphasizes ethnogenesis as a process of diaspora whereby dispersed groups are in a perpetual state of community-making outside of, but in reference to, a homeland. I focus on an analysis of the Angel assemblage of Ramey Incised pottery, a power-laden Cahokian object, and determine that Angel Ramey exhibits local paste signatures in what are otherwise primarily Cahokian-style pots. Further, I contextualize artifactual connections with socio-spatial practices of Angel communities and demonstrate that aligning residential structures and communal features to a Cahokian cosmography was a principal part of community-identity-making throughout the Angel polity. Ultimately, I argue that relationships with Cahokia motivated ethnogenesis in Angel communities.

**Keywords** Diaspora · Ethnogenesis · Cahokia · Angel · Cosmology · Relational · Assemblage · Community

## Introduction

The rise of Cahokia, the largest precontact Native American city north of Mexico, at AD 1050 just south of the confluence of the Missouri and Mississippi rivers involved the large-scale mobilization and far-flung movement of peoples, objects, and practices. Populations from distant locales across the midcontinent and midsouth immigrated or made pilgrimages into the city while Cahokian emissaries and missionaries traveled far

Chapter 8 was originally published as Malouchos, E. W. Journal of Archaeological Method and Theory (2020) 27:128–156. https://doi.org/10.1007/s10816-020-09443-0.

✉ Elizabeth Watts Malouchos
   eliwatts@indiana.edu

[1] Glenn A. Black Laboratory of Archaeology, Indiana University, 423 North Fess Avenue, Bloomington, IN 47401, USA

and wide with Cahokian politico-religious objects to spread a Cahokian lifeway (Alt 2002, 2006, 2018; Ashley and Thunen 2020; Butler 2017; Mehta and Connaway 2020; Pauketat 2004, 2013; Pauketat et al. 2015; Skousen 2018). These centripetal and centrifugal movements were recurrent for a century and a half whereby integrative activities and religious events continued to draw city-dwellers, rural residents, and foreigners together and Cahokian persons, ideas, and power-laden items Mississippianized the hinterlands. At the onset of the thirteenth century, significant shifts in politico-religious organization were concomitant with a sharp decline in Cahokia's population (Baltus 2014, 2015; Pauketat 2004). The making, maintenance, and un-making of the Cahokian community were fueled by the long-distance locomotion of Cahokian ways of being (Emerson et al. 2020).

The flows of people, places, things, practices, and ideas out of Cahokia have yet to be explored through a lens of diaspora theory. To interrogate the concept of a Cahokian diaspora, I follow a framework put forth by Craig Cipolla (2017) that emphasizes ethnogenesis as a diasporic process and diasporic communities as relational assemblages (*sensu* Harris 2013, 2014). Accordingly, I approach diasporic communities as sets of relations constituted by human and other-than-human community members that are in perpetual states of community-making, that is, new collective identities are forged as former group identities are negotiated outside of, but always in reference to a homeland. Framing diasporic processes as ethnogenic and relational provides a more nuanced avenue for identifying archaeological correlates of diaspora; through these approaches, subtle similarities and transformations in everyday community-identity-making can be traced between homeland and displaced communities in the deeper past. In order to evaluate diaspora in Mississippian communities, I consider the myriad ways that identity politics were materially negotiated. In the context of diasporic studies that have relied heavily on ceramic analyses (Orser 1998; see also Owens 2005), I broaden my analysis to consider how vernacular architectural practices relate to the material constitution of social identities. Engaging diaspora in this way affords a reimagining of the far-flung connections between Cahokia and the Angel polity of the Ohio River Valley in what is now southwestern Indiana (Fig. 1).

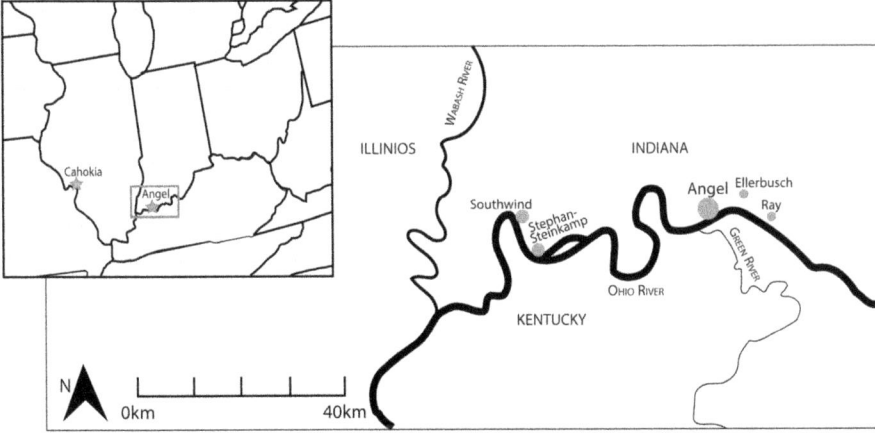

**Fig. 1** Cahokia, Angel, and excavated sites of the Angel polity in the Ohio River Valley of southwestern Indiana (from Hilgeman 2000 Fig. 1.7)

Angel is one of the largest Mississippian mound centers in the midcontinent and the last large Mississippian polity on the northeastern Mississippian frontier. Although Cahokian-style artifacts are documented at Angel Mounds, connections between the mound centers have been largely dismissed. In order to identify the connections between Cahokia and the Angel polity and evaluate if these relationships might be diasporic, I first reassess Cahokian-made or Cahokian-style prestige items recovered at Angel Mounds. I focus on an analysis of the Angel assemblage of Ramey Incised pottery, arguably Cahokia's most famous "calling card." I demonstrate the Angel Ramey assemblage shares attributes with both classically Cahokian Ramey and the majority of the locally produced Angel ceramic assemblage; Angel Ramey exhibits local paste signatures in what are otherwise primarily Cahokian-style pots. I suggest considering alternative scenarios that move beyond explanations of imitation in which Cahokian or local-but-knowledgeable potters construct Ramey vessels to entangle local substances with Cahokian cosmological ideologies.

The construction of and transformations in the built landscape were integral to the emergence of the Cahokian city-community-homeland (Alt 2019; Baires 2017; Betzenhauser 2011, 2017; Pauketat 2013, 2019; Pauketat and Alt 2003, 2005). Manipulation of traditional spatial discourses was part of the process of Mississippianization in many far-flung places, central in establishing Cahokian-related identities outside of the homeland (Alt and Pauketat 2011; Bardolph 2014; Millhouse 2012; Zych 2013). Therefore, I contextualize artifactual connections with socio-spatial practices of the Angel polity, specifically how residential and communal spaces were configured across the Angel landscape. I introduce new community organization data from the Stephan-Steinkamp site that demonstrate the practice of aligning residential structures and communities to a lunar movement was a principal part of community-identity-making throughout the history and across the broader landscape of the Angel polity. In doing so, this study offers a fresh take on material connections between the two centers and establishes a significant similarity in their celestially sculpted landscapes. The incorporation of local elements in Cahokia-style pots and aligned lunar landscapes tied Angel communities to a Cahokian cosmology for over three centuries. I argue that relationships with Cahokia and the centrifugal movements of Cahokian cosmological ideologies and practices were fundamental to ethnogenesis in the Angel polity.

## (Re)defining Diaspora

In the seminal chapter, "Diaspora and Identity in Archaeology: Moving beyond the Black Atlantic," Ian Lilley (2004:1) traces the etymology of the word diaspora to its ancient Greek origins: dia, meaning "across," and speirein, "to scatter." The root verb "speiro" specifically describes the scattering or sowing of seeds, emphasizing an ancient agricultural connotation. The sense of propagation evoked is relevant in considering the myriad anthropological treatments of diaspora. In fact, Rogers Brubaker (2005) characterizes the proliferation of the diaspora concept across academic disciplines as a "'diaspora' diaspora." Speaking to archaeology specifically, Lilley (2004:1) suggests that the conglomerated body of diaspora theory "makes it more rather than less useful" as it offers archaeologists a great number of intellectual avenues to consider past population dispersals at the "human scale of experience" (see also,

Cohen 2015:xv). The diffuse boundaries of diaspora theory have fueled debates regarding what constitutes a diaspora and which experiences and groups are appropriate to label as diasporic (*e.g.* Anthias 1998:557; Brubaker 2005, 2017; Lilley 2004:1; Tölölyan 1996:8). However, diaspora scholar Robin Cohen (2015) remarks that the concept of diaspora should not "be confined and tethered by one historical experience" (xv). In North American contexts, diaspora theory emerged from archaeological studies of African-American experiences (Armstrong 1999). Initially, diaspora was archaeologically identified through Africanisms, transatlantic continuities in material and cultural heritage, like the identification of cosmographic motifs originating in the southwest African coast inscribed on colonoware pottery in America (Ferguson 1992). Diaspora scholarship in archaeological discourse has since broadened to include historical and contemporary Jewish, Irish, and Removal Period Native American communities.

Whether scholars frame diaspora as a type of community, a social condition, or the experience of only limited groups, three criteria remain prominent in the literature: dispersion, homeland orientation, and boundary maintenance (Brubaker 2005:5–6; see also Cipolla 2017; Cohen 1997; Clifford 1994; Lilley 2004; Safran 1991). Brubaker notes that *dispersion* is arguably the most crucial criterion and the most readily apparent, wherein diasporic communities begin in one place, the homeland, but wind up somewhere else. The criterion of *homeland orientation* describes affinities for the homeland remaining an important source for situating identity in dispersed communities, for example, maintaining a connection to the homeland through collective memories, myths, or origin stories referencing the homeland, or maintaining a desire to return, or nostalgia for the homeland. The third criterion, *boundary maintenance*, entails the preservation and continuity of group identities in host communities or displaced landscapes.

Archaeologies of diaspora are generally predicated upon historically documented diasporic dispersals from which then the material correlates of diaspora are derived; the diaspora concept has mostly remained absent from theory regarding the archaeology of the precontact Americas (c.f. Cipolla 2017). However, Bruce Owen (2005:48-49) argues that the central elements of diaspora can be discerned in the deeper archaeological record. According to the three primary criteria he defines the following material correlates: (1) dispersals are evident in the abrupt appearance of materials and artifact styles in hinterland regions with origins in the homeland or through shared biological markers with homeland populations, (2) homeland orientation is demonstrated through the preservation of homeland iconography and trade goods, and (3) boundary maintenance is tangible in distinctive visible material markers of homeland group identities or ethnicity.

Despite its ubiquity in the literature, *boundary maintenance* has been critiqued for overemphasizing the continuity of discrete identities and discounting situations in which interactions with new peoples, places, things, and ideas result in the formation of new cultural identities and novel materiality (Brubaker 2005, 2017; Cipolla 2017). Indeed, contemporary social theory emphasizes that social identities are dynamic, multivariate, and fluid; the construction of identities is situational and in a perpetual state of redefinition through lived experiences (Barth 1969; Bhabha 1994; Insoll 2007; Jones 1997). The mutability of social identities is amplified in culture contact scenarios as interactions between new groups and ways of being give rise to tensions between unfamiliar and potentially competing social identities. In comparison, the concept of boundary maintenance essentializes the complex and constant construction of identities and implicates stability in what are highly volatile situations that can produce seismic shifts in identity politics (Brinkerhoff 2008; see also Wilson et al. 2020).

Craig Cipolla (2017) recently challenged the diasporic criterion of boundary maintenance charging archaeologists instead to recognize the processes of ethnogenesis inherent in diasporic situations, new communities and group identities are situated in a constant state of flux outside of the homeland. Barbara Voss (2015: 1, see also 2008) describes moments of ethnogenesis that, "signal the workings of historical and cultural shifts that make previous kinds of identification less relevant, giving rise to new forms of identity." Ethnogenesis in diasporic contexts can be understood as the emergence or transformation of new social identities whereby spatially incongruous communities negotiate the making and remaking of collective identities outside of, but in reference to, a homeland (Weik 2014). Cipolla (2017) suggests that focusing on processes of ethnogenesis, rather than boundary maintenance, better represents the reality of dynamic past indigenous communities. Expanding diaspora discourse to consider precontact communities engages long-term indigenous histories and demonstrates that diasporic processes and experiences are not limited to historical and post-colonial experiences (Cipolla 2017, 2018).

Furthermore, Cipolla (2017) advocates approaching diasporic communities though a framework of relational ontology to better capture the situational construction of social identities and ethnogenesis attendant in diasporic situations. Through a lens of ontological alterity, the social world is constituted not only by humans but also by agentive non-humans (Alberti and Bray 2009; Bird-David 1999; Harvey 2006). Human and non-human actors alike are entangled in intricate networks of relationships in which all things are related or have the potential to connected (Alberti and Marshall 2009; Hodder 2011; Ingold 2011). Transcending anthropocentric relationships, communities are "more-than-human sociality" (Harris 2013: 185), sets of relations that emerge through the connections among persons, places, and things (see also Pauketat 2013). Accordingly, Oliver Harris (2013, 2014) proposes framing communities as assemblages, made up interdigitated relationships of humans but also non-human actors (2014:77; DeLanda 2006; Deleuze and Guattari 2004; see also Bennet 2010; Hamilakis and Jones 2017; Pauketat 2013, 2019). Harris' approach situates identity-making and community-making as ever-emerging entangled processes irreducible to their constituent parts (2014: 89). Community-making involves the intentional gathering and assembling of bodies, materials, substances, and powers bound together by their relationships with each other.

Diaspora, when approached through a relational framework, transforms from a list of traits and material attributes to an exploration of how displaced peoples actively reassembled themselves with the peoples, places, and things of both their homelands and host worlds. A relational approach articulates the processes of diaspora, mainly, communal identity-making and ethnogenesis, as ongoing through lived experiences and daily material practices (Pauketat 2013). Communities emerge from a set of relations and diasporic communities are the processes and relationships of coming into being (Baltus and Baires 2020). Under Harris' formulation, we should question who and what constitute diasporic communities and how community actors are assembled in meaningful ways: "archaeological finds turn up in different kinds of contexts, we can

consider how they mediate connections between those contexts and link them into a single assemblage" (2014: 91).

In order to explore how diasporic conditions might articulate in Cahokian, Angel, and Mississippian histories, I draw from the works of several of the theorists just discussed and employ a three-tier approach to diaspora. First, following Lilley (2004) and Cohen (2015), I advocate broad definitions of diaspora necessary to consider the myriad processes related to movement, culture contact, and identity-making in the Mississippian world. Second, I adopt a new approach to diaspora offered by Cipolla (2017) that focuses on the dynamic process of ethnogenesis, the making and remaking of collective identities, rather than static boundary maintenance in diasporic scenarios. Third, following Harris (2013, 2014), I conceptualize Mississippian communities as complex assemblages of peoples, places, things, and powers. Herein, diaspora is a process of community-making whereby diasporic communities fracture, transform, and constantly negotiate material identifies in foreign lands. This allows me to capture the complexities of communal identity-making in the Mississippian world and how Cahokian material and spatial ontologies were entangled with the Angel landscape. Below, I turn to a discussion of the emergence of the Cahokian homeland and connections with the Angel polity of the Ohio River Valley.

## Ethnogenesis in the Cahokian Homeland

The importance of relationships with non-local populations during Cahokia's emergence have long been identified through the wide distribution of Cahokian-made objects and the presence of foreign materials and objects at Cahokia and outlying communities in the wider American Bottom region (Bareis and Porter 1984; Holley 1989; Kelly 1991). Archaeologists have traced Cahokian connections through the far-flung distribution of symbolically charged Cahokian politico-religious objects in distant locales like the Trempealeau complex in west-central Wisconsin (Pauketat et al. 2015) and Carson Mounds in the Yazoo Basin of Mississippi (Mehta and Connaway 2020). Likewise, large numbers of peoples from places like southwestern Indiana and northeastern Arkansas immigrated to Cahokia bringing with them materials and practices traditional to their foreign homelands (Alt 2002, 2006, 2018; Pauketat 2004; Slater et al. 2014; Skousen 2018). Susan Alt (2002, 2006, 2018) argues that the inward movement of immigrants to Cahokia and the comingling of diverse traditions and practices is precisely what afforded the innovation of new cultural forms (*sensu* Bhabha 1994) that incited Cahokia's ethnogenesis. Similarly, Timothy Pauketat (2013) envisions early Cahokian aggregations as an intentional practice of bundling (*sensu* Zedeño 2008), in which gathering and repositioning the traditional ways that people, places, things, and powers related made way for the establishment of a new cosmic realm and a new Cahokian city-community (see also Alt 2019; Baltus 2018; Pauketat and Alt 2018). He credits the bundling of persons and materials within these particularly realigned and cosmologically positioned landscapes with bringing a new Cahokian community into being. Melissa Baltus and Sarah Baires (2020) suggest that the Cahokian coalescence was instigated by an inverse diaspora of sorts, whereby a Cahokian homeland was constructed through the amalgamation of distant foreign homelands.

The translocal mobilizations of persons, objects, and practices precipitated the rapid transformation of collective identity practices at Cahokia—from the way potting clay was tempered, to how buildings were constructed, to how the regional landscape was inhabited. In particular, spatial relations were dramatically reconfigured as the built environment was reinvented during Cahokia's establishment (Baltus and Baires 2020; Betzenhauser 2011, 2017; Dalan 1997; Dalan et al. 2003; Emerson 1997; Emerson et al. 2020; Pauketat 2004, 2013; Pauketat and Emerson 1997, 1999). The massive scale of Cahokia's monumental cityscape was underpinned by an organizational principle that oriented mounds, plazas, and monuments along an axis 5° east of north (Pauketat 2013; Romain 2015, 2018). This axial alignment was constructed in reference to the movements of the moon and reflected a mirror image of cosmic organization (see also Baires 2017; Pauketat et al. 2017). In the Cahokian countryside, important shrine complexes like the Emerald Mounds site were similarly constructed according to lunar principles (Pauketat 2013). Immigrants, pilgrims, and new or potential religious converts traveling to the American Bottom from the east would have arrived at the Emerald complex first, a landscape sculpted with 11 mounds aligned to lunar standstills, orienting newcomers and visitors to the Cahokian cosmos as they continued their journey to the city (Skousen 2018). Moreover, everyday socio-spatial practices were also reimagined; in the city, traditional arrangements of annular courtyard groups were replaced with orthogonally aligned plaza groups (Collins 1990, 1997; Mehrer and Collins 1995; Pauketat 1998a, 2004, 2013). In fact, Pauketat (1998a, 2001, 2008) suggests that the disruption and appropriation of pre-Cahokian traditional spatial discourses supported the reinvention of a new communal and cosmic ethos to be established at Cahokia (see also Dalan 1997; Dalan et al. 2003; Pauketat and Emerson 1997). The directionality of Cahokia's cosmographic landscape aligned a new social spatiality and informed the bodily dispositions of inhabitants, pilgrims, and visitors.

## Angel History and Connections with Cahokia

Connections between the American Bottom and southwestern Indiana were established during Cahokia's fluorescence through interactions with peoples of the Yankeetown culture, a Late Woodland/Emergent Mississippian predecessor to Angel culture near the confluence of the Wabash and Ohio Rivers (Figs. 1 and 2) (Redmond 1990). The presence of uniquely decorated Yankeetown pottery has been documented in early Cahokian contexts across the American Bottom; Yankeetown ceramics are most prominent in the adjacent uplands, but have also been documented at Cahokia, East St. Louis, and BBB Motor, among other prominent floodplain sites (Alt 2006; Bareis and Porter 1984; Brennan 2016; Pauketat 2004). In the uplands, significant numbers of Yankeetown decorated wares have been recovered: Alt (2018) reports 5% of ceramic assemblage at the Knoebel site were Yankeetown wares.

In southwestern Indiana, Yankeetown-Mississippian relationships are much less apparent. The geographic and temporal boundaries of Yankeetown culture overlap significantly with that of the Angel polity (Greenan and Garniewicz 2010). Unlike Cahokian scenarios, an infinitesimal percentage of the Angel Mounds ceramic assemblage is represented by Yankeetown decorated sherds ($n = 24$ of 1.82 million)

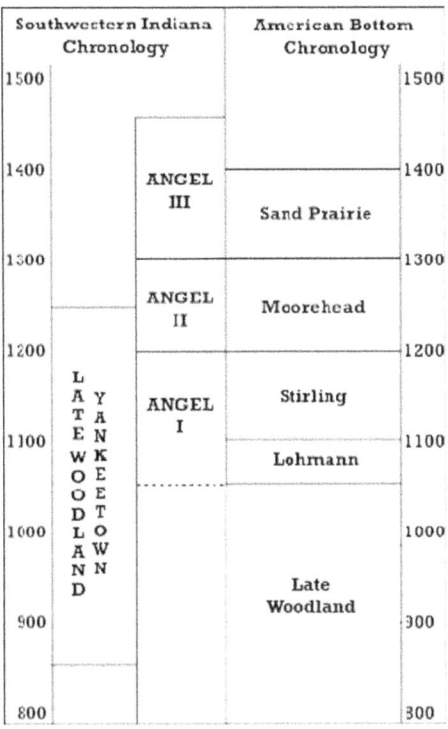

**Fig. 2** Mississippian period chronologies comparing the southwestern Indiana region of the Angel polity with the American Bottom region of Cahokia

(Hilgeman 2000; McGill 2013). Tacking back and forth between research in the American Bottom and southwestern Indiana, Alt (2018) observed that Yankeetown decorated ceramics are found in early Mississippian contexts much more frequently in the American Bottom than in any Mississippian contexts in southwestern Indiana. The absence of substantial Yankeetown ceramics at Angel has been used to argue that Mississippian Angel culture was an intrusive settlement that replaced or displaced Yankeetown populations (Hilgeman 2000; Honerkamp 1975; Monaghan and Peebles 2010; Peterson 2010).

Located on the banks of the Ohio River just east of modern-day Evansville, Indiana, the Angel Mounds civic-ceremonial center (40 ha) was comprised of 11 earthen mounds enclosed by several iterations of semi-circular palisade fortification walls (Figs. 1 and 3a) (Black 1967; Peterson 2010). During the first half of the twentieth century, large-scale excavations under the auspices of Glenn A. Black not only targeted monumental architecture and public spaces at Angel but also uncovered a large densely occupied residential neighborhood on the eastern half of the site termed the "east village" (Black 1967). Nearly 4% of the site has been excavated and nearly 2.5 million artifacts have been collected producing a ceramic assemblage totaling over 1.82 million objects (Hilgeman 2000; McGill 2013; Peterson 2010).

The Angel chronology is generally divided into three sub-phases based on ceramic seriation, but research in the last decade has provided radiometric data that have refined our understanding of the timing of events at Angel (Fig. 2) (Hilgeman 2000; Krus 2016; Monaghan and Peebles 2010; Monaghan et al. 2013; Peterson 2010). The Angel

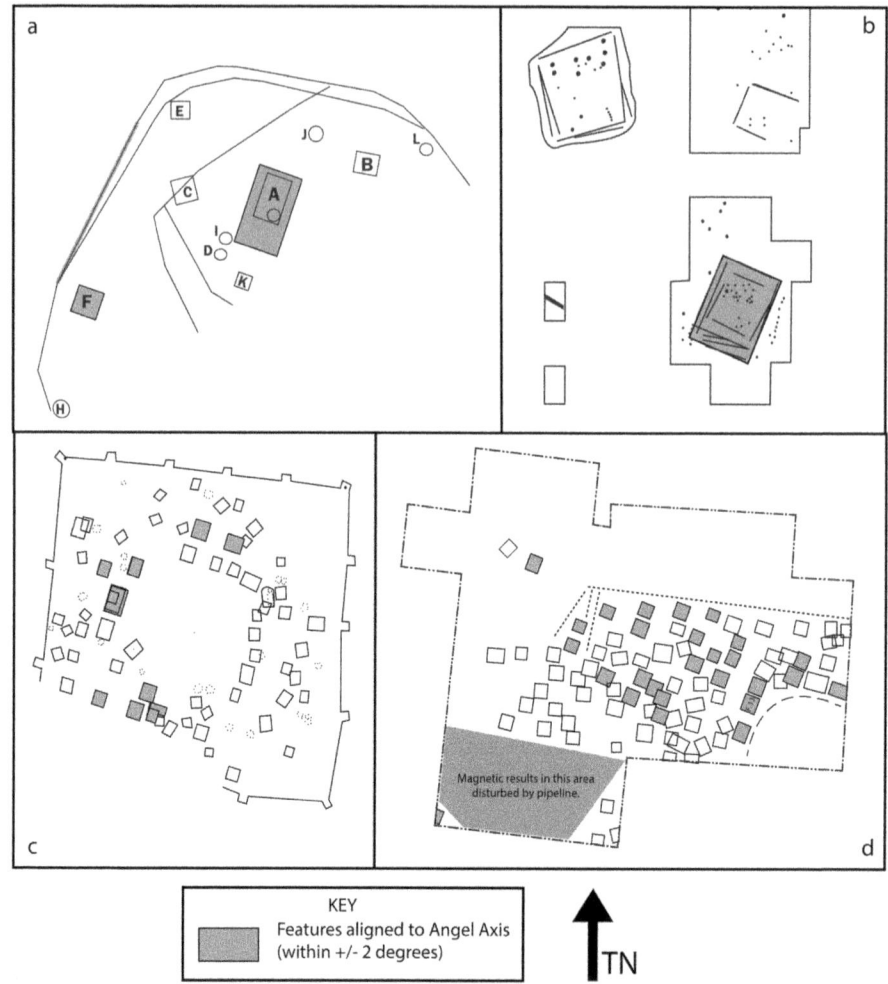

**Fig. 3** Angel polity community organization and repetition of the Angel axis in monumental and residential architecture: **a** Mound A, Mound F, and a western portion of the palisade at Angel Mounds (from Black 1967, Fig. 14), **b** rebuilt structure at Ellerbusch (from Green 1977, Fig. 5), **c** excavated structures at Southwind (from Munson 1994, Fig 5.1), and **d** magnetically detected structures at Stephan-Steinkamp

I phase represents the founding of the Angel town just before AD 1050 with the onset of construction of platform Mounds A and F (Fig. 3a) (Monaghan and Peebles 2010; Monaghan et al. 2013). However, there is no clear evidence of permanent habitation at the site during this initial phase (Hilgeman 2000; Peterson 2010). By AD 1200 and the Angel II phase, Angel was occupied by an estimated ~200–3000 residents and the town was fortified by the erection of the first outer palisade wall (Krus 2016; Peterson 2010). AD 1450 marks the end of the Angel III phase and the abandonment of Angel Mounds, accompanied by final capping mound layers placed atop Mounds A and F (Black 1967; Monaghan and Peebles 2010; Monaghan et al. 2013; Peterson 2010).

Surface surveys identified outlying Angel phase sites defining an Angel polity along a 120 mile stretch of the Ohio River from the Wabash to the Green Rivers (Fig. 1) (Green and Munson 1978). However, excavations have been limited to four hinterland sites: two villages, the Southwind and Stephan-Steinkamp sites, one small hamlet, the Ellerbusch site (Green 1977; Green and Munson 1978; Hilgeman and Schurr 1987; Munson 1994), and a small cemetery, the Ray site (Ball 1996). Here, I discuss the results of my analysis of Angel Ramey Incised pottery and review the distributions of other Cahokian-style objects recovered from Angel Mounds and outlying excavated sites.

## Cahokian Calling Cards in the Angel Polity

Cahokian-made objects distributed across the midcontinent and midsouth, likened by Pauketat (2004: 120) to "calling cards," include Ramey Incised pots, Cahokia-style chunkey stones, Cahokia-notched arrow points, long-nosed-god-maskettes, flint-clay figurines, and Mill Creek chert hoes (see Fig. 4 for examples from Angel Mounds). Ramey Incised pots, Cahokia-style chunkey stones, and Cahokia points have been found in the Angel polity; thus far, there is no evidence of long-nosed-god-maskettes or flint-clay figurines in southwestern Indiana. The small numbers of Cahokian artifacts have generally been discounted in comparison to the large material assemblages at Angel Mounds. All Angel region collections discussed below are curated at Indiana University's Glenn A. Black Laboratory of Archaeology.

## Ramey Incised Pots

Identified in far-flung locales across the Mississippian world, Ramey Incised pots are considered perhaps the most parsimonious artifactual evidence of interactions with Cahokia (Pauketat 2004). Archaeologists have long recognized Ramey Incised pots as

**Fig. 4** Examples of Cahokian "calling cards" uncovered at Angel Mounds: **a** Ramey Incised rim sherd, **b** Cahokia-style chunkey stone, **c** Cahokia-notched point, and **d** fragment of a Mill Creek hoe (Used with permission from the Trustees of Indiana University)

an important ritual item inscribed with iconography depicting powerful ideologies about cosmological order (Fowler and Hall 1975; Griffith 1981; Hall 1991; Pauketat and Emerson 1991; O'Brien 1972; Vogel 1975). The suite of imagery created by the broad trailed incised lines has been interpreted as both upperworld and underworld symbolism: convoluted, curvilinear, and geometric motifs are associated with sun, fire, rainbows, birds, and movements of wind, smoke, and dance (Emerson 1989, 1997; Pauketat and Emerson 1991) as well as the moon, serpents, movements of water, shell, ogees, and feminine life forces (Emerson 1989; Galloway 1997).

Beyond the cosmological associations of the iconography, Pauketat and Thomas Emerson (1991) postulated that the pots themselves are cosmographic. The vertical and horizontal fields created by the distinct jar morphology (sharp-angled shoulders with globular bodies) represent the upper and lower worlds and the quadriform incised designs symbolized the quadripartition of the cosmos along the cardinal directions. For Pauketat and Emerson, Ramey Incised pots did not merely evoke cosmological realms in their design but embodied cosmological order. Ramey users traversed realms in the process of accessing the vessel's contents and by doing so were inculcated with Cahokian religious ideology (see also Pauketat 2004, 2013). Until recently, the function of Ramey vessels as containers was undertheorized. Jessica Miller (2015) analyzed carbonization patterns evident in Ramey pots and demonstrated that Ramey Incised and Powell Plain (Ramey's unincised complement) were used in the decoction of teas and/ or medicines. Chemical signatures of Black Drink, the highly caffeinated drink made from yaupon holly leaves historically recorded in southeastern Indian renewal ceremonies and purification rituals, have been detected in another Cahokian ritual ware but may have been brewed in Ramey Incised and Powell Plain pots (Crown et al. 2012; Hudson 1979).

The powerful iconography (and potentially potent contents) of Ramey pottery found in far-flung locations has been interpreted as communicating Cahokian identities and ideologies (Emerson 1989, 1997; Friberg 2017; Hall 1991; Pauketat 2004; Pauketat and Emerson 1991, 1997). As such, Ramey pottery is viewed as integral to the processes of the Mississippianization of the greater midwest and southeast, foundational in sharing and establishing Cahokian lifeways and worldviews. Pauketat has discussed the agency of Ramey pottery acting as religiously charged mnemonic souvenirs accompanying visitors and pilgrims returning to their homelands and also as missionizing objects used by Cahokian politico-religious emissaries and proselytizers in the conversion of religious disciples in the hinterlands (Pauketat 1998b, 2004:124; 2013).

At Angel Mounds, only 100 sherds of 1.82 million collected have been identified as foreign wares (Hilgeman 2000). 90 Ramey Incised sherds, as identified by Sherri Hilgeman (2000), have been uncovered from excavations, 89 of which were located for this study (see also Peterson 2010). Ramey represents a miniscule percentage of the overall assemblage ($n = 90$ out of 1.82 million). However, when taken into the context of the small numbers of foreign ceramics ($n = 100$), the Cahokian influence is more significant: 90% of the sherds identified with a foreign origin at Angel are Ramey Incised. The fragmentary nature of the Angel Ramey assemblage as well as the variable combinations of design elements across Ramey motifs and quadri-repetition of Ramey designs make parsing a minimum number of vessels difficult. Based on qualitative analysis, I offer a more conservative estimate of at least 31 distinct Ramey vessels at Angel Mounds. However, the results below are figured by individual sherd count to

remain consistent with Hilgeman's analysis of the Angel decorated assemblage (Hilgeman 2000:173).

The majority (89%) of Angel Ramey was uncovered throughout the east village, likely from residential household contexts. However, one Ramey sherd was found in Mound A and two in Mound F for a total of 2% of the assemblage deposited in mound contexts. 9% of Ramey were uncovered from Feature 37 in the east village, one of the earliest non-mound features at Angel dating to AD 1150 (Peterson 2010). Feature 37, a large amorphous pit, contained thousands of artifacts including a significant percentage of all of the decorated pottery recovered from Angel, bone pins and awls, and over 2000 pieces of bone (Buchanan and Wernette 2016). This unusual detritus indicates extradomestic feasting and communal or foundational events. The sherds in Feature 37 likely represent three or four different vessels, 10% of the minimum number of Ramey vessels identified.

For this study, I analyzed the Ramey assemblage from Angel Mounds paying close attention to technological styles and paste composition. The fragmentary nature of the Angel Ramey assemblage makes some characterizations difficult; there are only two small rims and the vast majority of the incised motifs are incomplete. However, the small sample of rims does indicate that Angel Ramey rims were everted and angled rather than rolled. This morphological detail suggests manufacture at around AD 1200 concomitant with the slowing of production of Ramey at Cahokia, and what is thought to have been the first substantial habitation at Angel (Baltus 2014; Holley 1989; Krus 2013; Monaghan and Peebles 2010; Peterson 2010). Additionally, I calculated the rim-protrusion-ratios (RPR) for Angel Ramey rims, a method developed by George Holley (1989) to seriate shifts in the morphology of Cahokian jars (see also lip protrusion index Pauketat 1998a). The RPR is the ratio of the wall thickness below the rim lip to the rim lip length; jar rim protrusion becomes more pronounced later in the Cahokian sequence represented by decreasing RPR values through time. RPRs of both Angel Ramey rims fall into the ranges seen at Cahokia and the American Bottom: the RPR value (0.5294) of rim X11B-4763 corresponds to a classic Stirling date (AD 1100–1200) while rim X11C-875 has a low RPR value of (0.2727) indicative of late production corresponding to the Moorehead phase (AD 1200–1300) (Fig. 2).

Due to the incomplete state of the iconography, it is difficult to precisely define the motifs present. However, the broad trailed incised lines on Angel Ramey are consistent with the freeform but deliberate design execution on much of the Ramey found throughout the American Bottom (Griffith 1981). The majority of decorative motifs (94%) are curvilinear designs representing scrolls, volutes, or arcs. Five sherds, while quite fragmentary, are incised with nested triangles or chevrons. The scrolls, arcs, and volutes that are the most common motifs in the American Bottom are also the motifs exhibited at Angel whereas chevron, arc, and curvilinear motifs are more common in the northern midwest hinterland regions (Lower Illinois River Valley, Central Illinois River Valley, Apple River Valley, Upper Mississippi River Valley, and southeastern Wisconsin) (Emerson 1991; Friberg 2017; Millhouse 2012; Mollerud 2016; Richards 1992; Richards and Zych 2018; Zych 2013). Cahokian and American Bottom assemblages exhibit more diversity in motifs while designs are more homogenous at sites farther removed from Cahokia (Richards 1992); this uniformity in hinterland motifs may indicate a more singular strategy in the Mississippian conversion of the midcontinent (Baltus 2014). Moreover, Baltus (2014) observed an increase in the uniformity of Ramey motifs at and after AD 1200 that may demonstrate a shift or simplification in message as compared to the high degree of variability in motifs depicted earlier on at Cahokia.

At Cahokia, Ramey surfaces finished with burnishing are typical (Holley 1989) while at Angel, only 30% of the Ramey assemblage is burnished. Similarly, upwards of 94% of Cahokian Ramey Incised pottery is slipped, smudged, or a combination thereof (Mollerud 2016:135), while at Angel, only 45% of Ramey shows evidence of slipping, smudging, or slip/smudging. The predominance of plain (unslipped, unsmudged, and unburnished) surfaces in foreign Ramey assemblages is common throughout the wider Cahokian hinterlands (Friberg 2017; Mollerud 2016). Additionally, six Angel Ramey sherds (7%) have incised lines over surfaces that were first cord-marked and then smoothed over. Cord-marking and smoothed-over-cord-marking are common surface treatments on Late Woodland Yankeetown wares (Redmond 1990), are consistently present but in slight percentages (*i.e.* ~1%) in Mississippian Angel wares (Black 1967:468; Munson 1994), and very common in Cahokian wares (but not Ramey pottery) during the Moorehead phase (Holley 1989).

Sherri Hilgeman (2000) characterized Angel Ramey as too dissimilar to fit cleanly in either typical Cahokian or Angel assemblages. Based on personal communication with American Bottom archaeologists, Hilgeman described Angel Ramey as not as "well finished" as Cahokia Ramey (2000:109), referring to the coarser-tempered pastes and unburnished surfaces of Ramey in the Angel assemblage. Hilgeman also noted that the angular necks and sharp shoulders of Ramey jars were not typical of the more globular jars from Angel. Hilgeman categorized Angel Ramey as a distinct variety of Ramey, *Green River*, and interpreted Angel Ramey as both local copies and possible imports in her brief discussion.

While I agree with Hilgeman's (2000) assessment that Angel Ramey is neither classically Cahokian in surface finish and temper nor typically Angel in decorative design and morphology, the everted rims, angular shoulders, and broad trailed designs of the majority of the Angel Ramey assemblage are consistent with Cahokian styles. However, one aspect of the Angel Ramey assemblage clearly establishes local origins: the pastes of the vast majority of Angel Ramey contain regular hematite inclusions. Local Ohio River Valley clays that naturally contain the ferrous inclusions were favored in the Angel ceramic assemblage (Fig. 4a) (McGill 2013; Redmond 1990; see also Brennan 2014). Hematitic pastes are infrequent in Cahokian assemblages, if not virtually unknown at many sites across the American Bottom (Baltus 2014; Porter 1964). The majority of the Angel Ramey assemblage (93%) is tempered with shell exclusively, but there are six examples with grog and/or grit admixtures; this is consistent with the predominance of shell tempering in the wider Angel ceramic assemblage (McGill 2013). Moreover, Cahokian Ramey Incised jars are almost exclusively shell tempered and demonstrate less paste diversity, that is, a smaller percent of non-shell inclusions, than other Cahokian jars (Holley 1989; Pauketat and Emerson 1991; Porter 1964). While other technological and decorative aspects of Angel Ramey are similar to Cahokian-style wares, local paste recipes were clearly preferred.

No Ramey Incised pottery has been found at the Southwind, Ellerbusch, or Stephan-Steinkamp sites, however, two Ramey sherds representing two different vessels were found at the Ray site, a small, possibly Early Mississippian cemetery upriver from Angel (Ball 1996). The Ray site Ramey exhibits volute motifs incised on the rounded, rather than angular, shoulders of more globular Angel-style jars. At Angel, six sherds (7%) were similarly incised on more globular rounded shoulders rather than angled necks. The pastes of both Ray Ramey sherds are hematitic and consistent with local Angel wares.

In the wider Ohio Valley, a very modest number of Ramey Incised sherds have been reported from the Annis ($n = 2/16078$, Hammerstedt 2005) and Andalex ($n = 3/19837$ (Niquette et al. 1991) sites across the Ohio River in Kentucky, Kincaid Mounds down the Ohio River in southern Illinois (n = $3/\sim 15,000-\sim 100,000$ Cole et al. 1951:105), and Wickliffe Mounds at the confluence of the Ohio and Mississippi rivers in Kentucky ($n = 2/172054$, Wesler 2001). Farther up the Ohio along the Mississippian and Fort Ancient frontier, Ramey Incised sherds have been found at the Mississippian Prather site (Munson et al. 2006) and Fort Ancient culture State Line and Turpin sites (Cook 2008).The majority of the Ramey in the wider Ohio Valley seem to be locally made, although Cahokian-made imports have been identified at Annis, Wickliffe, and Kincaid (Cole et al. 1951; Hammerstedt 2005; Wesler 2001).

The rare occurrence of Ramey Incised pottery in the Ohio Valley has been interpreted as demonstrative of weak connections with Cahokia, particularly in comparison to more abundant connections to more northerly centers and sites in the Illinois and Upper Mississippi river valleys (Kelly 1991:67). For example, at Kincaid, Ramey represents at most 0.02% percent of the ceramic assemblage (Cole et al. 1951). However, more recently Pauketat (2013: 156) noted that Kincaid's organizational azimuth aligns to a minimum northern moonrise similar to the lunar orientations guiding the Cahokian and Angel landscapes (see discussion of architectonics below). The higher frequency of Ramey pottery at Angel could indicate stronger ties between Cahokia and Angel than with other centers and sites in the Ohio River Valley. However, perhaps like Angel, connections between Cahokia and Kincaid and other Ohio Valley centers and sites have been undertheorized and have not been situated within the broader contexts of architectural practices and the built landscape.

## Imports, Imitations, or Entanglements?

The standardization of technological style in Ramey vessels within the American Bottom region suggests a restricted number of producers and elite-controlled production, consumption, and dissemination (Pauketat and Emerson 1991; Hall 1991). Outside of the Cahokian heartland, most Ramey assemblages are constituted of combinations of Cahokian-made and locally made Ramey Incised pots. Locally produced wares are identified through their distinct recombination of Ramey decorative motifs with local potting styles. In culture contact situations in the northern hinterlands, Ramey designs were often integrated with traditional Late Woodland jar morphologies and design aesthetics to create new "hybrid" forms (Bardolph 2014; Delaney-Rivera 2000; Emerson 1991; Friberg 2017; Hall 1962; Knudson 1967; Millhouse 2012; Mollerud 2016; Richards 1992; Zych 2013). Scholars discuss these hybridized vessels as reflective of culture contact on the Mississippian frontier as newly established or newly multi-vocal communities variously adopted, rejected, or adapted Cahokian practices (*e.g.* Bardolph 2014; Friberg 2017; Millhouse 2012). For Christina Friberg (2017), hybrid vessels represent "cosmic negotiations" whereby traditional Late Woodland worldviews were incorporated or reinterpreted with Cahokian cosmological principles.

                                     Springer

In other cases, Cahokian-style Ramey motifs, vessel morphology, and surface treatments were consolidated with local paste recipes. Ramey pottery outside of the American Bottom is commonly constituted by shell temper mixed with other tempering agents (grit and or grog) or local traditional tempers are utilized as a wholesale substitution for shell. In the Cambria Locality of the Minnesota Upper Mississippi River Valley, Katy Mollerud (2016:305) reports the most significant difference between Cahokian-made and locally made Ramey is the replacement of shell temper with grit in what are otherwise "faithful emulations" (Mollerud 2016:305). Compositional analyses of hinterland Ramey assemblages have been integral in the identification of Cahokian-made Ramey Incised pots versus locally produced Ramey wares (Boszhardt and Stoltman 2016; Hammerstedt 2005; Mollerud 2016; Stoltman 1991; Stoltman et al. 2008). For example, Robert Boszhardt and James Stoltman (2016) examined thin-sections of four Ramey Incised vessels at the Iva site in the La Crosse Locality of the Wisconsin Upper Mississippi River Valley. Petrographic analysis revealed that the paste and temper compositions of two Ramey vessels were consistent with American Bottom pottery and were imported. The remaining two Iva site Ramey vessels, while Cahokian in form and decorative design, were made with local paste recipes.

Locally manufactured Ramey vessels are often characterized as copies, imitations, and emulations. Discussions of social emulation in historic archaeology frame imitation as an attempt "to replicate the behaviors and to adopt the material culture of others, especially those with perceived higher socioeconomic standing" (Bell 2002:253; see also Fine and Leopold 1990). The prevailing expectation with emulative behavior is that en vogue trends were introduced by elite classes and subsequently adopted or imitated by commoners as a stratagem in upward mobility (Bell 2002; Johnson 2010). In the case of Ramey Incised pottery at Angel Mounds, the traditional narratives of emulative effects do not fit well. There is no indication of status differentiation linked to Ramey pottery at Angel; Ramey is primarily (89%) found in residential, if not domestic, contexts of the east village rather than elite or monumental spaces. Moreover, some locally produced Ramey vessels were finely made by skilled and knowledgeable potters, consistent with Cahokian-made Ramey in vessel form and decorative design. If local pastes and untreated surfaces are the primary differences in locally made Ramey Incised pottery assemblages, could this indicate that Cahokian potters traveled to hinterland locales, made Ramey pottery of local materials, and instructed local potters (Friberg 2017; Pauketat 2004; Watts Malouchos 2016)? Processes of imitation and emulative effects at Angel were more complex than traditional models credit.

Speaking to indigenous-colonial encounters in the Great Lakes region, Meghan Howey (2011) posits that indigenous mimesis served to mediate colonial power relations. She argues that, "even if the copying is imperfect, it can nevertheless be very effective copying in acquiring the power of the original" (2011:331). She argues that the appropriation of power over something can be achieved through imitation and interprets a native-made ceramic skeuomorph of a European copper kettle as mimesis to stave off the upheaval attendant with European contact. Howey's nuanced interpretation of mimicry as power dynamic better aligns with locally produced Ramey in the Cahokian hinterlands. The fact that vessels are not classically Cahokian and likely were not dispersed from the American Bottom does not make them any less ideologically charged or their powers less potent. Perhaps locally recreating Ramey vessels harnessed

 Springer

traditional powers and cosmological forces in a deeper way, entangling the local substances used in the creation of vessels with the Cahokian cosmos, imbuing not only the makers, users, and viewers of the vessel but also the place and landscape with cosmic powers (see also Richards and Zych 2018). Approaching Ramey Incised pots within a relational framework allows us to understand how Ramey pots were powerful actors disseminating Cahokian ideologies, not only through their potent iconography, but through the comingling of homeland and foreign bodies (human and otherwise) (Alt 2018; Baltus and Baires 2012; Baltus 2018; Pauketat 2013; Pauketat and Alt 2018). Reimagining Ramey pottery as the gathering of powerful ideas, elements, places, and histories, rather than simply the whole-pot-final-product, affords commensurate powers and agency to both Cahokian-made imports and locally made hinterland reproductions.

### Other Cahokian Calling Cards at Angel: Chunkey Stones, Cahokia Points, and Mill Creek Hoes

Chunkey stones, similar to the rolling discs used in the ethnohistorically recorded chunkey game, originate in the American Bottom and adjacent regions during the Late Woodland period as early as AD 600 (DeBoer 1993; Pauketat 2004; Zych 2015). Warren DeBoer (1993) and Pauketat (2004), respectively suggest that chunkey stones were (re)appropriated by Cahokian elites as part of the city's foundation. Late Woodland chunkey stones are found in pits and midden contexts whereas there is a shift to ceremonial contexts at the onset of the Mississippian period, for example, feasting deposits underlying Cahokia's Mound 51 and the elaborate mortuary deposits in Mound 72. Robert Hall (1997) linked the chunkey game to Cahokian cosmology by likening the rolling of the chunkey stone to the movement of a celestial disc across the sky. Pauketat (2004) further suggested that chunkey stones might have established or reaffirmed Cahokian cosmological principles through public participation in chunkey gaming events (see also Alt and Pauketat 2007; Pauketat and Alt 2003). At Angel, Black (1967) noted 17 stone discoidals and 26 ceramic discoidals; two of the stone discoidals and one of the ceramic discoidals are made in the Cahokian chunkey style with biconcave or cupped faces (Fig. 4b). No chunkey stones or similar ceramic discoidals have been recovered at other Angel region sites.

Triangular Cahokia points, most famous for the immaculate examples interred in Cahokia's Mound 72, manifest in several varieties; notched styles are a more obvious indicator of a Cahokian origin. At Angel, at least two Cahokia-notched points have been recovered: one in Mound F and one in residential contexts of the east village (Fig. 4c). I would argue that there are at least two other examples from the east village that are worn Cahokia-notched rather than cluster types from the Central Mississippi Valley as they have been previously been identified (Justice 1987). Of the 1335 whole Mississippian points collected during the Black era at Angel, a mere six points have been identified as foreign. However, Cahokian-style notched points account for 67% of the foreign point assemblage (Black 1967; Herrmann 2013). Outside of Angel, two examples of Cahokia-notched points were recovered from surface and plowzone contexts at Ellerbusch, however, no Cahokia points have been found at Southwind or Stephan-Steinkamp.

While Cahokia's control of the political economy of Mill Creek hoes sourced in southern Illinois has been debated (Cobb 1989, 2000; Pauketat 2004:120), it is apparent that they were an important material component of the Cahokian lifeway evidenced through their ubiquity across the American Bottom and association with Cahokian contact in hinterland locales. At Angel, Black (1967) reports 15 hoes and fragments and 325 hoe flakes, 79% of which are Mill Creek (Fig. 4d) (see also Munson 1994). At Southwind, one complete hoe, 10 hoe fragments, and 43 hoe flakes were recovered, 91% percent of which are Mill Creek. Thirty-four hoe flakes were recovered from Ellerbusch, 92% of which are Mill Creek. To date, 23 hoe flakes have been identified in excavated feature contexts at Stephan-Steinkamp, 56% made of Mill Creek chert. The overwhelming and sustained preference for Mill Creek in southwestern Indiana is telling considering the regional increase in preference for Dover chert sourced from western Tennessee after AD 1200 at many sites and centers in the Ohio River Valley (Cobb 2000). The contemporaneous Kincaid and Wickliffe mound centers downriver from Angel near the confluence of the Ohio and Mississippi rivers witnessed an increase in preferences for Dover chert, despite their very close proximities to the Mill Creek quarries (Cole et al. 1951:133; Wesler 2001).

## Angel Architectonics

As previously noted, many scholars have discussed that Cahokian-made prestige goods and Cahokian ritual items were not the only media that disseminated a Cahokian ideology and that transformations in the built landscape and vernacular architecture drove the ethnogenesis of the Cahokian world (Alt 2017; Alt and Pauketat 2011; Baires 2017; Betzenhauser 2011, 2017; Pauketat 2013; Pauketat and Alt 2003, 2005). Cahokian identities were enacted through the built landscape and the ways in which people inhabited and performed daily activities in those spaces. Therefore, we must contextualize the traditional Cahokian "calling cards" to better understand the dynamic communities and broader landscapes in which these things are entangled. For the remainder of this paper, I detail patterns in the construction of space in Angel polity communities by elucidating patterns in the orientations of residential structures and communal features. Outside of Angel Mounds, Southwind, Ellerbusch, and now the Stephan-Steinkamp are the only sites with significant community plan data and associated radiometric dates from architectural contexts (Green 1977; Hilgeman and Schurr 1987; Munson 1994).

### Angel Alignments

Thomas Wolforth (1994) and later Staffan Peterson (2010) were the first to delineate the dominant organizational axis at Angel estimated at between 22° and 24° east of true north following the long axis of the rectangular base of Mound A. Mound A is the most central, largest, and oldest mound at Angel; recent radiometric dates pinpoint that mound-building activities at Mound A began prior to AD 1050 (Monaghan and Peebles 2010). All tangents of the Angel axis intersect in the center of the conical mound addition on the southeastern summit of Mound A (Fig. 3a). The Angel axis is reflected not only in Mounds A but also Mound F, mound top structures on Mounds A,

F, B, D, and J, a portion of the western palisade wall (Peterson 2010). At Angel Mounds, only 1-off mound residential structure of a total of 89 excavated during the Black era aligns with the Angel axis for a total of 1% of off mound structures aligned to the Angel axis. There are no physiographic features at or around Angel that share the orientations of the Angel axis.

Archaeoastronomer William Romain (2014, 2019) recalculated the Angel alignments and more precisely pinpointed the axes at 22.9° with tangents at 112.9° and 292.9°. This slight correction has significant implications as the recalculation indicates Angel's alignments are more accurately tied to lunar movements, specifically the northern minimum standstill. The northern minimum, or minor, standstill marks the inside range of the moon's most northerly movement on the horizon that occurs every 18.6 years (Pauketat 2013). The northwestern azimuth of Mound A at 292.9 degrees marks the moonset of the northern minimum standstill (Romain 2014, 2019). This orientation to the movements of the moon likely references physical, historical, and religious connections with Cahokia where the 5° eastern offset aligns the city and religious landscape to a lunar standstill (Emerson et al. 2020; Pauketat 2013; Pauketat et al. 2017; Romain 2015, 2018; see also Baires 2017). The Angel axis follows the foundational Cahokian cosmography, perhaps tapping into more ancient Woodland period cosmologies that associate the moon with fertility and female powers (Pauketat 2013; Pauketat and Alt 2018).

## Southwind

The Southwind site was a small village (2 ha) located near the western edge of the Angel polity just over 70 km downriver from Angel (Fig. 1). Based on the ceramic assemblage and radiocarbon dates, Southwind was inhabited during the Angel I and early Angel II phases from prior to AD 1100 to AD 1250 (Fig. 2) (Munson 1994; Striker 2009). Southwind was comprised of 64 rectangular structures, some rebuilt in place several times. Structures were situated around an ovate plaza surrounded by a rectangular bastioned palisade (Fig. 3c). Munson (1994) and later Peterson (2010) reported the repetition of the Angel axis in the largest structure and ovate plaza at Southwind. In fact, 11% of structures are oriented within ± 1° of the Angel axis, 17% of structures are oriented within ± 2°, and nearly one-third of the structures at Southwind orient with a general Angel axis grain. Additionally, the long axis of the rectangular palisade is situated 6° east of true north, within one degree of Cahokia's 5° city-wide organizational axis.

## Ellerbusch

The Ellerbusch site was a small hamlet just 3 km northeast of Angel (Fig. 1) (Green 1977). Three structures were uncovered, two rebuilt multiple times (Fig. 3b). Based on a calibrated radiocarbon date of AD 1156, Ellerbusch dates to the middle of the Angel I phase (Fig. 2). One of three structures is oriented 22° east of true north. One wall of this structure was rebuilt four times after the initial construction episode. Forty percent of the structures at Ellerbusch are oriented 22° east of true north following the Angel axis and 60% of structures follow the general grain of the Angel axis.

                                                           Springer

## Stephan-Steinkamp

Located on the Ohio River just over 60 km downriver from Angel, the Stephan-Steinkamp site was initially characterized as a small, early village contemporaneous with the Angel I phase and the Southwind and Ellerbusch sites (Figs. 1 and 2) (Hilgeman and Schurr 1987). Recently, I completed a 3-ha magnetic gradiometry survey of the Stephan-Steinkamp site in order to better understand community organization and how communal identities were materialized through the built landscape in the Angel polity. My gradiometry survey revealed only a portion of the community plan, indicating that the Stephan-Steinkamp site is much larger than originally hypothesized. The survey documented at least 83 densely packed rectangular (likely residential) structures, an open central plaza, and a linear anomaly delimiting the northern edge of the site, potentially representing a palisade or ditch fortification (Fig. 5). Most striking is the overall orientation of residential structures and the community plan.

Using ArcGIS 10.4.1, I calculated the azimuths of the magnetically detected structures at Stephan-Steinkamp correcting for magnetic declination. Of the 83 magnetically identified rectangular structures, 27 structures or 33% align within ±2 ° of the Angel axis (22.9° with tangents at 112.9° and 292.9°) (Fig. 3a, d and Fig. 5). An additional 24 structures are aligned with the general northeast/southwest organizational grain for a total of 61% of structures that strictly or more generally adhere along the Angel axis. The portion of the plaza detected seems to follow the alignment as well. At this time, it

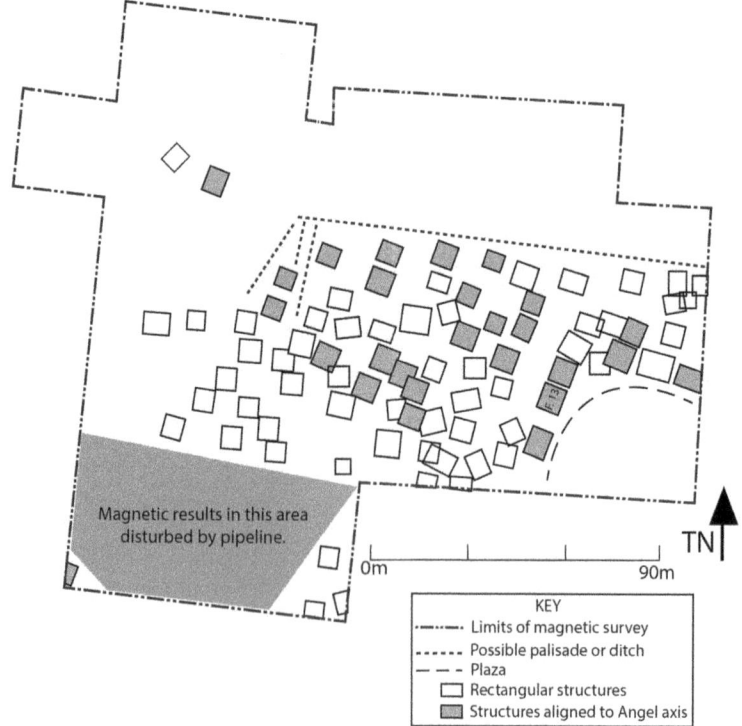

**Fig. 5** Interpretation of the Stephan-Steinkamp community plan resulting from the author's magnetic gradiometry survey

is unclear if the linear anomaly along the northern edge of the site is a palisade wall or ditch. However, the anomaly is aligned 96° east of true north, corresponding to the orientation of Southwind's rectangular palisade and within one degree of the 5° axial cardinal offset underpinning the Cahokian cityscape.

Subsequent ground-truthing excavations of structure Feature 13 revealed it was built a total of five times, that is, it was rebuilt almost exactly in place four times, every build in alignment with the Angel axis. A carbonized nutshell from either the first or second iteration of structure Feature 13 returned a median calibrated date of AD 1346 (2-sigma range of AD 1298–1413). Given the estimated use-life of a Mississippian structure at 12–17 years per build (Pauketat 2003:46) and the calibrated range, Feature 13's first of five constructions would not likely date prior to AD 1275 and the last rebuild of the structure would likely post-date AD 1400. The fourteenth-century timeframe for structure Feature 13 likely corresponds to the establishment of the village given its prominent place along the plaza, number of rebuilds, and absence of superimposing or intruding features. Contextualized with three other calibrated dates from architectural contexts in the AD 1340s, the timing of occupation of the Stephan-Steinkamp site is situated solidly in the Angel III phase making it the only Angel III phase habitation site investigated outside of Angel Mounds.

## Copy or Cosmography?

Although Cahokian and Angel axial alignments both reference movements of the moon, the lunar trajectories of Cahokia's cityscape and the Emerald shrine complex track a different standstill and occur at entirely different azimuths than Angel Mounds (Pauketat 2013). Donna Nash (2017:94) argues that "Unlike the emulation of a motif on a ceramic vessel or personal clothing, architectural configurations would have been difficult to copy unless a person participated in construction." Such precise architectural alignments could not be easily emulated and would have required execution by knowledgeable persons, particularly in the case of lunar azimuths as standstill intervals span nearly two decades.

The Angel axis created a sacred geography wherein everyday movements through, around, and between aligned structures and mounds would have physically enacted a Cahokian cosmography. The repetition of alignments in both monumental and residential architecture across the Angel polity connected Angel social and spatial orders to a Cahokian cosmography, a reorganization of the cosmic order on a regional scale. Just as alignments structured bodily dispositions at Cahokia, alignments assembled Angel communities with Cahokian ideas, powers, and histories embedding these relationships and spiritual dispositions in the local landscape (Pauketat 2013; see also Fowles 2009).

## Angel Ethnogenesis and the Cahokian Diaspora

Here, I summarize the chronological and material connections between Cahokia and the Angel polity before revisiting Angel communities in the context of core diaspora criteria.

As Cahokia was experiencing its Big Bang near AD 1050, Yankeetown peoples from southwestern Indiana were immigrating to the American Bottom (Alt 2002, 2006,

                                     Springer

2018). At the same time, the dominant organizational axis of Angel was emplaced through the construction of Mounds A and F, but the Angel Mounds site remained a vacant ceremonial center (Monaghan and Peebles 2010; Peterson 2010).

By AD 1150, Cahokia was reaching its peak population (Pauketat 2004). At the same time at Angel, locally produced Ramey Incised pottery was created, used, and deposited in Feature 37 likely as part of a communal or feasting event (Peterson 2010). In the wider Angel polity, the Southwind and Ellerbusch communities were established by orienting significant percentages of residential structures to the Angel axis (Green 1977; Munson 1994).

Much of the American Bottom was depopulated by AD 1250 as Cahokia experienced a prolonged abandonment during the thirteenth and fourteenth centuries (Baltus 2014, 2015; Pauketat 2004). At the same time, the Angel site experienced its first substantial occupation and locally made Ramey Incised pottery was discarded in residential contexts of the east village (Peterson 2010). By AD 1300, Southwind and Ellerbusch (Green 1977; Munson 1994) were no longer inhabited while the earliest structures and central plaza at Stephan-Steinkamp were likely under construction, aligned to the Angel axis.

After AD 1350, Cahokia and the American Bottom were almost entirely depopulated (Pauketat 2004). Meanwhile, the Angel axis was reaffirmed at Stephan-Steinkamp by the continued aligned construction of significant portions of the community. After AD 1400, Mounds A and F at Angel were capped with a final layer of fill and Angel Mounds was abandoned by AD 1450 (Monaghan et al. 2013).

Do the artifactual, architectural, and chronological linkages at Angel indicate a Cahokian diaspora? To answer this, first, I refer back to the general diaspora criteria outlined at the beginning of this paper.

1. *Dispersion:* There is ample evidence to demonstrate longstanding connections between the American Bottom and the Yankeetown culture of southwestern Indiana during Cahokia's emergence (Alt 2002, 2006, 2018). If, as Baltus and Baires (2020) posit, Cahokia's emergence created an inverse diaspora, did Yankeetown immigrants or their descendants eventually return to their homelands of origin along the Ohio River with Mississippian ways of life, religion, and cosmography (see also Emerson et al. 2020)? Additionally, Cahokian-made or Cahokian-style objects, particularly Ramey Incised pottery, suggest sustained connections during the early years of Angel Mounds: 9% of Angel Ramey was recovered from Feature 37 dating to AD 1150 (Peterson 2010). The everted rim morphology of Angel Ramey suggests manufacture after AD 1200. Although locally produced, many Angel Ramey vessels were made by skilled and knowledgeable potters consistent with Cahokian-made Ramey in vessel form and decorative design pointing to a scenario in which some Angel Ramey pots could have been created by Cahokian emigrants. Moreover, the prolonged abandonment of Cahokia during the 13th and 14th centuries corresponds with the timing of the first substantial residential occupation of Angel Mounds, the center's subsequent population growth, and the founding of the late Angel Stephan-Steinkamp village.

2. *Homeland orientation*: At Cahokia, reconfiguring and reimagining the built landscape—from residential architectural techniques, to monuments, to the

organization of towns and cities—was central to the creation of the Cahokian world and a new Cahokian identity (Alt 2006, 2017; Alt and Pauketat 2011; Baires 2017; Betzenhauser 2011; Pauketat 2013; Pauketat and Alt 2005; Skousen 2018). If physcially aligning community landscapes, domiciles, and the daily dispositions of resident bodies (human and otherwise) was integral to the creation of a Cahokian community, so to would it be outside of the Cahokian homeland. Being Cahokian was embodied in the homeland and farther afield through everyday practices enacted in lunar aligned landscapes. The construction of the Angel axis in reference to lunar trajectories oriented Angel communities along the same organizational principles as the city of Cahokia and the Cahokian cosmos. The alignments would have emplaced Cahokian ideologies and histories in the Angel landscape. Angel communities were literally and figuratively oriented toward a Cahokian homeland: everyday movements through, around, and between aligned structures and monumental architecture would have physically reinforced connections to a historical homeland or mythological place of cosmological origin, perhaps evoking a sense of nostalgia for ancestral times and places (see also Buchanan 2020).

3. *Ethnogenesis*: Communities and group identities are continually constructed and negotiated through patterned material and social practices. Identities are not something people and groups have; rather, identities are something people and groups do (*sensu* Pauketat 2008:240). Therefore, communal identities were enacted through the built landscape and the ways in which people inhabited and performed daily activities in those spaces. In the Angel polity, communities were realized through everyday interactions with powerful cosmological architecture that assembled Angel and Cahokian genealogies. The establishment of the Angel axis as a principal feature during early community-making at Angel, Southwind, and Ellerbusch and during the late remaking of the Stephan-Steinkamp community indicates that Cahokian cosmology figured prominently into the foundations of communal identities. Moreover, a significant proportion of locally produced Ramey was recovered from Feature 37, a pit feature coeval with the earliest habitation of Angel Mounds. In the Angel polity, the positioning of local people, places, and things to a Cahokian cosmography brought the Angel world into being.

## Concluding Thoughts

Emerson et al. (2020) argue that expatriates "willfully rejected" Cahokian identities following the decline of the city. However, the evidence presented here regarding the Angel polity does not fit this scenario, even at face value, the traditional diaspora prerequisites are met (*e.g.*, Owens 2005). Dispersals are evident in Cahokian cosmological iconography in the form of Ramey Incised pottery found at Angel Mounds. Other Cahokian-made and Cahokian-style artifacts (chunkey stones, notched points, and Mill Creek hoes) are present across the Angel polity indicating sustained connections or trade with the Cahokian homeland. Multiple scales of the built landscape are oriented, like Cahokia, to a lunar standstill, aligning Angel landscapes literally and figuratively to the Cahokian homeland.

Like Baltus and Baires (2020), this work acknowledges diaspora as a process of becoming. In this way, ethnogenesis is inherent in the flux of diasporic experiences in foreign lands; traditional identity practices are mediated and new ways of being are materialized outside of the homeland (Cipolla 2017). Moreover, understanding the relationality of communities and how other-than-human agents figured in community-making offers a more nuanced consideration of how diasporic communities were materially disassembled and reassembled in the deeper past. When Angel community-making is considered ethnogenic and relational, the linkages with Cahokia demonstrated herein are even more powerful.

For Angel communities, it was not the mere presence or ownership of Cahokian-made objects that perpetuated connections to Cahokia, rather, it was the entangling of local communities (human and non-human constituents alike) with Cahokian cosmic powers. Much more than cheap imitations, locally manufactured Ramey Incised vessels were the physical embodiment of the recombination of Angel and Cahokian worlds. Likewise, Angel communities engaged the Cahokian cosmos by aligning their buildings and communal landscapes to the moon, assembling and binding local histories and identities with Cahokian cosmic forces. While, as Baltus and Baires (2020) note, we cannot assume that the meanings of Ramey iconography or lunar alignments remained fixed, at Cahokia or Angel, it is clear that a Cahokian ontology was integral to Angel ethnogenesis and remained important to constructing the Angel landscape and informed community-making for nearly three centuries.

The material practices of Angel communities, discussed here as interdigitated and multidimensional processes of community-making, offer compelling evidence for a potential Cahokian diaspora during the thirteenth and fourteenth centuries, wherein connections with Cahokia motivated Angel ethnogenesis. This study demonstrates that the connections between Angel and Cahokia have been underestimated and that Angel communities created relationships with Cahokia by configuring their physical and social landscapes to a particular Cahokian cosmogram. The evidence here indicates stronger ties with Cahokia than the mere artifact counts of "calling cards" at Angel would suggest. Movements of peoples, things, practices, and ideas with cosmic associations were key to Cahokian ethnogenesis, and these cosmic movements in the Ohio River Valley set ethnogenesis in motion in Angel communities.

**Acknowledgments**   Research at the Stephan-Steinkamp site was supported by the Indiana University Glenn A. Black Laboratory of Archaeology, Indiana University Department of Anthropology David C. Skomp Fund, and the generosity of Kenneth Burgdorf and family. Many thanks to my fellow co-organizers and contributors to the original session at the 2017 Southeastern Archaeological Conference and this special issue. Thank you to Dr. Susan Alt for the thoughtful comments on the conference draft of this paper and thanks to all the original session discussants (Dr. Vincas Steponaitis, Dr. Lynne Sullivan, Dr. Susan Alt, and Dr. Peter Peregrine) for your lively discussion of archaeologies of diaspora and the Mississippian world. Three anonymous reviewers provided thoughtful comments and suggestions that supported the transformation of this work from conference musings to article. Special thanks to my dear husband, Giannis Malouchos, for sharing his expertise in Ancient Greek language.

## Compliance with Ethical Standards

**Conflict of Interest**   The author declares that she has no conflict of interest.

# References

Alberti, B., & Bray, T. L. (2009). Animating archaeology: of subjects, objects and alternative ontologies. *A Special Section for Cambridge Archaeological Journal, 19*(3), 337–441.

Alberti, B., & Marshall, Y. (2009). Conceptually open-ended methodologies. *Cambridge Archaeological Journal, 19*(3), 344–356.

Alt, S. M. (2002). Identities, traditions, and diversity in Cahokia's uplands. *Midcontinental Journal of Archaeology, 27*, 217–236.

Alt, S. M. (2006). The power of diversity: the roles of migration and hybridity in culture change. In B. M. Butler, & P. D. Welch (Eds.), *Leadership and polity in Mississippian society* (pp. 289–308). Carbondale: Center for Archaeological Investigations, occasional paper no. 33. Southern Illinois University.

Alt, S. M. (2017). Building Cahokia: transformation through tradition. In C. T. Halperin & L. Schwartz (Eds.), *Vernacular architecture in the Americas* (pp. 141–157). London: Routledge.

Alt, S. M. (2018). *Cahokia's diverse farmers.* Tuscaloosa: The University of Alabama Press.

Alt, S. M. (2019). From weeping hills to lost caves: a search for vibrant matter in greater Cahokia. In S. M. Alt & T. R. Pauketat (Eds.), *New materialisms ancient urbanisms.* London: Routledge.

Alt, S. M., & Pauketat, T. R. (2007). Sex and the southern cult. In A. King (Ed.), *The southeastern ceremonial complex* (pp. 232–250). Tuscaloosa: University of Alabama Press.

Alt, S. M., & Pauketat, T. R. (2011). Why wall trenches? *Southeastern Archaeology, 30*(1), 108–122.

Anthias, F. (1998). Evaluating 'diaspora': deyond ethnicity? *Sociology, 32*(3), 557–580.

Armstrong, D. V. (1999). Archaeology and ethnohistory of the Caribbean plantation. In T. A. Singleton (Ed.), *I, too, Am America: studies in African-American archaeology, 173–192.* University of Virginia Press.

Ashley, K., & Thunen, R. L. (2020). St. Johns river fisher-hunter-gatherers: Florida's connection to Cahokia. *Journal of Archaeological Method and Theory, 27*(1), 1–21.

Baires, S. E. (2017). *Land of water, city of the dead: religion and Cahokia's emergence.* Tuscaloosa: University of Alabama Press.

Baltus, M. R. (2014). Transforming material relationships: 13th century revitalization of Cahokian religious-politics. Unpublished Ph.D. Dissertation, Department of Anthropology, University of Illinois at Urbana-Champaign.

Baltus, M. R. (2015). Unraveling entanglements: Reverberations of Cahokia's big bang. In M. E. Buchanan & B. Jacob Skousen (Eds.), *Tracing the relational: the archaeology of worlds, spirits, and temporalities* (pp. 146–160). Salt Lake City: University of Utah Press.

Baltus, M. R. (2018). Vessels of change: everyday relationality in the rise and fall of Cahokia. In *Relational engagements of the indigenous Americas: alterity, ontology, and shifting paradigms.*

Baltus, M. R., & Baires, S. E. (2012). Elements of ancient power in the Cahokian world. *Journal of Social Archaeology, 12*(2), 167–192.

Baltus, M. R., & Baires, S. E. (2020). Defining diaspora: A view from the Cahokia homeland. *Journal of Archaeological Method and Theory, 27*(1).

Ball, S. (1996). The ray site: Angel phase mortuary behavior at an outlying site. Paper presented at the Midwest Archaeological Conference, Milwaukee, Wisconsin.

Bardolph, D. N. (2014). Evaluating Cahokian contact and Mississippian identity politics in the late prehistoric central Illinois River valley. *American Antiquity, 79*, 69–89.

Baries, C. J., & Porter, J. W. (Eds.). (1984). *American bottom archaeology: a summary of the FAI-270 project contribution to the culture history of the Mississippi River valley.* Urbana: University of Illinois Press.

Barth, F. (Ed.). (1969). *Ethnic groups and boundaries.* Boston: Little Brown.

Bell, A. (2002). Emulation and empowerment: material, social, and economic dynamics in eighteenth- and nineteenth-century Virginia. *International Journal of Historical Archaeology, 6*(4), 253–298.

Bennett, J. (2010). *Vibrant matter: a political ecology of things.* Duke University Press.

Betzenhauser, A. M. (2011). Creating the Cahokian community: the power of place in early Mississippian sociopolitical dynamics. Unpublished Ph.D. Dissertation University of Illinois, Urbana.

Betzenhauser, A. M. (2017). Cahokia's beginnings: mobility, urbanization, and the Cahokian political landscape. In G. D. Wilson (Ed.), *Mississippian beginnings.* Gainesville: University of Florida Press.

Bhabha, H. K. (1994). *The location of culture.* New York: Routledge.

Bird-David, N. (1999). Animism" revisited: personhood, environment, and relational epistemology. *Current Anthropology, 40*(S1), S67–S91.

Black, G. A. (1967). *The angel site: an archaeological, historical, and ethnological study.* Indianapolis: Indiana Historical Society.

Boszhardt, R. F., & Stoltman, J. B. (2016). Petrographic analysis of late woodland and middle Mississippian ceramics at the Iva site (47Lc42). *Onalaska, Wisconsin, Midcontinental Journal of Archaeology, 41*(2), 93–126.

Brennan, T. K. (2014). Mississippian community-making through everyday items at Kincaid mounds. Unpublished Ph.D. Dissertation, Department of Anthropology, Southern Illinois University, Carbondale.

Brennan, T. K. (Ed.). (2016). Main street mound: a ridgetop monument at the East St. *Louis Mound Complex* (Illinois state archaeological survey, research report 36). Urbana-Champaign: Prairie Research Institute, University of Illinois.

Brinkerhoff, J. M. (2008). Diaspora identity and the potential for violence: toward an identity-mobilization framework. *Identity, 8*(1), 67–88.

Brubaker, R. (2005). The 'diaspora' diaspora. *Ethnic and Racial Studies, 28*(1), 1–19.

Brubaker, R. (2017). Revisiting "the 'diaspora' diaspora". *Ethnic and Racial Studies, 40*(9), 1556–1561.

Buchanan, M. E., & Wernette, M. (2016). Angel mounds feature 37 preliminary faunal results. Unpublished report for Indiana University Office of Vice Provost for Research on file at the Glenn A. Black Laboratory of Archaeology.

Buchanan, M. E. (2020). Diasporic longings? Cahokia, common field, and nostalgic orientations. *Journal of Archaeological Method and Theory, 27*(1).

Butler, A. M. (2017). *The Mission should you accept it: the built space of a Mississippian Mission.* Indianapolis: Paper presented at the Midwest Archaeological Conference.

Cipolla, C. N. (2017). *Native American diaspora and ethnogenesis.* Oxford Handbooks Online.

Cipolla, C. N. (2018). Earth flows and lively stone. What differences does 'vibrant'matter make? *Archaeological Dialogues, 25*(1), 49–70.

Clifford, J. (1994). Diasporas. *Cultural Anthropology, 9*(3), 302–338.

Cobb, C. R. (1989). An appraisal of the role of Mill Creek chert hoes in Mississippian exchange systems. *Southeastern Archaeology*, 79–92.

Cobb, C. (2000). *From quarry to cornfield: the political economy of Mississippian hoe production.* Tuscalossa: University of Alabama Press.

Cohen, R. (1997). *Global diasporas, an introduction.* Seattle: University of Washington Press.

Cohen, R. (2015). Foreword. In Sigona N., Gamblen A., Liberatore G., Neveu Kringelbach H. (Eds.) Diasporas re-imagined: spaces*, Practices and Belonging*, Oxford: University of Oxford.

Cole, F. C., Bell, R., Bennett, J., Caldwell, J., Emerson, N., MacNeish, R., Orr, K., & Willis, R. (1951). *Kincaid: a prehistoric Illinois Metropolis.* Chicago: University of Chicago Press.

Collins, J. M. (1990). *The archaeology of the Cahokia mounds ICT-II: Site structure, Illinois cultural resources study no. 10.* Springfield: Illinois Historic Preservation Agency.

Collins, J. M. (1997). Cahokia settlement and social structures as viewed from the ICT-II. In T. R. Pauketat & T. E. Emerson (Eds.), *Cahokia: domination and ideology in the Mississippian world* (pp. 124–140). Lincoln: University of Nebraska Press.

Cook, R. A. (2008). *SunWatch: fort ancient development in the Mississippian world.* The University of Alabama Press.

Crown, P. L., Emerson, T. E., Gu, J., Hurst, W. J., Pauketat, T. R., & Ward, T. (2012). Ritual black drink consumption at Cahokia. *Proceedings of the National Academy of Sciences, 109*(35), 13944–13949.

Dalan, R. A. (1997). The construction of Mississippian Cahokia. *Cahokia: domination and ideology in the Mississippian world*, 89–102.

Dalan, R. A., Holley, G. R., Woods, W. I., Watters, H. W., & Koepke, J. A. (2003). *Envisioning Cahokia: a landscape perspective.* DeKalb: Northern Illinois University Press.

DeBoer, W. R. (1993). Like a rolling stone: The chunkey game and political organization in eastern North America. *Southeastern Archaeology*, 83–92.

DeLanda, M. (2006). *A new philosophy of society: Assemblage theory and social complexity.* London: Continuum.

Delaney-Rivera, C. (2000). Mississippian and late woodland cultural interaction and regional dynamics: a view from the lower Illinois River valley. Ph.D. Dissertation: Department of Anthropology, University of California, Los Angeles.

Deleuze, G., & Guattari, F. (2004). *A thousand plateaus: capitalism and schizophrenia.* London: Continuum.

Emerson, T. E. (1989). Water, serpents, and the underworld: an exploration into Cahokia symbolism. In (Ed.) Galloway, P. *The Southeastern Ceremonial Complex: Artifacts and Analysis* (pp. 45-92). University of Nebraska Press: Lincoln.

Emerson, T. E. (1991). The Apple River Mississippian culture of northwestern Illinois. In T. E. Emerson & R. Barry Lewis (Eds.), *Cahokia and the hinterlands: Middle Mississippian cultures of the Midwest* (pp. 164–182). Urbana: University of Illinois Press.

Emerson, T. E. (1997). *Cahokia and the archaeology of power*. Tuscaloosa: University of Alabama Press.

Emerson, T. E., Hedman, K. M., Brennan, T. K., Betzenhauser, A. M., Alt, S. M., & Pauketat, T. R. (2020). Interrogating diaspora and movement in the greater Cahokian world. *Journal of Archaeological Method and Theory, 27*(1).

Ferguson, L. (1992). *Uncommon ground: archaeology and early America, 1650–1800*. Washington, DC: Smithsonian Institution.

Fine, B., & Leopold, E. (1990). Consumerism and the industrial revolution. *Social History, 12*(2), 151–179.

Fowler, M. L., & Hall, R. L. (1975). Archaeological phases at Cahokia. In *Perspectives in Cahokia Archaeology, Illinois archaeological survey, bulletin 10* (pp. 1–14). Urbana: University of Illinois.

Fowles, S. (2009). The enshrined pueblo: villagescape and cosmos in the northern Rio Grande. *American Antiquity, 74*(3), 448–466.

Friberg, C. M. (2017). Cosmic negotiations: Cahokian religion and Ramey incised pottery in the northern hinterland. *Southeastern Archaeology, 37*(1), 39–57.

Galloway, P. (1997). Where have all the menstrual huts gone? The invisibility of menstrual seclusion in the late prehistoric Southeast. In (Eds.) Claassen, C. & Joyce, R. *Women in Prehistory: North America and Mesoamerica* (pp. 47-62). University of Pennsylvania Press.

Green, T. J. (1977). Economic relationships underlying Mississippian settlement patterns in Southwestern Indiana and North-Central Kentucky. Unpubublished Ph.D. Dissertation, Department of Anthropology, Indiana University, Bloomington.

Green, T., & Munson, C. (1978). Mississippian settlement patterns in southwestern Indiana. In B. D. Smith (Ed.), *Mississippian settlement patterns* (pp. 293–330). New York: Academic Press.

Greenan, M., & Garniewicz, R. (2010). Investigations at the Yankeetown site (12W1). *Indiana Archaeology, 5*(1), 28–48.

Griffith, R. J. (1981). *Ramey incised pottery, Circular No. 5*. Urbana: Illinois Archaeological Survey.

Hall, R. L. (1962). *The archaeology of Carcajou Point*. Two volumes: University of Wisconsin Press, Madison.

Hall, R. L. (1991). Cahokia identity and interaction models of Cahokian Mississippian. In T. E. Emerson & R. Barry Lewis (Eds.), *Cahokia and the hinterlands: Middle Mississippian cultures of the Midwest* (pp. 3–34). Urbana: University of Illinois Press.

Hall, R. L. (1997). *An archaeology of the soul: North American Indian belief and ritual*. Urbana: University of Illinois Press.

Harvey, G. (2006). *Animism: respecting the living world*. New York: Columbia University Press.

Hammerstedt, S. (2005). Mississippian status in Western Kentucky: evidence from the Annis Mound. *Southeastern Archaeology, 24*(1), 11–27.

Hamilakis, Y., & Jones, A. M. (2017). Archaeology and assemblage. *Cambridge Archaeological Journal, 27*(1), 77–84.

Harris, O. J. T. (2013). Relational communities in prehistoric Britain. In C. Watts (Ed.), *Relational archaeologies*. London: Routledge.

Harris, O. J. T. (2014). (re) assembling communities. *Journal of Archaeological Method and Theory, 21*(1), 76–97.

Herrmann, E. (2013). Pre-Mississippian projectile points in Mississippian context at Angel Mounds. *Midcontinental Journal of Archaeology, 38*(2), 189–204.

Hilgeman, S. L. (2000). *Pottery and chronology at angel*. Tuscaloosa: University of Alabama Press.

Hilgeman, S. L. & Schurr, M. R. (1987). The 1986 IU/GBL excavations at the Stephan-Steinkamp site (12Po33). *Proceedings of the Indiana Academy of Science 102nd Annual Meeting* 96: 83-90.

Hodder, I. (2011). Human-thing entanglement: Towards an integrated archaeological perspective. *Journal of the Royal Anthropological Institute, 17*(1), 154–177.

Holley, G. (1989). *The archaeology of the Cahokia mounds ICT-II: Ceramics, Illinois cultural resources study no. 11*. Springfield: Illinois Historic Preservation Agency.

Honerkamp, M. W. (1975). The Angel phase: an analysis of a middle Mississippian occupation in southwestern Indiana. Unpublished Ph.D. Dissertation, Department of Anthropology, Indiana University, Bloomington.

Howey, M. (2011). Colonial encounters, European kettles, and the magic of mimesis in the late sixteenth and early seventeenth century indigenous northeast and Great Lakes. *International Journal of Historical Archaeology, 15*(3), 329–357.

Hudson, C. M. (1979). *Black drink: A native American tea*. University of Georgia Press.

Ingold, T. (2011). *Being alive: Essays on movement, knowledge and description*. Routledge.

Insoll, T. (Ed.). (2007). *The archaeology of identities: A reader*. London: Routledge.

Johnson, M. (2010). *English houses 1300–1800: Vernacular architecture, social life*. London: Longman.

Jones, S. (1997). *The archaeology of ethnicity: Constructing identities in the past and the present.* London: Routledge.

Justice, N. D. (1987). *Stone age spear and arrow points of the midcontinental and eastern United States: a modern survey and reference.* Bloomington: Indiana University Press.

Kelly, J. E. (1991). Cahokia and its role as a gateway center in interregional exchange. In T. E. Emerson & R. Barry Lewis (Eds.), *Cahokia and the hinterlands: Middle Mississippian cultures of the Midwest* (pp. 3–34). Urbana: University of Illinois Press.

Knudson, R. A. (1967). Cambria Village Ceramics. *Plains Anthropologist, 12*(37), 247–299.

Krus, A. M. (2016). The timing of Precolumbian militarization in the US Midwest and southeast. *American Antiquity, 81*(2), 375–388.

Lilley, I. (2004). Diaspora and identity in archaeology: Moving beyond the Black Atlantic. In L. Meskell & R. Preucel (Eds.), *A companion to social archaeology* (pp. 287–312). Oxford: Blackwell Publishers.

McGill, D. E. (2013). Social organization and pottery production at the angel mounds archaeological site. Unpublished Ph.D. Dissertation, Department of Anthropology, Indiana University, Bloomington.

Mehrer, M. W., & Collins, J. M. (1995). Household archaeology at Cahokia and its hinterlands. In J. Daniel Rogers & B. D. Smith (Eds.), *Mississippian communities and households* (pp. 32–57). Tuscaloosa: University of Alabama Press.

Mehta, J. M., & Connaway, J. M. (2020). Mississippian culture and Cahokian identities as considered through household archaeology at Carson, a monumental center in North Mississippi. *Journal of Archaeological Method and Theory, 27*(1).

Miller, J. R. (2015). Interior carbonization patterns as evidence of ritual drink preparation in Powell plain and Ramey incised vessels. *American Antiquity, 80*(1), 170–183.

Millhouse, P. G. (2012). The John chapman site and Creolization on the northern frontier of the Mississippian world. Unpublished Ph.D. Dissertation, Department of Anthropology, University of Illinois, Urbana-Champaign.

Mollerud, K. J. (2016). The Cambria connection: Identifying ceramic production and community interaction in late prehistoric Minnesota, AD 1050–1300. Unpublished Ph.D. Dissertation, Department of Anthropology, University of Wisconsin, Milwaukee.

Monaghan, G. W., & Peebles, C. S. (2010). The construction, use, and abandonment of angel site mound a: Tracing the history of a middle Mississippian town through its earthworks. *American Antiquity, 84*(323), 103–113.

Monaghan, G. W., Schilling, T., Krus, A. M., & Peebles, C. S. (2013). Mound construction chronology at angel mounds episodic mound construction and ceremonial events. *Midcontinental Journal of Archaeology, 38*(2), 155–170.

Munson, C. A. (1994). *Archaeological investigations at the Southwind site, a Mississippian Community in Posey County, Indiana.* Indianapolis: Manuscript on file at the Indiana Department of Natural Resources - Division of Historic Preservation and Archaeology.

Munson, C. A., Strezewski, M., & Stafford, C. R. (2006). *Archaeological investigations at the Prather site, Clark County, Indiana: The 2005 survey and excavations, IPFW archaeological survey reports of investigations 602.* Fort Wayne: Indiana University-Purdue University.

Nash, D. (2017). Vernacular versus state housing in the Wari empire: Cosmological clashes and compromises. Halperin, Christina, and Lauren Schwartz, eds. Vernacular *Architecture in the Pre-Columbian Americas.* Taylor & Francis.

Niquette, C. M., Kreisa, P. P, Clay, R. B., & Crites, G. D. (1991). *Excavations at the Andalex Village (15Hk22) Hopkins County, Kentucky.* Cultural resource analysts, Inc. contract publication series 91-03.

O'Brien, P. J. (1972). *A Formal Analysis of Cahokia Ceramics from the Powell Tract.* Illinois archaeological survey monograph no. 3, Urbana, Illinois.

Orser Jr., C. E. (1998). The archaeology of the African diaspora. *Annual Review of Anthropology, 27*(1), 63–82.

Owen, B. (2005). Distant colonies and explosive collapse: The two stages of the Tiwanaku diaspora in the Osmore drainage. *Latin American Antiquity, 16*(1), 45–80.

Pauketat, T. R. (1998a). *The archaeology of downtown Cahokia: the Tract 15A and Dunham Tract excavations.* (Illinois transportation archaeological research program studies in archaeology 1). Urbana: University of Illinois.

Pauketat, T. R. (1998b). Refiguring the archaeology of greater Cahokia. *Journal of Archaeological Research, 6*(1), 45–89.

Pauketat, T. R. (2001). *The archaeology of traditions: Agency and history before and after Columbus.* Gainesville: University Press of Florida.

Pauketat, T. R. (2003). Resettled farmers and the making of a Mississippian polity. *American Antiquity, 68*, 39–66.

Pauketat, T. R. (2004). *Ancient Cahokia and the Mississippians*. London: Cambridge University Press.

Pauketat, T. R. (2008). The grounds for Agency in Southwestern Archaeology. In M. D. Varien & J. M. Potter (Eds.), *The social construction of communities* (pp. 233–250). Lanham, Maryland: Altamira Press.

Pauketat, T. R. (2013). *An archaeology of the Cosmos: Rethinking agency and religion in ancient America*. London: Routledge.

Pauketat, T. R. (2019). Introducing new materialisms, rethinking ancient urbanisms. In S. M. Alt & T. R. Pauketat (Eds.), *New materialisms ancient urbanisms* (pp. 1–18). London: Routledge.

Pauketat, T. R., & Alt, S. M. (2003). Mounds, memory, and contested Mississippian history. *Archaeologies of memory*, 151-179.

Pauketat, T. R., & Alt, S. M. (2005). Agency in a postmold? Physicality and the archaeology of culture making. *Journal of Archaeological Method and Theory, 12*(3), 213–236.

Pauketat, T. R., & Alt, S. M. (2018). Water and shells in bodies and pots: Mississippian rhizome, Cahokian Poiesis. In E. Harrison-Buck & J. Hendon (Eds.), *Personhood & other-than-human agency in archaeology* (pp. 72–99). Boulder: University of Colorado Press.

Pauketat, T. R., Alt, S. M., & Kruchten, J. D. (2017). The emerald acropolis: Elevating the moon and water in the rise of Cahokia. *Antiquity, 91*(355), 207–222.

Pauketat, T. R., & Emerson, T. E. (1991). The ideology of authority and the power of the pot. *American Anthropologist, 93*, 919–941.

Pauketat, T. R., & Emerson, T. E. (1997). *Conclusion: Cahokia and the four winds* (pp. 269–278). Cahokia: Domination and Ideology in the Mississippian World.

Pauketat, T. R. & Emerson, T. E. (1999). Representation of hegemony as Community at Cahokia." in *Material Symbols: Culture and Economy in Prehistory*, edited by John E. Robb, 302–317. Carbondale: Center for Archaeological Investigations, Southern Illinois University.

Pauketat, T. R., Boszhardt, R. F., & Benden, D. M. (2015). Trempealeau entanglements: An ancient colony's causes and effects. *American Antiquity, 80*(2), 260–289.

Peterson, S. A. (2010). Townscape archaeology at Angel Mounds. Unpublished Ph.D. Dissertation, Department of Anthropology, Indiana University, Bloomington.

Porter, J. W. (1964). *Thin section description of some Shel[l] tempered prehistoric ceramics from the American bottoms*. Carbondale: Southern Illinois University Museum lithic laboratory, research report 7.

Redmond, B. G. (1990). The Yankeetown phase: Emergent Mississippian cultural adaptation in the lower Ohio River valley. Unpublished Ph.D. Dissertation, Department of Anthropology, Indiana University, Bloomington.

Richards, J. D. (1992). Ceramics and culture at Aztalan: A late prehistoric village in Southeast Wisconsin. Unpublished Ph.D. Dissertation, Department of Anthopology, University of Wisconsin, Milwaukee.

Richards, J. D., & Zych, T. J. (2018). A landscape of mounds: Community Ehtnogenesis at Aztalan. In T. R. Pauketat & B. H. Koldehoff (Eds.), *Archaeology and ancient religion in the American midcontinent* (pp. 304–342). Tuscaloosa: University Alabama Press.

Romain, W. F. (2014). *Ancient astronomers of the eastern woodlands: Watson brake to Cahokia. Paper presented at the Midwest archaeological conference*. Illinois: Champaign-Urbana.

Romain, W. F. (2015). Moonwatchers of Cahokia. In (Eds.) Pauketat, T. R., & Alt, S. M. *Medieval Mississippians: The Cahokian World*. Santa Fe: School for Advanced Research press.

Romain, W. F. (2018). Ancient Skywatchers of the eastern woodlands. In T. R. Pauketat & B. H. Koldehoff (Eds.), *Archaeology and ancient religion in the American midcontinent* (pp. 304–342). Tuscaloosa: University Alabama Press.

Romain, W. F. (2019). *Ancient Skywatchers of the Mississippi Valley. Lecture presented at the the the Maya exploration center*. Ohio: Chillicothe.

Safran, W. (1991). Diasporas in modern societies: Myths of homeland and return. *Disapora: A Journal of Transnational Studies, 1*(1), 83–99.

Skousen, B. J. (2018). Rethinking archaeologies of pilgrimage. *Journal of Social Archaeology, 18*(3), 261–283.

Slater, P. A., Hedman, K. M., & Emerson, T. E. (2014). Immigrants at the Mississippian polity of Cahokia: strontium isotope evidence for population movement. *Journal of Archaeological Science, 44*, 117–127.

Stoltman, J. B. (1991). Ceramic petrography as a technique for documenting cultural interaction: An example from the upper Mississippi Valley. *American Antiquity, 56*, 103–120.

Stoltman, J. B., Benden, M. D., & Boszhardt, R. F. (2008). New evidence in the upper Mississippi Valley for Premississippian cultural interaction with the American bottom. *American Antiquity, 73*, 317–336.

Striker, M. A. (2009). Archaeological investigations at the Southwind site (12PO265), Posey County, Indiana. Project No. 07–55101. Report on file at the Indiana Department of Natural Resources-Division of Historic Preservation and Archaeology, Indianapolis.

Tölölyan, K. (1996). Rethinking diaspora(s): Stateless power in the transnational moment. *Diaspora: A Journal of Transnational Studies, 5*(1), 3–36.

Vogel, J. O. (1975). Trends in Cahokia ceramics: Preliminary study of the collections from tracts 15A and 15B. In Perspectives in Cahokia archaeology: Illinois archaeological survey bulletin 10, edited by James A. Brown, pp. 32–71. Urbana: University of Illinois.

Voss, B. L. (2008). *The archaeology of Ethnogenesis: Race and sexuality in colonial San Francisco.* Berkeley: University of California Press.

Voss, B. L. (2015). What's new? Rethinking ethnogenesis in the archaeology of colonialism. *American Antiquity, 80*(4), 655–670.

Watts Malouchos, E. (2016). Connecting to Cahokia: Reconsidering material connections between angel and the American bottom. In *Paper presented at the 73rd annual southeastern archaeological conference.* Athens: GA.

Weik, T. M. (2014). The Archaeology of Ethnogenesis. *Annual Review of Anthropology, 43*(1), 291–305.

Wesler, K. (2001). *Excavations at Wickliffe mounds.* Tuscaloosa: The University of Alabama Press.

Wilson, G. D., Bardolph, D. N., Esarey, D., & Wilson, J. J. (2020). Early Mississippian diasporas of the north American midcontinent. *Journal of Archaeological Method and Theory, 27*(1).

Wolforth, T. (1994). *An examination of alignments between prehistoric constructions and solar alignments, In (Ed.) Munson, C. a. Archaeological Investigations at the Southwind Site, A Mississippian Community in Posey County Indiana.* Indianapolis: Manuscript on file at the Indiana Department of Natural Resources - Division of Historic Preservation and Archaeology.

Zedeño, M. N. (2008). Bundled worlds: The roles and interactions of complex objects from the north American Plains. *Journal of Archaeological Method and Theory, 15*(4), 362–378.

Zych, T. J. (2013). The construction of a mound and a new community: an analysis of the ceramic and feature assemblages from the northeast Mound at the Aztalan site. Master's thesis, Department of Anthropology, University of Wisconsin – Milwaukee.

Zych, T. J. (2015). The chunkey game. In T. R. Pauketat & S. M. Alt (Eds.), *The Medieval Mississippians* (pp. 71–73). Santa Fe: School for Advanced Research Press.

**Publisher's Note** Springer Nature remains neutral with regard to jurisdictional claims in published maps and institutional affiliations.

Milton Keynes UK
Ingram Content Group UK Ltd.
UKHW020743231123
433129UK00008B/504